Managing Complex Educational Change

Why is educational change becoming more complex? Are there patterns in this complexity? How may managers cope effectively with complex educational change?

This book investigates initiatives to reorganise school systems, involving highly emotive closures and mergers. It reveals how reorganisation was a complex change to manage because it was large-scale, componential, systematic, differentially impacting and context-dependent. These characteristics affected management tasks, generating ambiguity in the change process that limited managers' capacity to control it. The authors offer four management themes as realistic strategies for coping with complex educational change:

- Orchestration
- Flexible planning and co-ordination
- Culture building and communication
- Differentiated support.

Managing Complex Educational Change is essential reading for all concerned with educational change – managers in schools and colleges, students on advanced courses, trainers, local and regional administrators, academics and policymakers. The research has general implications for the theory and practice of managing complex change.

Mike Wallace is Professor of Education at the University of Bath. **Keith Pocklington** is Co-Director of CREATE Consultants.

Managing Complex Educational Change

Large-scale reorganisation of schools

Mike Wallace and
Keith Pocklington

London and New York

First published 2002
by RoutledgeFalmer
11 New Fetter Lane, London EC4P 4EE

Simultaneously published in the USA and Canada
by RoutledgeFalmer
29 West 35th Street, New York, NY 10001

RoutledgeFalmer is an imprint of the Taylor and Francis Group

© 2002 Mike Wallace and Keith Pocklington

Typeset in Bembo by
Keystroke, Jacaranda Lodge, Wolverhampton
Printed and bound in Great Britain by
St Edmundsbury Press, Bury St Edmunds, Suffolk

British Library Cataloguing in Publication Data
A catalogue record for this book is available from the British Library

Library of Congress Cataloging in Publication Data
A catalog record has been requested

ISBN 0–415–20096–2 (hbk)
ISBN 0–415–20097–0 (pbk)

Contents

Figures

Tables

Foreword

Complexity is not an easy concept to work with. As Wallace and Pocklington discuss, complex educational change operates on a grand scale, it consists of diverse, overlapping components, it reaches across education system levels, it affects stakeholders very differently, and it is heavily influenced by contextual factors. *Managing Complex Educational Change* is a rare and intriguing book. It is unique among studies that use a theory of complexity in order to unravel real cases of educational reform – cases which take into account the content of policies and the multilevels of action and interaction among stakeholders.

Other studies have used the 'Triple I' model of initiation, implementation and institutionalisation to analyse single innovations (Fullan, 2001a). Wallace and Pocklington use this same model in a much more sophisticated way. They first examine *context*, which by definition requires them to take into account multiple innovations impinging on local education authorities. They then work through the dynamics of actual policy innovations across the three stages of initiation, implementation and institutionalisation. The result is an insightful appraisal of the real complexity of educational reform.

Managing Complex Educational Change is pursued through the dynamic interplay of theory and practice. The end result is that the authors are able to develop a theory of knowledge that is truly grounded in the reality of multifaceted reform, while at the same time accessible to the reader and amenable to action. They conclude with a powerful framework that cross-links the five characteristics of complexity (large-scale, componential, systemic, differentially impacting, and contextually dependent) to four 'change management themes'.

The four themes are: first, the metatask of orchestration (absolutely key in order to work on coherence-making in response to the endemic problem of multiple innovations colliding – see Fullan, 2001b); second, flexible planning and co-ordination (again, crucial when change unfolds in a non-linear fashion, and must be adapted to during the journey); third, culture building and communication (in which vision-building is a continuous process); and fourth, differential support which must be targeted to the range of stakeholders and capacities and evolving needs.

Managing Complex Educational Change lives up to its title. It draws us into the real world of messy, multifaceted educational change, leads us through a journey of learning, and leaves us with an understanding of the truly complex phenomenon of educational reform. We are left with a greater appreciation of educational change, and a set of ideas, tools and insights for taking productive action. Above all, it leaves us with hope as we realise that even complexity is not beyond our reach of understanding.

Michael Fullan
Ontario Institute for Studies in Education
University of Toronto
February 2002

References

Fullan, M (2001a) *The New Meaning of Educational Change* (3rd Edn), New York: Teachers College Press and London: RoutledgeFalmer.

Fullan, M (2001b) *Leading in a Culture of Change*, San Francisco: Jossey-Bass.

Preface

The primary purpose of this book is to move forward the theoretical understanding of contemporary educational change by identifying patterns in its complexity with management implications, and by exploring the extent and limits of its potential manageability. The secondary purpose is to generate practical themes for rendering complex educational change as manageable as possible inside the inherent limits. To achieve these purposes we draw on our recent research into what we have conceived as a complex educational change, an investigation of large-scale reorganisation of schools in England during the late 1990s. The findings constitute the source of the patterns in complexity and of the change management themes we identify. We suggest that they may have wider applicability beyond reorganisation of schools to other complex changes elsewhere, and offer an agenda for further research.

Given our ambitions for the book, it was never going to be simple to write. Focusing on the complexity of a major educational change presented us with quite a challenge, initially as investigators and later as would-be communicators. In reporting on research into the reorganisation of schools we faced an inescapable tension. We wanted to remain faithful to the complexity of the change process by portraying something of its intricacy, ambiguity, interconnectedness, and convoluted causality. To do so it was necessary to employ an eclectic conceptual framework with a multiplicity of elements in synthesising our findings to reveal patterns in that complexity. We were aware that finely detailed portrayal of such a complex phenomenon risked inducing information overload through a surfeit of factual minutiae. Conversely, synthesis and explanation risked inducing conceptual overload through a surfeit of free-floating abstractions whose derivation from findings and their applicability to other contexts might remain undemonstrated.

We took up the challenge of addressing complexity head-on as a first step in moving away from what we regard as overly reductionist single-perspective or atheoretical analyses of educational change. There a simplistic account of the complex reality experienced by practitioners is too often the price paid for clear description and straightforward prescription. Yet focusing on the nature of complexity itself can alleviate the problem of reductionism only to a certain degree. It is a truism that any portrayal is bound to be selective and any synthesis will be limited to the range of concepts and generalisations that can feasibly be grasped. Here we hope to have reached a fruitful compromise between detailed reporting and conceptualisation.

We are centrally concerned with managing complex educational change. Large-scale reorganisation of schooling, in a particular context, is interpreted as one instance of this phenomenon. It provides an empirical starting point for inductive exploration of complex educational change, but its wider relevance has yet to be tested. We have addressed ourselves to an international audience and so have assumed that readers may not be familiar with the English education system at the time of our research. It should be borne in mind that our treatment of the national and local policy context of reorganisation is confined to whatever seemed most relevant to the management of this complex change. A partial summary of the system of state education in England during the 1990s is set out at the beginning of the book as a reference point for readers. But we have covered only those elements of the system structure and the stakeholders involved in the school reorganisation initiatives we studied. Several elements of the system were undergoing change during the time of our research, such as the national agency for school inspection. Others have changed since, like the grant-maintained schools policy and the legislative framework governing school reorganisation – not least because ministers of the present British central government have endeavoured to solve the kinds of problem following from their predecessors' policies that featured in this investigation. A series of matrices throughout our account of reorganisation provide further reference points. They constitute summaries that frame the detailed exploration of different aspects of its complexity.

It is also a truism that complex educational change is non-linear. Yet a book describing it has to be linear as there must be an order of presentation that minimises repetition. As a result, we have employed extensive cross-referencing to highlight where earlier topics are picked up in later chapters. Our hunch is that characteristics of complexity and their management implications identified in the present study may be applicable at some level of abstraction to other changes in other contexts. We invite readers engaging with this text to consider the extent to which these generalisations may resonate with their experience of other changes in the field of education or elsewhere.

Our research was funded by a grant from the Economic and Social Research Council (reference number R000236059). We are indebted to the many informants in central government, the two research LEAs and the eighteen of their schools where we conducted case studies, and especially to the senior LEA officials and headteachers who enabled us to work in their organisations. All our informants willingly gave up the time required for our interviews despite their frequently heavy workload. Their readiness to talk frankly about their experiences enabled us to explore complexities of reorganisation in some depth. Jan Gray, the project manager at the School of Education at Cardiff University, transcribed the large number of interview summary tapes. Keith Pocklington undertook case studies in one LEA and its schools, conducted a preliminary analysis of all the case study data, wrote thematic summaries of the findings, formulated some of the supporting exemplification, and commented on draft chapters. Mike Wallace directed the project, developed the conceptualisation of complex educational change, undertook case studies in the other LEA and its schools, synthesised the data, and composed the text for this book.

Keith Pocklington wishes to express his deep appreciation for the boundless patience displayed by Jan Ascoli. She provided much practical support, working on countless drafts of analytic summaries and illustrative examples, highlighting inconsistencies and instances of repetition, and waging war on jargon and acronyms. Mike Wallace would like to acknowledge Alison Wray's intellectual contribution to the conceptualisation of the research, her help with clarifying issues when perplexity ruled, and her timely reminders that there is more to life than book-writing.

Acronyms and abbreviations

CE	Church of England
CEO	chief education officer
DES	Department of Education and Science
DFE	Department for Education
DfEE	Department for Education and Employment
DoE	Department of the Environment
GM	grant-maintained
HMI	Her Majesty's Inspector
LEA	local education authority
LMS	local management of schools
MOE	more open enrolment
MP	Member of Parliament
Nimbyism	not in my backyard
OFSTED	Office for Standards in Education
RC	Roman Catholic
SMT	senior management team
SN	standard number
VA	voluntary aided
VC	voluntary controlled
VPR	voluntary premature retirement

1 Change gets complicated

This book makes a start on addressing three questions with great significance for the future of education. Why is educational change becoming increasingly complex? Are there patterns in this complexity? How may managers cope effectively with complex educational change? As a basis for seeking some preliminary answers to these general questions, we will focus on the specific complex educational change represented by large-scale initiatives in England to reorganise schools during the last decade.

There can be little question that processes of social change are becoming more complex. For change is not what it used to be, whether in education or other areas of the public sector. And these days, there is a lot more of it about. Take educational provision in Britain. Time was when publicly funded education here amounted to a 'national service, locally administered' and Griffiths (1971: 7) could comment that 'the English educational system is decentralised, untidy and, compared with European [sic] systems, unique in its relative freedom from control by the central government'.

In the domain of compulsory schooling, most planned change originated with professional staff (faculty) in organisations at the periphery of the education system. They were empowered to try out their own ideas; to choose from a menu of curriculum innovations developed by specialists whose publications were marketed in schools and colleges; and to pick from a range of in-service training courses run by professional advisers employed by the local education authority (LEA – the intermediate, district administrative level of the education system between central government and individual institutions). Although staff were technically accountable to the school governing body responsible for oversight of their work, most governors simply 'rubber stamped' their decisions. A career in teaching was a safe bet with prospects of job security for professional life, considerable autonomy over what went on inside the classroom and long holidays.

Occasionally the customary stability of schoolteachers' working life could be rudely interrupted by LEA initiatives to reorganise educational provision in the area, with central government backing as required in law. The postwar selective system for older students consisted of grammar schools for the academically most able and secondary modern schools for the rest. From the 1960s comprehensive schools serving the full ability range largely replaced this system. LEA officials were invited by central government ministers (DES 1965) to indicate their plans for comprehensivisation. The 'light touch' ministerial approach reflected the tradition of LEA control over state schooling (Griffiths 1971: 73):

> There was a permissiveness and conciliatory air about the whole thing; the Secretary of State 'requests' local authorities to prepare and submit their plans; he 'urges' them to consult him and 'hopes' or 'expects' that certain developments will occur. Part of this was a sort of ministerial badinage, but it also suggested that the delicate partnership between central and local government must be decorously maintained, and that the facts of the situation prohibited any quick or easy adoption of reorganisation schemes.

Accretion of reorganisation arrangements based on individual LEA preferences led to 'the most extraordinary melanges' of schools within an LEA with different ages of student transfer between schools, giving rise to a 'growing need for the eventual rationalisation of the entire system of secondary education' (Griffiths 1971: 98). The longstanding two-tier arrangement of primary and secondary schools where students transferred at the age of 11 was replaced in some LEAs by three-tier systems with middle schools for students aged 8–12 or 9–13. They were in part a pragmatic solution to the problem of maximising the use of existing buildings between a neighbouring grammar and secondary modern school, neither being large enough to cater for the full ability range of students. A grammar school often became a comprehensive high school while the neighbouring secondary modern school became a middle school. Central government stipulations precluded new building where existing buildings of sound quality were available (Hargreaves 1983).

Demographic changes led to the creation of new schools, especially in expanding towns and cities, alongside closure of rural schools in areas of population decline. The 1960s 'baby boom', together with a national policy in 1972 to raise students' school leaving age, brought rapid expansion of the education system followed by contraction when the birth rate fell away in the 1970s (Briault and Smith 1980). The resultant excess capacity was unevenly distributed in schools, soon becoming a target for local and central government policymakers. Maintaining the surplus student capacity imposed a significant burden on local and national taxation. Since taxes are perennially unpopular with voters, politicians in local and central government stood to favour their electoral chances if they could reduce this expenditure or use the savings to improve education services. But the attraction for taxpayers of receiving better value for their money was more than offset by the principle of 'nimbyism' (not in my back yard) for those whose community's school came under threat of the LEA axe. Parents from communities affected frequently resisted LEA initiatives to close or to merge schools. Firm proposals had to be published locally and submitted to central government. Many were rejected, leaving LEA officials with the task of seeking a new solution to their surplus capacity problem (Ranson 1990).

It was never straightforward to manage sporadic major changes such as comprehensivisation or contraction initiated by national and local policymakers for implementation in schools. This was and is a sizeable education system, with authority distributed unequally between a variety of stakeholders at central government, LEA and school levels. Its history stretches back into the nineteenth century, so traditions dating back many years might easily be transgressed by contemporary changes in new structural arrangements and educational practices.

Reorganising schools in a complex education system

The pattern of governance for most publicly funded schools determines stakeholders' involvement across the three main administrative levels of the English education system (Table 1.1). By the 1990s, the period covered by our study, cumulative changes in democratic government nationally and locally and in the administration of state education had brought about the following arrangement. At central government level, *ministers* from the elected majority political party regulated the nature, overall resourcing, and governance of the national system of state-funded education. They could legislate to create parameters for reorganisation. Professional *civil servants* acted as their executives, based in the central government department responsible for education. (The brief and the name of this department changed twice during the period covered by our research and has changed once since, but its involvement with reorganisation was unaffected. To avoid confusion, we have referred to it throughout as the Department for Education and Employment (DfEE), its name from 1995 to 2001.) *Her Majesty's Inspectors* (HMI) acted as ministers' 'eyes and ears', providing independent advice based on their monitoring of educational provision across the country. Legislation in 1992 led to the establishment of a new central government agency for inspection of schools, the Office for Standards in Education (OFSTED). The agency continued to be administered by a core group of HMI, but most school inspections were now contracted to inspection teams whose members had received OFSTED training.

Ministers were drawn from the ranks of *Members of Parliament* (MPs), which included their colleagues in government and members of other political parties in opposition. All MPs represented a constituency (most LEAs contained several). They provided a direct link between national government and school communities, being in a position to bring concerns arising at that level to ministers' attention.

At local government level, *councillors* or 'elected members' in the majority political party formed the *ruling group* of each local *council*, with jurisdiction over a borough or county district. The *leader of the council* (a member of the ruling group) chaired council meetings. Each borough or county council was responsible for local taxation which part-funded schooling through its LEA. The council had an education committee chaired by a councillor from the ruling group, with membership drawn from all councillors. Members of the education committee could make recommendations to be ratified by the full council. LEA

Table 1.1 Structure of the English education system relevant to school reorganisation (mid-1990s)

Main stakeholders	Source of authority	Contribution to operation of the education system
Central government (national) level		
Secretary of State and other ministers in the Department for Education and Employment (DFEE)	Members of Parliament from the political party gaining a majority of seats in Parliament at the last general election	Determining the nature and resourcing of state educational provision on behalf of central government
ministers in the Department of the Environment (DoE)	Members of Parliament from the political party gaining a majority of seats in Parliament at the last general election	Regulating the level of local government taxation, so affecting LEA expenditure on school provision
Civil servants	Central government employees	Acting for ministers in developing and implementing central government policies (the DFEE territorial team had a regional brief)
Her Majesty's Inspectors (HMIs)	Central government employees	Monitoring the quality of educational provision and advising central government ministers (district HMIs had a regional brief) administering the national system of school inspection within The Office for Standards in Education (OFSTED), a central government agency
Constituency Members of Parliament (MPs)	One representative for each constituency who gained a majority of votes at the last general election, a member of the political party in government or one in opposition	Responding to concerns expressed by voters in their constituency, lobbying local councillors and central government ministers on their behalf
LEA (local government) level		
Local councillors in the ruling group of the local council	Members of the political party gaining a majority of local council seats at the last local election	Developing and implementing local government policies within central government parameters
Local (borough or county) council	One representative for each ward within the borough or county who gained a majority of votes at the last local election, a member of the political party of the ruling group or one in opposition, diocesan representatives	Local government body whose responsibilities included local taxation and educational provision within central government parameters

Education committee of the local council	Members of the local council and diocesan representatives	Developing and implementing local government policies relating to educational provision
LEA officials (officers and inspectors)	Local council employees	Acting for the local council in developing and implementing local government policies relating to educational provision
Local school staff union representatives	Representatives of union members (e.g. teachers, headteachers) in schools	Representing the interests of union members in negotiation with LEA officials and local councillors

School level

Governing body	Representatives of stakeholder groups connected with each school (LEA, staff, parents, local community)	Overseeing the management of each school, including the operating budget and staff selection
Headteacher	LEA employee	Managing the school within the oversight of the governing body, some teaching
Other teaching and support staff	LEA employees	Teaching and learning, managing and providing ancillary support under the leadership of the headteacher

Regional diocesan authority for church schools operating at LEA level (CE, RC)

Diocesan board of education	Representatives of stakeholder groups connected with the religious character of church schools	Responsibilities include church school provision, religious education in church schools
Diocesan representatives	Employees of the diocesan board	Acting for the diocesan board in managing church school provision

officials were professionals acting as executives for the council. They consisted of *officers* with responsibility for administering educational provision led by the *chief education officer* (CEO) and *LEA inspectors* concerned with monitoring and improving its quality. One duty of LEAs was to regulate the supply of student places, extending to reorganisation initiatives if deemed necessary. Formal links were established with school staff unions. Many staff were members of *trade unions* or professional associations, some of which had a representative drawn from members in each school. This person liaised with local union or professional association representatives who were consulted by LEA officials and councillors on matters affecting their union or professional association members.

At the individual school level, elected or co-opted members of the *governing body* for each school represented parents whose children attended the institution, the wider local community, the LEA (drawn primarily from councillors serving on the education committee), and school staff. A clerk to the governors – often an LEA official – serviced every governing body. Governors' responsibilities included appointing school staff according to an annual budget covering their salaries, set by the LEA within central government parameters. *Headteachers* (principals) attended school governing body meetings and could decide whether to accept governor status and therefore the entitlement to vote on governing body decisions. They were responsible for the day-to-day running of their school within the oversight of the governing body.

A further administrative complication arose from the substantial number of *Church of England* (CE) and *Roman Catholic* (RC) *church schools*, originally established through church bodies or charitable trusts. The inheritance of distant educational history, they had become especially significant in reorganisation of schools. Central government legislation in 1944 brought these schools under state control as voluntary schools and so within the jurisdiction of LEAs, which were also responsible for setting up new county schools (Nice 1992; Mackinnon *et al.* 1996). Responsibility for administration of church schools in each LEA was shared with the CE or RC regional *diocesan authority* concerned. Each designated region or diocese spanned one or more neighbouring LEAs and was divided into many parishes, some containing church schools. Clergy and laypeople held administrative responsibility for diocesan authority concerns, typically chaired by the bishop of the diocese. Among them were *diocesan representatives*, responsible for education provision in schools supported by the diocese. At school level, the vicar (CE) or priest (RC) of the parish where a church school was located would commonly be the chair of governors. Voluntary schools were subdivided into *voluntary controlled* or *voluntary aided*, the latter retaining greater independence, mostly over religious matters, in return for provision of some financial support by the diocesan authorities (Table 1.2). (The full picture was even more complicated. A few schools whose governance was similar to that of voluntary aided schools were established by 'special agreement'. They are omitted from the table since none featured prominently in our research. For details see Nice 1992.)

Diocesan authorities had to be consulted over any LEA reorganisation initiatives affecting their church schools. While LEA proposals could be put forward to cease to maintain voluntary aided schools, governors alone could initiate proposals to close or open them or to change their status, say, from voluntary aided to voluntary controlled. Proposals for voluntary aided schools had to receive both governing body and LEA backing in practice.

Incremental development of the national education system increased the complexity of the context into which new educational changes were introduced. In the light of his study of British education policy making during the calm period of postwar consensus, Kogan (1978: 158–9) reflected:

> In the 1960s it seemed possible to state the aims and purposes of education and to find its means. Instead . . . sophisticated indeterminacy describes policy process as incremental and disjointed. It rejects rationalistic attempts to predict what people need and to find the means of achieving it.
>
> The educational planner cannot rely on any particular model of change. He [*sic*] must accept that changes are not linear. No fixed sequence of time

Table 1.2 Administration of 'county' and 'voluntary' schools in England during the mid–1990s

Administration	Type of School		
	County	Voluntary controlled (VC)	Voluntary aided (VA)
Origin	Established by the LEA	Established by a voluntary body (church authority). The large majority of VC schools are Church of England (CE)	Established by a voluntary body. About half of VA schools are Church of England (CE) and half are Roman Catholic (RC)
Responsibility for providing premises	LEA	Voluntary body	Voluntary body
Funding sources for new building	LEA (central government loan)	LEA (central government loan)	Voluntary body (85% through a central government grant, and a discretionary loan for the remaining 15%)
Financial arrangements for provision of schooling	LEA	LEA	The voluntary body is responsible for external repairs and maintenance, assisted by an 85% LEA grant. The LEA is responsible for running costs, internal repairs, and staff salaries
Formal control	LEA and governing body	LEA and governing body. Members of the voluntary body nominate one-third of governors	Governing body and LEA. Members of the voluntary body nominate two-thirds of governors, so controlling admission of students and staff appointments
Employment of staff	LEA	LEA	Governing body
Provision of religious instruction	Must offer non-denominational religious instruction to all students	Can offer denominational religious instruction to students whose parents request it	Can offer denominational instruction to all students
Authority to propose reorganisation	LEA	Councillors in the LEA may propose to cease to maintain a VC school, the governors may serve at least two years' notice on central government and the LEA	Councillors in the LEA may propose to cease to maintain a VA school, the governors may serve at least two years' notice on central government and the LEA

and logic as between the different components can be discerned. Within the policy process it is impossible to sort out causes from effects and components can be latent, biding their time for a change of circumstances, or dynamic, or simply never happen. Moreover, there is sedimentation of many of the more important elements. Institutions, curricula, resource distributions, buildings, all represent an accretion of historic commitments which need not be outmoded but which are the result of interaction between components of the past and the potent present.

Even then, policy shifts embodied more factors than policymakers could feasibly take into account, foremost being the legacy of past changes. Causal linkages between factors could be ambiguous, their expression and interaction unpredictable. Greater complexity was soon to follow.

The nature and scope of educational change were to alter dramatically here and in other western countries during the 1980s as government ministers turned to reforming education on a grand scale. In the UK, the year 1986 ushered in the present era of central government intervention in state education. Triggers for reforms included burgeoning public expenditure alongside perceived failure of the state education system – despite huge investment of public money in it – to provide the kind of skilled and flexible workforce which could compete with other advanced and newly industrialised nations in what was fast becoming a global economy. Consequently the era of small-scale, school-based innovations within a national service, locally administered, is long over. If ministers get their way the marketisation of state schools, centralisation of the curriculum, its assessment and surveillance, and modernisation of the teaching profession will turn the English education system into a 'community enterprise, nationally directed, steered and disciplined'. One certainty in the turbulent environment of perpetual reform is having to cope with externally driven changes, ever more complex and so more intractable to manage – not least because of the central government attempt to direct, steer, and discipline those at other education system levels held responsible for putting central government policies into practice.

Education professionals with management responsibility must cope with the unprecedented complexity of education reforms, the tasks of implementing them, and the new regime they imply. A sizeable minority also face the largely unpublicised and undocumented tasks of managing large-scale initiatives to reorganise schooling, whose interaction with reforms and other ongoing work piles complexity on to complexity. Few planned changes in education can arouse such hostility, make such a radical and even terminal impact on the career of teachers and headteachers, and have such a long term impact on parents, students, and their communities as these reorganisation initiatives. Managing change seems unlikely to get much more complicated and emotionally demanding than this. Reorganisation of schooling in an era of educational reform offers a paradigm case of complex educational change.

From acknowledging complexity to prescribing practice: missing links?

There is an urgent need to unpack the complexity of change to inform guidance for those who must deal with it. Fullan (1993), one of the first commentators to acknowledge how the nature of educational change was changing, has proposed that a new paradigm for understanding is needed that embraces its growing 'dynamic complexity'. Yet much practical advice on managing change has not so far kept pace with the shift in the complexity of change itself. On the one hand, there is no shortage of prescriptive models resting on the outdated assumption born of more stable times that change is potentially amenable to strong managerial control through rationalistic means (Wallace 1998a), couched in terms such as 're-engineering' (Davies 1997), or 'self-management' (Caldwell and Spinks 1988). Such models tend to be overly mechanistic, amounting to 'splendidly rational blueprints for an unreal world' (Hoyle 1986a: 15). If the managerial milieu ever was stable enough to allow narrow specification of the diverse and diffuse educational aims of school staff and governors, costing of means for their achievement, and uninterrupted progress towards their realisation, then it surely is no longer.

The bulk of this guidance ignores the policy 'big picture', source of so many constraints on managerial control (Whitty *et al.* 1998). UK reforms to marketise schooling were launched with accompanying ministerial rhetoric about empowering headteachers and governing bodies. The local management of schools (LMS) initiative gave them greater control over the operating budget and hiring of teachers, hitherto the province of LEAs. They could now dip into the finances to market their school to parents. Simultaneously, control over what students learned was centralised through the introduction of a mandatory National Curriculum and its assessment, backed by regular external inspection. Headteachers and governors certainly were empowered – to implement new central government requirements. Any who failed to do so could be identified through national tests and the beefed-up inspection regime, publicly 'named and shamed', and subjected to measures designed to bring them back into line. Decentralising control over inessentials (such as freedom to improve efficiency through creative budgeting) while centralising control over essentials (such as the curriculum) was part of a wider strategy across the public sector (Taylor-Gooby and Lawson 1993).

On the other hand, the small amount of guidance for managers in education (e.g. Fullan 1993, 1999) and elsewhere (e.g. Stacey 1992, 1996) which does commendably square up to 'dynamic complexity' has had to rely more on striking metaphor than hard evidence. Such writers tend to move straight from acknowledging the significance of complexity to appropriating various concepts, lifting them from their original context and applying them directly to another very different realm as a foundation of prescriptive 'lessons' for managing complex change. Given the current state of our knowledge, this strategy rests on a considerable conceptual and empirical leap of faith. First, the conception of complexity on which many writers draw originates with complexity and chaos theory in mathematics and its application in the natural sciences (Gleick 1988). They take key concepts such as 'self-organisation' and employ them impressionistically as loose metaphors to describe and prescribe human interaction in organisations. Take Stacey's (1996: 330) account of chaos theory's explanation of a laser beam. As a gas is heated, the molecules in it become more unstable, increasing their random movement until they come to a critical point where they:

> appear to communicate with each other and suddenly they organise themselves to all point in the same direction. The result is a laser beam casting its light for miles. The sudden choice of molecules all to point in the same direction is not predictable from the laws of physics. There is no central intention or law prescribing this behaviour; it emerges out of instability through a self-organising creative process.

Self-organisation inside an organisation is 'the spontaneous formation of interest groups and coalitions around specific issues, communication about those issues, cooperation and the formation of consensus on and commitment to a response to those issues' (Stacey 1996: 333). The prescription follows that senior managers in situations of some uncertainty should provide conditions which foster creative problem solving through spontaneous self-organisation.

It is possible to draw a parallel between behaviour of molecules in a heated gas and people coming together to tackle an issue they have identified by conceiving the former as a metaphor for the latter. But at what cost in terms of distortion or oversimplification? Minsky points out how metaphors merely draw our attention to some similarity between otherwise distinct entities. They are useful only where parallels are sufficient to offer a coherent set of connected insights into the entity to which they are applied. He refers to the concepts of any interpretive framework as a 'uniframe', noting that:

> Good metaphors are useful because they transport uniframes, intact, from one world into another. Such cross-realm correspondences can enable us to transport entire families of problems into other realms, in which we can apply them to some already well-developed skills. However, such correspondences are hard to find since most reformulations merely transform the uniframes of one realm into disorderly accumulation in the other realm.

> (Minsky 1985: 299)

The natural and social worlds are fundamentally different. The social world obeys a 'double hermeneutic' (Giddens 1976): actors under scrutiny, as well as analysts, come to their own interpretation of what is happening, and analysts' ideas can filter down to these actors and affect their behaviour. Actors possess 'agency' to the extent that they could do otherwise; they have some choice of alternative actions according to their interpretation of their situation.

Structuration theory (Giddens 1984) draws our attention to the way actors' behaviour is not narrowly determined, though their agency will have limits imposed by social structures that are themselves the largely unwitting product of agency. The seductiveness of Stacey's transport of uniframes from natural to social worlds rests on a linguistic sleight of hand disguising the resultant 'disorderly accumulation'. He minimises the gap between gaseous and human contexts by anthropomorphising the gas molecules! What sense does it make to imply that they 'communicate' with each other, 'organise themselves' or make a 'choice' to point in the same direction? Such language is used to make the analogy seem closer that managers can create conditions where other people in situations of uncertainty are likely to organise themselves spontaneously or to choose to work towards a shared goal. Chaos theory has proved an irresistible 'strange attractor' to many natural and social scientists who, according to Horgan (1997), are guilty of 'over-reaching': extending the application of the metaphor beyond the limits of its conceptual or empirical utility.

Second, even if we were to accept wholesale transport of uniframes from the natural to the social world, a question would remain over the applicability of such ideas between social contexts. Suppose that conditions for self-organisation can be created in the lightly regulated context of private sector organisations, although it smacks of wishful thinking to assume that workers will spontaneously congregate only around issues acceptable to managers. (A notorious incident in a British car factory during the 1970s springs to mind. Nightshift workers spontaneously collaborated in solving the issue of how to get some paid sleep. They brought in sleeping bags and set up camp by the assembly line.) The public sector is more heavily regulated and subject to much greater state intervention, so it cannot be a foregone conclusion that a strategy that works in, say, a multinational corporation will produce the same results in state schools.

Third, these conceptual difficulties point to the empirical one: the missing link here is evidence from the context to which the new ideas are applied. Such writers are short on the intermediate step of investigating patterns in the complexity of change and its management in the systems of organisations to which their advice relates. Evidence of this kind could provide the grounding for more fine-grained and context-sensitive guidance.

That is the starting point for our work. Our intellectual 'project' (Bolam 1999) is to develop the sort of 'knowledge for understanding' (Hoyle 1986a) that could in principle inform the future development of more realistic 'knowledge for action' than most current practical guidance. The latter tends to overplay the extent of managers' agency and underplay its limits. We ask the relatively impartial question 'what happens and why?' as a necessary precursor to the more strongly normative question 'how may practice be improved?'. Our focus is the intermediate step of exploring characteristics and the management of complex educational change, employing a pluralistic theoretical orientation originating in the social sciences. The analysis is inductive, illustrated by research into reorganisation of schooling in the context of education reform – our paradigm case of complex change. The book is a research report but the patterns in complexity we reveal may resonate with other contexts. We hope to contribute in the longer term towards practical guidance which more fully reflects the complexity of educational change that managers out there actually face. It must speak to their lived experience that managing complex change entails the endemic 'organisational pathos' (Hoyle 1986b) of struggling to manage the unmanageable. It should be constructed on a firmer conceptual and empirical foundation than yesterday's 'hyperrationalism' (Wise 1983), the outmoded legacy of an era when change was simpler, and what may be termed today's 'hyper-conceptualisation'. Theorists such as Stacey may have built a more sophisticated edifice of borrowed concepts embracing contemporary complexity, but the application of these concepts to other domains has over-reached the necessary empirical underpinning.

Researching large-scale reorganisation of schooling

Most recent British research relevant to managing change in schools has been reform-focused (Wallace and Weindling 1999), foregrounding a particular policy. The rest of ongoing work, including other reforms, is construed as context or background. Our study reversed that focus by foregrounding reorganisation, not generally conceived as a reform. Other ongoing work including the implementation of various reforms constituted the context for activities to manage reorganisation. The latter impacted reciprocally on everything else being managed. Large-scale reorganisation initiatives were under-researched. Yet studies of planning in schools undergoing reorganisation (Wallace and McMahon 1994) and a pilot study for our research suggested just how complex a change reorganisation could be. Interaction between central and local government policies (Wallace 1996a) impacted on LEA reorganisation initiatives, and mergers could prove problematic before and after reorganisation (Wallace 1996b).

These initiatives might entail an LEA-wide programme of school closures and mergers, significant expansion of schools, a change in the student age range for which schools catered (known as a 'change in character'), new building work and refurbishment of existing buildings. Staff in these schools might face years of job insecurity. Depending on individuals' age and the content of proposals for reorganising particular schools, their prospects might include:

- compulsory redundancy (unilateral termination of their employment by the LEA, which was formally their employer)
- voluntary redundancy (resigning from their post and accepting a sum in compensation equivalent to over a year's salary or wages)
- premature retirement (resigning from their post before the normal retirement age)
- redeployment (transfer to a surviving school) bringing the experience of learning to work with a new group of colleagues and students in the institutions surviving reorganisation.

Formally, reorganisation initiatives comprised two parts. First, formative LEA proposals to change provision of schooling were published and stakeholders in the locality were consulted. Firm proposals were drawn up and submitted to the Secretary of State at the DfEE. He or she decided whether they should be given central government approval, especially where they generated objections. Second, it was an LEA responsibility to put into effect uncontentious proposals and any others winning approval. This process was officially completed on the date set for reorganisation.

The substantive aim of the research was to investigate how large-scale LEA initiatives to reorganise schooling were managed in LEAs and schools in the context of policy changes affecting reorganisation. Accordingly, the study concentrated both on what happened across the administrative levels of the education system and on the short-term consequences for school management after reorganisation. A subsidiary aim was to provide an evidence base for conceptualising the management of complex educational change. Large-scale reorganisation of schooling involved co-ordinated 'multilevel' interaction among individuals and groups within and between LEA and school levels of the education system and, to a lesser extent, central government. An earlier study of the management of multiple innovations in schools (Wallace 1991a, 1992) had highlighted how disjunction between activities at different education system levels could ensue because of limited communication between them. The opportunity was presented here to track interaction between LEA and school levels. The theoretical orientation guiding data collection and analysis was eclectic. It is introduced here and elaborated in Chapter 3.

We focused on the expression of agency in patterns of interaction between various stakeholders caught up in reorganisation. These patterns reflected stakeholders' attempts to channel others' agency in the direction they favoured through encouragement, and to delimit others' agency by attempting to pre-empt or correct any action that might transgress the limits of this favoured direction. Expression of agency by one individual or group of stakeholders could expand or reduce the agency of others with whom they interacted. We also considered the delimitation of some or all stakeholders' agency by structural factors that set broad parameters for interaction. Factors were both ideological, connected with educational, managerial and legal assumptions, and economic. We sought inductively to identify characteristics of reorganisation contributing to its complexity as a change which had to be managed. We discuss these characteristics in Chapter 2 and indicate in Chapter 3 how they reflect the working of agency inside certain limits.

Interaction within these limits was analysed through a pluralistic framework building on previous studies of educational change (Kogan 1975; Ranson 1990) that examined how stakeholders interacted in pursuing their interests. It incorporated a combined cultural and political perspective on interaction (Wallace and Hall 1994; Wallace and Huckman 1999) which facilitated investigation of stakeholders' employment of power to shape the culture of others and, recip-rocally, cultural determinants of their uses of power. The flow of interaction, especially across education system levels, was conceived as occurring within an extensive network (Nohria 1998) of stakeholders directly or indirectly related to each other. Fullan's (1991, 2001) conception of the origin, process and outcomes of single innovations guided our scrutiny of the dynamics of interaction as the reorganisation initiatives unfolded.

The context of reorganisation included other policies that affected LEA initiatives. Such policies and the reorganisation initiatives themselves entailed policymakers at different system levels selecting means of persuading others to put policies into practice. Means were categorised, following McDonnell and Elmore (1991), as a set of 'policy instruments'. We explored the efforts of stakeholders at local and school levels to mediate policies with which they disagreed by viewing their response as a form of 'counter-policy' (Wallace 1998b).

The thrust of reorganisation and these policies was regarded as part of the 'managerialist' project adopted in many western governments to increase efficiency and effectiveness in their public sector (Pollitt 1993; Clarke and Newman 1997). It is driven by increasingly harsher global economic conditions, imposing narrower limits on interaction within the reorganisation initiatives. Yet the state did not act monolithically in pursuing this project, internal contradictions generating further constraints on those charged with responsibility for seeing reorganisation through. Several British central government reforms were designed to curtail LEA formal powers yet, paradoxically, LEA officials and councillors were still expected to bring about large-scale reorganisation with much diminished authority over headteachers and governors. The complexity of managing reorganisation initiatives stemmed in part from the confrontation between the new order of authority devolved from LEAs to schools and the longstanding professional culture shared among LEA officials and school staff. Endurance of this culture in the face of reforms ending the old order of strong LEA control over schooling empowered officials to fulfil their responsibility for reorganisation despite their loss of authority.

A contradictory central government reform policy within the managerialist project significantly inhibited reorganisation initiatives from 1988. Parents, school staff, and governors were encouraged to 'opt out' of LEA control of their school by applying to the Secretary of State for grant-maintained (GM) status, whereby the school would be funded directly by central government at an advantageous rate (Bush *et al.* 1993). This policy provided a potential route for escaping closure or merger under LEA reorganisation proposals. Where this strategy was successful, surplus student capacity in the locality was perpetuated in these newly created GM schools. LEA officials and councillors responding to central government pressure to reorganise had to accept the risk of losing schools to the new GM sector.

Design and methods

The Economic and Social Research Council funded the research from January 1996 to September 1998. Our methods of investigation were qualitative: focused, interpretative case studies (Merriam 1988) at LEA and school levels, informed by techniques of data analysis developed by Miles and Huberman (1994) including the use of matrices to summarise findings. We negotiated access to investigate reorganisation initiatives already under way in a small metropolitan borough LEA containing an industrial town and outlying rural areas and in a large county LEA with both rural districts and market towns.

Initiatives in both LEAs comprised sequential annual phases of reorganisation in different areas. The Secretary of State had announced the decision on LEA proposals for the final phases of reorganisation just before the project began. We concentrated on activity to manage reorganisation in these schools and the experience of staff affected. Contemporaneous data collection in the borough covered more than a year before the reorganisation date of 1 September 1997 for the final phase and the succeeding term. In the county, data were collected in the term preceding reorganisation of the final tranche of schools on 1 September 1996 and for over a year afterwards. We also adopted a complementary retrospective focus on LEA proposal development and consultation activity and local community responses that had led up to submission of formal proposals.

Criteria for selecting schools reflected our concern to explore the complexity of reorganisation. We prioritised those institutions in the final phases that were scheduled under LEA proposals to undergo the most radical changes. More could be learned in these situations than in the institutions where scheduled changes were minor. Our sample included schools subject to linked proposals for groups of institutions in the same locality, and proposals which might encompass closures, mergers and extensive building programmes. It was important to include schools catering for younger and older students, as they tend to differ markedly in size and organisational complexity. Two schools in the county LEA were included where applications had been made to become grant-maintained to avoid LEA proposals. (No borough schools were in this category.) The eighteen case-study schools prior to reorganisation are listed and their fate under LEA proposals or escape through the GM route are summarised in Tables 1.3 and 1.4. After reorganisation, the number of case-study schools reduced to ten.

The reference to governance indicates whether each pre- or post-reorganisation institution was a *county*, *voluntary controlled*, or *voluntary aided* school, and therefore whether the appropriate diocesan authority was involved in negotiation over reorganisation proposals (see also Table 1.2). Additional contextual information in the borough was gathered on two expanding first schools and two closing middle schools in the same group or 'pyramid' as the case study institutions. In this LEA, grouping of schools into pyramids for administrative purposes was based on the locality or 'catchment area' to be served by each high school. Typically a high school received students from several nearby middle schools. They received their students in turn from a larger number of neighbouring first schools. Prior to reorganisation the research pyramid consisted of seven first schools, four middle schools and the high school, the latter operating on two sites as the outcome of a past merger (Figure 1.1). Contextual information in the county was gathered in one expanding high school. We also investigated

Table 1.3 Borough LEA case-study school sites and reorganisation arrangements

Area of borough LEA	School (and governance)	Pre-reorganisation school name	Reorganisation arrangements	Post-reorganisation school name
In the same pyramid of 7 first schools, 4 middle schools and 1 high school	13–18 high, split-site (county) 9–13 middle (county)	Hillside High Endale Middle	One existing high school site closed. Hillside High School expanded to become an 11–18 secondary school by receiving 11–13 year-old-students from the four closing middle schools in the pyramid. When Endale Middle School closed, its site became the 11–14 site of Hillside Secondary School	Hillside Secondary
	4–9 first county 9–13 middle (county)	Sedge First Sedge Middle	Both schools closed and were merged on Sedge Middle School site to create a new 4–11 primary school. 11–13-year-old students transferred to the secondary school. LEA officials disposed of the ex-Sedge First School site	Headland Primary

Note
Reorganisation took place over two years, completed in 1997.

retrospectively the involvement of central government civil servants with LEA proposals. Criteria for selecting informants were:

- at central government level – involvement in assessing proposals from the two LEAs
- at LEA level – centrality in managing reorganisation proposals and the implementation of those approved by central government, the range of responsibilities for management tasks affecting case study schools, and the range of stakeholders concerned with reorganisation proposals
- at school level – centrality in managing the implementation of reorganisation proposals, and the range of impacts on staff affected by reorganisation.

The excellent access to informants we were given enabled us to undertake an extensive programme of semi-structured interviews and to assemble a large

Table 1.4 County LEA case-study school sites and reorganisation arrangements

Area of county LEA	School (and governance)	Pre-reorganisation school name	Reorganisation arrangements	Post-reorganisation school name
Eastern area	4–8 first (CE VC)	Beacon First	All four schools closed and were merged on the former Brook Middle School site to form a new 4–11 voluntary aided primary school, using the former Beacon First School site as an annexe. LEA officials disposed of the former Highlane First School and former St Joan First School sites	Ridge Primary (annexe)
	4–8 first (CE VC)	Highlane First		
	4–8 first (RC VA)	St Joan First		
	8–12 middle (CE VA)	Brook Middle		Ridge Primary (main site)
	4–8 first (county)	Down First	The LEA merger proposal led to a successful application for Down First school to become a GM 4–8 school, subsequently a 4–7 infant school. Down Middle School became a 7–11 junior school	Down GM Infant
	8–12 middle (CE VA)	Down Middle		Down Junior
North-eastern area	4–8 first (CE VC)	Capston First	Both schools closed and were merged on the former Farfield First School site to form a new 4–11 voluntary controlled primary school. LEA officials disposed of the former Capston First School site	Bigtree Primary
	4–8 first (CE VC)	Farfield First		
Central area	4–8 first (CE VA)	Newell First	Both schools closed and were merged on a new site to form a 4–11 voluntary aided primary school. LEA officials disposed of the former Newell First School site. Moor First became an independent school	Newell Primary
	4–8 first (CE VC)	Moor First		Moor (independent)

Table 1.4 (Continued)

Area of county LEA	School (and governance)	Pre-reorganisation school name	Reorganisation arrangements	Post-reorganisation school name
Southern area	4–11 primary (county)	Lake Primary	Both schools closed and were merged on Lake Primary School site to form a new 4–11 county primary. LEA officials disposed of the former Lowrise Primary School site	Lake Primary
	4–11 primary (county)	Lowrise Primary		
	4–11 primary (CE VC)	Dale Primary	The LEA merger proposal led to a successful application for Dale Primary School to become GM. Southlip Primary remained unchanged	Dale GM Primary
	4–11 primary (CE VC)	Southlip Primary		Southlip Primary

Note
Reorganisation took place in one year, with transfer of all students in 1996.

document archive. We aimed to interview representatives from all the main stakeholder groups while also tracking the process of managing reorganisation within and between system levels. Most informants were interviewed once whilst a minority were interviewed up to five times, depending on their centrality in managing aspects of reorganisation across the fieldwork period. Indicatively, we interviewed two LEA officers in the borough on five termly occasions because they were responsible for reallocating staff in the pyramid that included our case study schools. Their work on this task continued beyond the reorganisation date until the fate of all displaced staff was settled. The headteacher of the high school was also interviewed termly before and after reorganisation because he was responsible for preparation and also for developing the school after reorganisation. Those informants we interviewed on one occasion included:

- central government civil servants at the DfEE who had assessed case study LEA proposals
- senior local councillors who had played a key part in formulating proposals
- LEA officials with specialist responsibility for an aspect of reorganisation
- diocesan authority representatives who negotiated the fate of schools for which they shared control with the LEA
- local teacher and headteacher union representatives seeking to protect their members whose careers and working conditions were affected by reorganisation

Pyramid of schools *before* reorganisation (the four case-study schools have a bold outline)

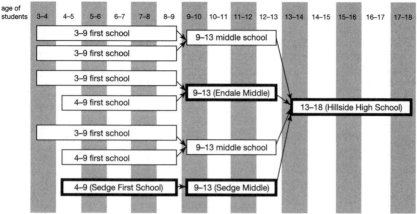

Pyramid of schools *after* reorganisation (the two case-study schools have a bold outline)

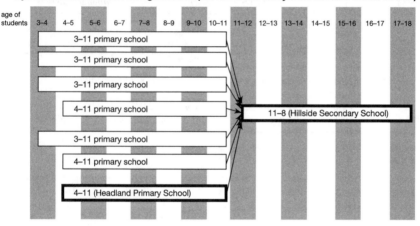

Figure 1.1 Borough LEA pyramid of schools containing case-study school sites

- teachers who had recently experienced redeployment
- school site managers (janitors) whose jobs, and in one instance whose home on the school campus, were threatened by LEA merger proposals
- chairs of governors from closing schools.

In all, 325 confidential interviews were conducted with 188 informants: a fifth with LEA officials; three-quarters with school staff and governors; the remainder with central government civil servants (Table 1.5).

Our integrated approach to data collection and analysis facilitated progressive focusing as the study unfolded. We derived the research questions from the

Table 1.5 Profile of interviews

LEA level	LEA officials and others interviewed								
	Senior officer	Officer	Senior inspector	Inspector	Senior councillor	Union represen-tative	Diocesan represen-tative	Pressure group leader	Total
Borough									
Number of informants	6	6	1	3	2	2	1	–	21
Number of interviews	12	11	1	3	2	2	1	–	32
County									
Number of informants	5	12	1	6	2	3	2	1	32
Number of interviews	8	19	4	10	2	3	2	1	49

Central government level	Senior Inspector (OFSTED)	Inspector (regional base)	Official (DFEE Territorial Team)	Total
Informants interviewed	1 once	1	3	5

School level	Schools in the borough				Schools in the county			
	Head-teacher	Other senior staff	Other staff	Governor	Head-teacher	Other senior staff	Other staff	Governor
Sp 96	4	–	–	–	8	–	–	1
Su 96	4	9	6	2	16	1	15	10
	first part of reorganisation September				reorganisation completed September			
Au 96	4 (+2)	9	4	2	7 (+1)	1 (+3)	16	8
Sp 97	4(+2)	8	9	–	1	1 (+6)	5 (+2)	–
Su 97	4	6	8	1	6	2	18	3
	reorganisation completed September							
Au 97	2	10	6	1	– (+1)	–	–	–
Total	22 (+4)	42	33	6	38 (+2)	5 (+9)	54 (+2)	22
	(Figures in parentheses refer to interviews with two middle school and two first school headteachers in the same pyramid of schools)				(Figures in parantheses refer to interviews with the headteacher and other staff of a secondary school undergoing a change in character)			
Number of informants	= 49 (borough)				= 81 (county)			
Number of interviews	= 107 (borough)				= 132 (county)			

Note

Time: Sp = spring term, Su = summer term, Au = autumn term

literature, the pilot study and our pluralistic perspective, to which detailed interview questions related. We tape recorded interviews and took fieldnotes, then prepared summary tapes by referring to the interview schedules, fieldnotes, tapes and documents. These summaries, including our interpretations and direct quotations to back them, were transcribed and collated. They formed the basis for within-site and cross-site analysis. We developed matrices to display data and scanned the data set to identify themes and to explore the contextual complexity of particular interactions. With each informant we negotiated a confidentiality agreement that no individual, school or LEA would be identified in publications arising from the study. Officials of the two LEAs declined our offer of feedback after fieldwork was completed. Senior officials most centrally involved in the LEA case studies and, where contactable, headteachers of case-study schools featuring prominently in the book were invited to comment on a draft of the relevant chapters.

Strengths and limitations of the research

Getting to grips with such a complex change is hard research work producing many challenges and compromise decisions. A qualitative approach appeared to offer the best chance of exploring the diversity of concerns, feelings, levels of awareness, actions and experiences of the people at different system levels who struggled to make sense of the reorganisation process. Since making meaning lies at the heart of educational change (Fullan 2001), it was essential that we put ourselves in the privileged position of gathering the perceptions of people at each system level. Whilst we ended up knowing less than any informants about their unique experience of reorganisation, we did gain a unique overview of the aggregate of experiences and their reciprocal impact. The theoretical orientation and pilot study enabled us to focus the research from the outset and work inductively, remaining open to surprises which data collection soon brought, and being ready to modify our plans accordingly.

The corollary of adopting an exclusively qualitative approach and concentrating on a few case studies was that our depth of understanding was bought at the expense of generalisability in the sense of our findings being representative of reorganisation experiences elsewhere. Nevertheless it should be borne in mind that the reforms impacting on reorganisation were national and so probably affected other reorganisation initiatives at the time. The similarities between strategies for managing reorganisation in two contrasting LEAs suggest that, while there was room for agency in following alternative courses of action and response, it was narrowly delimited by structural forces reflected in reform policies. We disseminated our findings with practical implications at a national conference for LEA officials and others responsible for managing reorganisation initiatives. They confirmed that what we had witnessed resonated with their experiences. Our priority had been to deepen our understanding of what made managing this change so complex. But we had an eye to identifying the kinds of factors and patterns likely to be reflected in complex changes elsewhere and so tentatively to suggest that they might have more general relevance to the management of complex educational change.

Other limitations of the study are worth noting. First, fieldwork did not start until the Secretary of State's decision had been announced on the final tranche of LEA reorganisation proposals. Our retrospective interviewing risked bias from informants' selective memory of events, possibly over-emphasising the dramatic. But it brought the advantage that informants were willing to disclose their agendas and their contribution to what had occurred because the fate of schools was no longer a live issue.

Second, our presence at case-study sites contributed to a modest 'halo' effect. We adopted a stance of impartiality towards the subjects of our study, attempting to avoid intrusion of our own political ideologies. We also had no personal stake in the outcomes of the reorganisation process we witnessed. Nevertheless, the overview we came to possess was not fully shared by our informants. The 'inside knowledge' we gained extended to individuals' judgements about each other's performance. We accepted an obligation as a condition of access to respond to requests to give generalised feedback while respecting confidences. Very occasionally we were aware that our feedback statements had made a minor impact on management practice, as where one of us alerted an LEA official to a conflict over the redistribution of resources from a closing school, enabling steps to be taken that resolved the issue.

Finally, our approach inevitably restricted the variety of data collected and our interpretation of it. We relied on what informants said about what they and others did without observing for ourselves. Wherever possible we sought corroboration by cross-checking different accounts of the same situation and referring to documentary evidence. In addition, our sociological orientation meant that psychological variables, such as 'personality clashes', were interpreted solely in terms of their social and political determinants and effects. We stepped well beyond the data in drawing general conclusions about managing complex change. They should be regarded as speculations for others to test.

Where do we go from here?

The book is directed towards answering the central question: how did a network of stakeholders within and between education system levels employ their agency within structural boundaries to manage the complex change process embodied in large-scale reorganisation of schooling?

The next two chapters complete our introduction to the field of enquiry. Chapter 2 opens with the small picture of two rural schools in the county LEA whose fates were linked. It portrays how powerfully reorganisation may impact on members of a community and other stakeholders with a hand in deciding the fate of their village school. From there the focus broadens as we unpack successive layers of the local, national and international contexts forming the bigger picture impinging on this microcosm of reorganisation. Our account provides an illustrative basis for highlighting characteristics of the complexity of reorganisation with implications for its management. The patterns in complexity were identified inductively as the research proceeded through the iterative process of data collection and analysis. Chapter 3 describes in full our theoretical orientation heralded above.

The following four chapters explore in depth the complex change process embodied in reorganisation, indicating how the characteristics of complexity affected management strategies employed in LEAs and schools. Structural factors heavily constrained stakeholders' choice over whether to instigate or respond to reorganisation initiatives. But they left stakeholders with variable agency that was always sufficient to allow some choice over how to act. Chapter 4 provides an overview of reorganisation across the two LEAs. We discuss the origins of the LEA initiatives and the structural economic and educational factors driving them, describe the forms taken by these initiatives as a whole, and summarise their direct outcomes.

We adopt a similar structure for the three chapters dealing chronologically with stakeholders' expression of agency during each stage of the change process. We begin each by highlighting prospectively how characteristics of complexity would affect management strategies for the stage at hand. We discuss how tasks were performed to manage this stage across administrative levels of the education system. The account of strategies at LEA level is complemented by tracking two complex mergers, one between a large high school and middle school in the borough, the other between two small first schools in the county. A series of matrices provides a visual summary of who was responsible for which management tasks at each system level. We conclude by considering retrospectively how characteristics of complexity affected management strategies throughout the relevant stage. Chapter 5 deals with the initial highly contentious stage on which everything else hinged: interaction across the network of stakeholders at all three system levels connected with the management tasks entailed in putting initiatives in train, consultation and feedback, and central government decision-making on reorganisation proposals. Chapter 6 examines the interplay of management tasks within and between LEA and school levels to prepare for reorganisation once central government approval was received. The aftermath of reorganisation at LEA and school levels is taken up in Chapter 7, reporting on the LEA effort to capitalise on the opportunity for promoting school improvement in the institutions surviving reorganisation, and discussing short-term tasks to get newly reorganised schools running smoothly and longer-term tasks to develop effective educational provision.

Chapter 8 concludes the book. We consider how 'knowledge for action' might be appropriately developed in the light of findings from our 'knowledge for understanding' project. The first part of the chapter is cautionary. The argument is put forward that practical guidance should not demonstrably overstep the boundaries of agency that managers may feasibly be expected to possess. Rather it should be realistic about how much and how little is controllable, knowable, and reconcilable in complex situations in which managers are likely to find themselves. It is probable that they will face severe limits to the manageability of complex educational change. We exemplify some of these limits by examining three ways in which the potential manageability of complex educational change is likely inherently to be restricted, supported with illustrations from our data. The final part of the chapter is more upbeat. We tentatively offer some general practical themes emerging from the data and so context-sensitive to the complexity of school reorganisation initiatives. We speculate that they may also be applicable at a high level of abstraction to other complex changes in education and elsewhere and suggest that they form a promising starting point for further research and the development of practical guidance.

2 Unpacking complexity

What puts the complexity into complex educational change? Given the variety of forms that educational changes may take in diverse contexts, it seems unlikely that a comprehensive set of defining characteristics could be identified. An all-inclusive definition would have not only to distinguish educational changes that are complex from those that are not but also embrace all circumstances to which the label 'complex' might apply. Owing to its multifaceted nature, complex educational change is as straightforward to define summarily as it is impossible exhaustively to unpack in its fine detail. One dictionary definition of the adjective 'complex' is: 'composed of more than one, or of many parts; not simple or straightforward; intricate; difficult' (Chambers 1998: 336). The central feature of complex educational change, therefore, is its duality as a single entity – the change itself (such as reorganisation of schooling), and a set of constituent parts (such as the people with different specialist expertise involved in reorganisation and their interaction inside and across administrative levels of the education system). Conceiving complex educational change as a duality implies that the entity has sufficient unity to merit being labelled as a particular change, while there is enough interrelationship between its constituent parts to produce that degree of unity: the entity and its constituents are two aspects of the same phenomenon.

There can be no sharp distinction between simple and complex educational changes. They may be more usefully conceived as ranging along a continuum from the simple, as in teachers' routine experience of receiving a new class of students, to the highly complex – witness large-scale reorganisation. As the complexity of educational change increases, so does the range of parts that make it up and the amount of interaction between them. Complex educational changes are not all of a piece. Some features may be more or less universal, such as the significance of forms of interaction other than face-to-face between people involved. Others may be particular to the content and context of the change at hand (such as the significance of church schools for LEA reorganisation initiatives in England). So, while it is impossible to specify all the parts whose contribution generates the complexity of any complex educational change, it is plausible to identify characteristics of complexity, some of which may have applicability beyond the context of reorganisation.

We claimed earlier that educational change is becoming more complex and that there is a lot more of it about. Compared with the school-initiated change of the past, there is also a lot more about it. Complex educational change relocates individual teachers and their schools as pawns in a system-wide game. Here we begin to explore their experience as part of something much bigger, of which they have variable but always limited awareness despite its often-dramatic effect on their work and career. The account centres on the school level, examining the fate of two small rural case-study schools in the county LEA. Reorganisation proved unusually conflictual and made a particularly strong impact on their staff and communities. From there, the focus broadens to consider how change for those directly involved formed part of the LEA-wide initiative affecting hundreds of institutions and how the initiative constituted part of a national and international phenomenon. Finally, drawing on this example, we outline characteristics of reorganisation as a complex educational change and point to their management implications.

The small picture: reorganisation changes lives

Newell and Moor were two villages near the border of the county, each served before reorganisation by a small voluntary controlled first school, the legacy of Church of England provision since the 1840s (Table 2.1). Villagers in Newell consisted predominantly of working-class families who had lived there for generations, residing alongside middle-class newcomers. Their counterparts in Moor were more uniformly middle-class incomers who could afford the picturesque old houses there. Contrasting policies of their parish council (the community council for a village which makes recommendations to the county council about matters such as granting planning permission for building houses) had resulted in contrasting patterns of village development.

While Newell was expanding through low-cost housing development which had attracted families with young children in recent years, Moor was not. There development had been confined to filling gaps between existing dwellings with high-quality, expensive homes. Housing policies had affected the intake of students. The number attending Newell First School had more than doubled in the past seven years, most students living in the village. The number had similarly increased at Moor First, but a substantial minority of students resided outside the village. The schools also contrasted starkly: Newell was housed in the original schoolhouse and a temporary classroom, both rather dilapidated, on a cramped site by a well-used road; Moor had the benefit of an old but permanent building in good condition on a more spacious site whose access road was not a through route, so carrying little traffic.

The first intimation that these small schools might be threatened with closure was raised in 1991. Members of the two communities were invited to participate in an LEA public consultation exercise on the principle of reorganisation to unify the age when students transferred between schools across the LEA, incorporating the possibility of reducing the number of schools in the primary sector at the same

Table 2.1 Context of Newell and Moor villages and their schools before and after reorganisation

Contextual feature	Newell	Moor
Location	Rural, 3 miles from Moor, 4 miles from the border with a neighbouring LEA	Rural, 'picture postcard' village, 3 miles from Newell, 1 mile from the border with a neighbouring LEA
Demographic change	Village residents were mixed 'indigenous' working class and incoming middle class, the population was expanding, the parish council policy was to encourage housing development attracting young families	Village residents were mainly incoming affluent middle class, the population was static, the parish council policy was to restrict new housing to infill between existing houses

Schools immediately before reorganisation

School name	Newell First School	Moor First School
Student age range	4–8	4–8
Governance	VC	VC
Capacity (student places)	60	60
Number of students enrolled	49	37
Profile of students	A large majority lived in Newell village	A small majority lived in Moor village, a minority resided in an adjacent LEA
Teaching staff	Headteacher (full-time, 3 days per week teaching load), senior teacher (full-time), teacher (part-time)	Headteacher (full-time, 3 days per week teaching load), teacher (full-time), teacher (part-time)
Number of student classes	2	2
Date when the school was founded	1843	1849
Buildings	The original schoolhouse, one temporary classroom, in poor condition	The original schoolhouse with a wing built in the 1950s, in good condition
Site	Cramped with little potential for expansion of school buildings	Spacious with considerable potential for expansion of school buildings

Schools immediately after reorganisation

School name	Newell Primary School	Moor Independent School
Student age range	4–11	4–11
Governance	Voluntary aided	Independent (free provision for students from Moor or nearby village, fees were charged for others)

Table 2.1 (Continued)

Contextual feature	Newell	Moor
Capacity (student places)	120	60
Number of students enrolled	90	14
Profile of students	A majority lived in Newell, a minority lived in nearby villages including Moor	A majority lived in Moor or a nearby village, a minority lived elsewhere
Teaching staff	Headteacher (full-time), senior teacher (full-time), two teachers (part-time)	Headteacher (full-time), teacher (full-time), teacher (part-time)
Number of student classes	3 (planned to increase to 4 by 1999)	2
Date when the school was founded	1996	1996
Buildings	New building	Unchanged
Site	A new spacious site on what was Newell village playing field	Unchanged

time. Their uncertainty was heightened when the LEA initial formative proposals were published two years later. The proposal relating to Newell and Moor suggested that both schools should close and students should travel to an infant or junior school to be established in a village four miles from Newell and seven from Moor. This move transgressed the widely held belief that the school was central to the life of the village and that young children should not have to travel far. One principle underpinning the proposals had special significance: 'to plan for primary schools to cater for a minimum of 90 pupils'. Fewer than ninety students then attended both schools combined, precluding a case being made to retain the status quo. The consultation document stated: 'It is recognised that the proposal above offers no prospect of village education outside [the village with the infant and junior school]. Therefore, the local education authority wish to invite alternative suggestions as to how best to organise cost effective educational provision in this area.' The impact on the two communities was profound, engendering rivalry as members of each community attempted to save their own village school.

Mobilisation of the Newell community was swift. A public meeting was called in the village hall to gauge community feeling, and the almost unanimous view emerged that the school should be retained. Members of the parish council conducted a questionnaire survey of every household in the village, revealing that 98 per cent would support a fight to save the school. A Steering Committee was formed to counter the LEA proposal. Its fourteen members gave broad community representation: governors, parents, teaching staff, the church and the parish council. The strength of their determination was indicated by the headteacher:

> I think most people had written us off . . . this village set out to prove that there was a great deal more to be said about it [reorganisation] before a decision was made . . . They [LEA officials] reckoned without this tremendous steering group and the tremendous support we had from the community.

There followed an extensive publicity campaign, lobbying of influential figures, representation at public sessions of the county council, and background research to establish that the population of the village was expanding. A written report making the case for retaining a school in the village was presented to officials at the public consultation meeting to seek views on their initial formative proposals. Arguments against the LEA proposals included: children as young as 4 would have to be bused considerable distances; the scope for community education would be undermined; and, in emotive terms, 'above all, the closure of village schools would rip the heart out of local rural communities', for 'a village without a school is like a home without a hearth'. It was recommended that a primary school serving the 4–11 age range should be created either by extending the present buildings or by building a new institution on another site in the village.

The Moor campaign was lower key. The governors and the headteacher took the lead with assistance from selected members of the community, so the campaign had less extensive representation than at Newell. They rejected the initial formative proposal on similar grounds, recommending instead that a primary school should be provided in one of the two villages. Their school would be ideal because an extension could be built on adjacent available land, the premises were in sound condition, and access was safer than at Newell as the road was not a through route. Building an extension to this school would be cheaper than the Newell Steering Committee proposal to build a new school. Their report included a statement of the intention to apply for voluntary aided status for the extended school.

Teachers experienced stress because of the uncertainty over their own future. The extra work of preparing a response and coping with enquiries from parents exacerbated the strain for the headteachers, each of whom had a regular class teaching commitment for three days per week. One noted: 'You had to reassure them . . . trying to allay people's fears but also trying to calm them down', while 'staff got very worried and upset, so you had to talk things through'. Their stress increased when the joint LEA and diocesan authority revised formative proposals were announced. Consultation had included intensive private negotiation between officials and diocesan representatives, and now a merger between the two schools was suggested. The one at Newell should become a VC infant (4–7) school, expanded on its present site to take ninety students; the one at Moor should close. This proposal was rejected at a shared public consultation meeting

held at Moor for both communities. Members of the Newell Steering
Committee argued that it would not guarantee long-term viability of the school.
The institution would remain small and would not cater for older students of
primary school age. Moor First School governors argued against the implication
that their own village would lose its school.

The diocesan representative met the governors of both schools and indicated
that the church would be willing to underwrite a change of status for either
school to become voluntary aided. The potential of this offer to support their
case was immediately realised by members of the Newell Steering Committee
but not by the Moor First School governors. The LEA was responsible for
building costs for a VC school by borrowing from central government (see Table
1.2). For a VA school 85 per cent of building and refurbishment costs would
be eligible for central government grant while the remainder would have to be
found by the diocesan authority.

A further revised joint LEA and diocesan authority formative proposal was put
forward suggesting another form of merger: for a VA primary school to be
established in either of the two villages while the other village school closed.
Since the diocesan authority was ready to take on a VA school in either
community and so would be responsible for funding 15 per cent of any building
work, its representative should liaise with the two communities in deciding the
location. According to one informant: 'That set one village against the other,
which was a dreadful thing to do.' Members of the Newell Steering Committee
who had close links with the parish council negotiated with council members
to release the village playing field as the site for a new school. The parish council
owned some allotments (of land rented out to gardeners) in an area scheduled
for housing development. It was agreed that they could be sold off now. Some
of the money could be used to make a gift to the diocesan authority equal to the
15 per cent contribution to building work for which it was liable. A very strong
case was then presented to the diocesan authority whose financial circumstances
did not allow substantial investment in building:

- a financially viable, larger institution
- sufficient places for students in the locality whose parents might wish them
  to attend a church school
- voluntary aided status, giving the diocesan authority greater control over
  education provision in the area
- brand new buildings and facilities with the prospect of low maintenance
  costs
- and all for free!

Governors at Moor First School continued pressing their proposal to extend
the present school building, assuming that any demand on the diocesan authority
purse from building work should be as modest as possible. A two-classroom
extension would cost less than the new four-classroom building advocated by the
Newell Steering Committee. But the Newell parish council offer now meant that

money was no object for the diocesan authority. The diocesan representative visited the two schools with an architect to assess building requirements. He noted that the key criterion was not financial, but the principle of the diocesan authority ensuring adequate distribution of church school places in viably large rural schools across the LEA. The choice was simple. Newell was where the students were: the number enrolled was higher; more students lived in the village than lived in Moor, so fewer would have to travel far to school if the latter were to close; the school age population of Newell was growing, at Moor it was now static.

The decision to opt for a VA primary school on a new site at Newell was formalised and submitted to central government for approval. Members of the Newell Steering Committee stood to achieve their objective. What might be conceived as their strong 'self-organisation' (though initially to resist officials) was set to repay their effort. While they had organised themselves specifically to counter officials' efforts, through a series of interactions with other stakeholders their sole interest in saving their school turned out also to suit the interest of councillors and diocesan representatives who held the power of decision. The Newell Steering Committee had played by implicit LEA and diocesan authority rules, adopting what one informant termed a stance of 'good, solid, reasoned argument' relying on hard evidence rather than emotionally charged demonstrations. This approach helped to establish a climate of readiness to listen amongst the target audience. The range of stakeholders represented among committee members strengthened their credibility when claiming to have the community behind them. Members worked closely as a team, contributing their specialist expertise, whether connected with negotiation, planning applications, local government, or the mass media. A small core group planned the overall strategy while keeping the rest of the community updated and seeking their continued support.

The success of a journalist committee member's endeavour indicates the significance of specialist contributions. She used her professional knowledge to publicise the cause through the local, national, and even international media. Media correspondents working at the national level followed up this story, providing the Newell Steering Committee with free publicity.

Second division

In contrast, the governor-led campaign at Moor was perceived by one involved to have been hampered by its identification with the school rather than the community. The campaigners had been wrong-footed by relying on their better school buildings and a traffic-free site with potential for expansion. Many Moor campaigners felt a sense of 'bereavement' when the central government decision was announced some three months later than anticipated, approving the LEA and diocesan authority firm proposal. A rift opened up between the headteacher and those governors who were ready to accept defeat and other governors and their supporters who wanted to fight on.

The chair of the governing body led the resistance, assisted by the school secretary, campaigning for nursery provision to be offered in the premises and later for the school to become independent. They boycotted meetings to prepare for students to attend the new school at Newell and invited members of a pressure group set up to resist closure proposals elsewhere to attend a campaign meeting in the village hall. The meeting was highly conflictual. Those who did not accept the campaigners' tactics judged them to be behaving reprehensibly. This conflict affected the temporary governing body for the new school at Newell because it was legally required to incorporate representatives from both existing governing bodies.

The central government decision did nothing to ease the stress for teaching staff in the two schools. Both headteachers now had to oversee preparations for closure. The headteacher at Newell First School lived in the village. She eventually decided to accept the LEA offer of early retirement available to any headteacher of eligible age whose school was to be closed: 'I don't think I would have retired normally at this time . . . It's become very stressful for me . . . because I couldn't get away from it. I just feel tired.' She had found some new tasks very demanding: 'To suddenly have to deal with the press was very daunting . . . I had to very carefully prepare statements I could give them because otherwise they would have invented something else.' Her counterpart at Moor testified to the difficulty of coping with reorganisation:

> A lot of people are out of their depth because it's so new to all of us. I think that everybody would say they have met things about reorganisation that they've never had to think about before – and that's what out of your depth means . . . meeting new situations and having to tackle them with no experience behind you. Once you get too many of those, you are swimming in deep water.

The uncertainty over her employment was soon resolved after the headteacher at Newell First School decided to retire. Closing two VC schools and replacing them with one new VA school meant that for staff there was a change of employer from the LEA to the governing body (Table 1.2). Under such circumstances, European employment protection legislation obliged members of the temporary governing body to offer posts to existing staff in the first instance wherever possible. She successfully applied for the headship of the new school at Newell. This move landed her not only with the tasks of preparing for its opening alongside overseeing closure at Moor First School but also with the acrimony of those who judged her to have placed her self-interest before that of her own community. The headteacher commented:

> I have never in my life been under so much pressure . . . I am a person who does not work happily in conflict – I am a person who prefers to talk things through with people amicably and come to an amicable decision . . . I have found . . . since I made the decision that I would go along with things [the

central government decision] . . . I have been doing the tightrope walk because of relationships.

Professional relationships were maintained between the staff of the two schools throughout this period. Their overriding concern, once their employment was settled, was over the perceived threat of impending change and the imminent end to a settled era. A teacher observed: 'Things will never be the same again, and I think we will have lost something . . . that closeness . . . It's a very intimate atmosphere, you feel like a family.'

Staff who were teacher governors were caught up in meetings to prepare for closure or plan for the new school. One noted: 'I do feel put upon . . . we're very over-stretched. It has curtailed my family life and social life.' Teachers spoke of feeling trapped between opposing forces. As LEA employees they felt obliged to be loyal, so publicly supportive of reorganisation. But they also felt a duty to parents who did not believe that closing their school was in their children's interest.

The entire staff at Moor was affected by the tension between the headteacher and the group fighting to keep the school open. One teacher suggested that it was partly due to individuals' inability to contain their strong feelings: 'They've got to have somebody to blame, somebody to shout at, and she's [the headteacher] the only one [accessible] from the LEA.' She spoke of how paranoia took hold, so that people no longer knew who or what to believe. The safest option was to withdraw from unnecessary contact. The sense of professional isolation was reinforced by their unfulfilled expectation that officials should offer proactive support. One teacher complained:

> I don't feel as if we've had enough support from the LEA, knowing that this is one of the most difficult reorganisations in the county. I feel as if I've just been left to get on with my job . . . I know [the headteacher] has had a lot of support and that we're supposed to get the support through her, but there's some issues you can't talk to [her] about. I know they [officials] have said, 'If you need us just ring', but just occasionally it would be nice to have someone say: 'How are *you* today?'

Informants at school level had limited understanding of the reorganisation initiative as a whole but were very aware of the consequences for their situation. Several perceived that officials had been unrealistic in their planning. One alleged LEA U-turn was the message received early on that there would be more jobs than teachers after reorganisation. (The message that officials consistently attempted to convey was that there would be sufficient jobs for all *permanent* employees.) Staff reported that they had been assured that they need not worry, irrespective of whether they were on a permanent contract and facing redeployment or coming to the end of a temporary contract. Later they perceived that this message changed: there were more teachers than there would be jobs. Teachers on temporary contracts felt increasingly vulnerable.

In the autumn of 1996 the new VA Newell Primary School duly opened its doors – though not without an eleventh-hour panic precipitated by unfinished building work. Contingency plans had to be made, entailing the combined intake of the two former schools 'camping out' in the confined premises of the old Newell First School until building work was done. The headteacher's exceptionally heavy workload continued throughout the first year. She articulated her vision for the new school and worked with colleagues to establish routine procedures and develop the curriculum in unfamiliar surroundings, where snags over aspects of the building work continued to surface. Staff morale remained quite low until long after reorganisation. One informant likened the gradual undermining of the high morale of pre-reorganisation days to 'three to four years watching your prize cabbages nibbled away by caterpillars'.

The campaign that refused to die at Moor did reap rewards for its protagonists. They successfully raised the money to fund an independent primary school and gained permission from the owner of the estate to which the premises belonged to use them for this purpose. Education was free for students living in Moor and the nearest village a mile away while others' parents were to be charged. Moor Independent School survived its first year with a financial surplus despite fees being levied from the parents of only two students. The chair of the trustees, a local businessperson, was quoted in a newspaper as saying:

> Walking through the village hearing children playing in the playground just seems right. A village without a school is just not the same. Villagers put in hundreds of hours of their time although everybody is getting a bit frazzled. There was a lot of trepidation when we first started. A lot of people felt let down by the council but we want to put that behind us and be able to coexist with the Newell school.

However, the conflict generated by reorganisation left what promised to be an enduring legacy. The success of Moor Independent School was bought at the expense of Newell Primary, which failed to fill to capacity because the projected number of students from Moor First did not materialise.

The big picture: scope and economics of reorganisation

The interactions connected with reorganisation at Newell and Moor were part of something much larger. Though they were of major – even life-changing – importance to most people from the schools and their communities, they represented a tiny fraction of the interactions constituting the change brought about by the LEA initiative. The schools were just two of sixty-two in the central administrative area of the county affected by reorganisation at that time. Whereas the attention and emotions of staff and members of the two communities were largely consumed by the situation at Newell and Moor, managing reorganisation of their schools was merely one element of the staff workload. It was business as usual throughout, from the annual round of teaching and learning to the implementation of central government reforms.

Similarly, for almost all officials based at the next administrative level reorganisation was a significant but one-off project, taking place in the context of their other duties. Officials with planning or pastoral responsibilities for the central administrative area were most closely concerned with the two schools. The diocesan representative had a broader interest in the future of fourteen other church schools in this area alongside over sixty elsewhere in the county. Officials with specialist responsibility for, say, distribution of furniture and equipment dealt simultaneously with stocktaking and removals for the two schools alongside upwards of another two hundred across the county.

Senior officials orchestrated the entire initiative up to reorganisation, working closely with senior councillors serving on the education committee of the county council. The schools at Newell and Moor were reorganised alongside 180 others in four out of five county administrative areas on 1 September 1996. This was the culmination of an LEA project whose genesis went back to the beginning of the decade, with thirty-two schools being reorganised in 1994 in the fifth administrative area. Overall, around fifty officials and as many councillors, professional association and diocesan representatives, 250 headteachers, several thousand of their school staff colleagues, and over a thousand governors had contributed to managing the reorganisation initiative at LEA and school levels. All experienced face-to-face contact with a few other stakeholders, and had indirect contact with rather more. None had dealings with everyone involved in managing the change across the LEA. Yet through their combined efforts, whether to support or counter LEA proposals, the reorganisation initiative was brought to fruition largely as LEA strategists envisaged.

The initiative as a whole was one of several countrywide representing LEA responses to a national policy thrust to reduce surplus capacity. The county was one of over a hundred LEAs in England at the time, all subject to policy changes brought in by highly interventionist central government ministers. The initiative which generated such conflict in Newell and Moor was one of the most ambitious projects to remove surplus capacity of those undertaken in around 70 per cent of English LEAs during the first half of the decade (Audit Commission 1996). During that period the estimated 1.5 million surplus places (DFE 1992) were reduced through a combination of LEA reorganisation initiatives and a modest upturn in the school age population to below 0.9 million (Audit Commission 1997).

Central government inspectors and civil servants vetted the bulk of LEA reorganisation proposals surviving public consultation. They took into account implications for provision of education and for financing any new building work where any LEA loan or diocesan authority grant had been requested. A minister took their advice into account in deciding whether to approve these proposals on behalf of the Secretary of State. The joint firm proposals for Newell and Moor were in a batch of 187 assessed by a small group of perhaps twenty HMI and DfEE civil servants. None, apart from the district HMI, had more than fleeting acquaintance with any of the people whose working lives or whose children's education would be so deeply affected by their efforts where approval was given. As with LEA officials and school staff, school reorganisation was just one aspect of their work.

LEA reorganisation initiatives did not arise spontaneously – there was little hint of LEA 'self-organisation' here. They were a response to mounting central government pressure. Ministers financially squeezed LEAs with a substantial proportion of surplus student places by denying them access to central government funds unless they undertook to reduce their surplus. In the county, changing the age at which students transferred between schools and reducing the number of schools in the primary sector offered a means of achieving the required reduction. The 1993 Education Act added the threat that ministers now had authority to step in and do the job of LEAs for them. The Secretary of State could direct LEAs to bring forward reorganisation proposals and, if they failed to comply, draw up proposals instead (DFE 1994).

These policy moves were no more spontaneous either. Central government watchdogs, whose briefs included monitoring central and local government expenditure on state schooling and promoting better value for money from such services, had published a series of reports from the mid-1980s calling for the high level of surplus student places to be reduced (National Audit Office 1986; Audit Commission 1984, 1986, 1988, 1990). The Treasury was exerting increasing pressure on the central government spending departments responsible for public services, including education, to rein in expenditure (Deakin and Parry 1993). Indeed the push to reduce surplus school capacity in the state education sector was part of a wider strategy undertaken by this and many other western governments since the 1970s. The aim was to restrain the burgeoning increase in public spending which had long outstripped the level of economic expansion needed to sustain it, leading to a chronic financial crisis (Pollitt 1993; Foster and Plowden 1996).

So a root cause of school reorganisation is economic. Wealth is generated by the private sector, part of which must be invested in social reproduction. State education contributes to social reproduction by ensuring the supply of a skilled and compliant labour force in shifting economic circumstances. There is a limit to the proportion of wealth that can be invested in social reproduction before it undermines business profitability. A consequence of capitalist economics is that there are always likely to be resource constraints for state education since it is a necessary cost for a system whose imperative is profit, not other social goods (Hargreaves 1983).

By the 1980s the proportion of wealth needed for social reproduction in western nations to cope with ever increasing demands for public services was getting out of hand. Either taxation would have to be increased or the efficiency of public service provision would have to be improved, reducing public expenditure for the same level of services. Both left- and right-wing governments made such efforts, indicating that the causes of the financial crisis lay deeper than political party ideology. Governments were spurred on in the project of 'reinventing government' by management gurus such as Osborne and Gaebler (1992), whose analysis of initiatives to marketise the US public sector suggested that the state could downsize its involvement by decentralisation and privatisation of services. Their panacea was 'entrepreneurial government', a form of service provision driven by more businesslike principles.

Central government in the UK was no exception to this international trend. The county reorganisation initiative was affected by national policy changes designed to promote entrepreneurship in state schools while curtailing LEA authority to manage local provision of schooling. The pressure to downsize through reorganisation was a direct consequence of the central government thrust to reduce public expenditure by ceasing to maintain so many half-empty buildings. Promoting the GM (grant-maintained) sector, where schools were directly funded by central government, was a decentralisation policy designed to empower parents and governors to remove schools from local government control. As we shall see, one stimulus for attempting to attain GM status was to escape LEA reorganisation proposals, especially for closure. This new sector offered parents more choice between a greater diversity of types of school in what was conceived as an educational marketplace where neighbouring schools were to compete for custom. The advent of the local management of schools (LMS) initiative in the early 1990s removed from LEAs the authority to appoint staff, now exclusively the province of governing bodies.

Reorganisation was affected also by a second economically driven international imperative. The context for it, as discussed in Chapter 1, was one of multiple education reform directed towards the instrumental aim of improving the nation's ability to compete in a global market (Brown and Lauder 1996). While reorganisation at Newell and Moor unfolded, staff there were also coping with reforms including the National Curriculum, its assessment, and the new system of regular external inspection. Conservative central government ministers of the day, like their New Labour successors, were trying to raise the standard of state education. The UK, in common with other developed western countries, could no longer compete with newly industrialised nations for the kinds of production possible with low-skilled workers earning a low wage. The alternative economic strategy emerging at the time of our study was to capitalise on the specialised knowledge, skills and technology that remain largely the domain of developed nations in producing top-quality, customised goods and services in areas such as biotechnology and microelectronics. A high standard of state education was required to produce a workforce with specialist skills and knowledge necessary to occupy the favoured 'high skill, high wage' niche in the world market.

Characteristics of complex educational change

To comprehend large-scale reorganisation of schooling as an instance of complex educational change, it is necessary to identify patterns amongst the myriad interactions within and between administrative levels of the education system that this change embodied. Since every interaction forms part of the context for others, it is equally important to consider links between these interactions and the institutional, local, national, and international contexts in which they were embedded.

We conclude the chapter with an exercise in unashamed reductionism, extracting characteristics of the complexity of educational change from the above account. They suggest profitable ways of analysing what managing change of this magnitude may require. Our typology is summarised in Table 2.2: there are five characteristics, each broken down into more detailed constituents. The characteristics and their constituents may be distinguished analytically but they do not exist independently of each other. All may be expressed differently and each relates to others. Our hunch is that the more complex an educational change, the more likely it will feature the five core characteristics in combination.

First, complex educational change is typically *large-scale*, impinging on the lives of many people. As members of a pluralist society, they are likely not only to have some stake in the content of the change but also to perceive it differently according to their varying circumstances. *A multitude of stakeholders with an extensive range of specialist knowledge and priorities* will probably be involved or affected, by design. The county reorganisation initiative necessitated changes in

Table 2.2 Characteristics of complex educational change with management implications

---

1   Large-scale
   • a multitude of stakeholders with an extensive range of specialist knowledge and priorities
   • the allegiance of stakeholders to partially incompatible beliefs and values, within limits

2   Componential
   • a diversity of sequential and overlapping components affecting different stakeholders at particular times
   • a multiplicity of differentiated but interrelated management tasks

3   Systemic
   • a multidirectional flow of direct and mediated interaction within and between system levels
   • an unequal distribution of power between stakeholders within and between system levels who are nevertheless interdependent
   • the centrality of cross-level management tasks

4   Differentially impacting
   • a variable shift in practice and learning required
   • variable congruence with perceived interests and its associated emotive force, altering with time
   • a variable reciprocal effect on other ongoing activities
   • variable awareness of the totality beyond those parts of immediate concern

5   Contextually dependent
   • interaction with an evolving profile of other planned and unplanned changes
   • impact of the accretion of past changes affecting resource parameters

---

the work and career of over a thousand school staff and in educational provision for many more parents and students. They were bound to possess very different first-hand knowledge, expertise, and priorities relating to the change, depending on their work responsibility or community situation, what they wanted out of reorganisation or what they wanted to protect. School staff at Newell and Moor were simultaneously worried about their job, preparing for closure, or making a new start. Parents were concerned that educational provision would continue to be available nearby and that their village would remain socially and economically viable. The diocesan representative wanted to improve the distribution and viability of church schools. Officials wished to win acceptance for proposals and avoid losing schools to the GM sector. Civil servants at the DfEE were exercised with financial implications of building work connected with proposals.

These stakeholders will probably hold *allegiance to a plurality of partially incompatible beliefs and values, within limits* of assumptions about their entitlement and constraints on alternative courses of action. LEA officials believed that their proposals would retain provision within a reasonable distance from the home of every school-age child around Newell or Moor. They judged that the educational experience offered would be of higher quality in a school that was large enough for staff to cover the full range of National Curriculum subjects effectively. When existing arrangements were threatened by the LEA proposals, many parents and other community members who accorded with the principle of reorganisation rallied around their shared 'nimbyist' belief in protecting the status quo for their children. One alternative was to set up private education, but no one questioned the legitimacy of officials launching the reorganisation initiative in the first place.

Second, complex educational change is *componential*, an entity made up of interrelated and differentiated parts which vary over time. The content of the change is likely to consist of a *diversity of sequential and overlapping components affecting different stakeholders at particular times*, a striking feature of the LEA reorganisation initiative. For Newell and Moor, the process, from publication of initial formative proposals to actual reorganisation, took three years and was still affecting the emerging institutions a year and a half later. The initiative was originally conceived in three annual phases, with Newell and Moor in the final one. There was a long period of overlap between phases, with the first approaching completion as planning began for subsequent ones. In early 1996 officials were offering aftercare to staff from schools surviving the first phase in one administrative area while implementing approved proposals in schools across the other four areas. Stakeholders might be going through contrasting experiences at any point. As staff at Newell and Moor prepared for closure, those in local secondary schools were preparing for expansion as they took the oldest students from middle schools in the area. For their colleagues in the first phase of reorganisation this part was just a memory.

The variety of components, perhaps coupled with their cumulative impact over time, will dictate that a *multiplicity of differentiated but interrelated management tasks* must be addressed. The headteachers at both Newell and Moor had to manage closure, squeezing in reorganisation-related management tasks on top of their full-time management and teaching activity. Once the latter was appointed as headteacher-designate of the new Newell Primary School, she also had to prepare for its opening, then cope with the aftermath. Officials responsible for the schools had to help draft proposals, manage public consultation meetings, support preparations for closure and opening, and monitor the situation after reorganisation. Senior officials had to orchestrate the whole process leading to reorganisation. DfEE civil servants had to manage the scrutiny of proposals.

Third, complex educational change tends to be *systemic*, taking place across two or more administrative levels of a large education system which both shapes and constrains the ways in which stakeholders interact. A cross-level change process will embody a *multidirectional flow of direct and mediated interaction within and between system levels*. The change process must involve interaction between individuals and groups based at different system levels where a change is initiated either centrally or at an intermediate system level for implementation at the periphery. Many interactions will take place via intermediaries who interpret the communications of stakeholders at one level seeking to impact on the actions of those at another level. The flow of interaction directly affecting Newell and Moor began with initial formative proposals planned at LEA level. They stimulated intense face-to-face interaction in the Newell and Moor communities and repeated exchanges between these people, officials, and the diocesan representative. A district HMI visited the schools and reported back to civil servants at the DfEE. They liaised with LEA officials and received documentation that included reports from the Newell Steering Committee and Moor governors. All these stakeholders experienced face-to-face interaction with others based at their system level with whom they were most closely associated. The channels for communication across levels were fewer, greater reliance being placed on documentary or electronic means. Participants in many interactions crossing system levels included intermediaries working on behalf of absent stakeholders. Officials who fronted public consultation meetings represented senior colleagues responsible for the content of proposals. The diocesan representative was answerable to the diocesan board of education. Its members made decisions in the light of his recommendations, including the one to create Newell VA Primary School. Much information transmitted from LEA to school level was disseminated through documents such as proposals written by LEA specialists. Everyone learned of the decisions taken on behalf of the Secretary of State, but very few people from other system levels had met the minister concerned.

Interaction across such an extensive network of stakeholders based at different system levels will almost certainly engender some ambiguity resulting from the unintended consequences of actions. They may be hidden from their perpetrators because they are not party to further interactions among stakeholders elsewhere stimulated by their endeavours. There is a strong propensity for unintended consequences to arise when action at one system level is taken to affect people at another. Nobody at either central government or LEA levels intended that

Moor would end up with an independent school as a consequence of their actions. There was significant unpredictability about the future path of the reorganisation initiative for much of the time: it was not a foregone conclusion that councillors would support their officials, that ministers' support for LEA proposals would outweigh their concern to promote the GM schools sector, or that all members of local communities would accept particular proposals without a fight.

There will be an *unequal distribution of power between stakeholders within and between system levels who are nevertheless interdependent.* The formal powers of stakeholders may differ widely, especially between levels of the education system. Yet none is powerless and ultimately even the formally most powerful change initiators are constrained by their dependence on the less formally powerful whose co-operation or compliance may be required where they actually implement the change. Members of the communities at Newell and Moor were initially consulted about the principle of reorganisation and subsequently about how reorganisation of their schools might be achieved. At this point they were not given free choice over whether or not they would like their own school to be reorganised. Senior LEA officials were authorised by councillors to direct their colleagues' contribution to the initiative. Authority to pressurise LEAs into undertaking reorganisation initiatives and require public consultation on proposals rested with central government. Authority to put pressure on central government rested with its own appointed watchdogs and Treasury. Economic conditions exerted pressure on the entire education system. Yet the outcomes at Newell and Moor demonstrated that local communities were not without power. Their members could have recourse to authority over school-level decisions and informal influence in gathering support for countering proposals. Conversely ministers relied on LEA and school staff to bring about reorganisation, while the latter relied on central government to support their case and on each other to implement whatever decision was made.

The *centrality of management tasks across system levels* follows from the aspiration of policymakers at one level to change education practice at other levels. Several LEA officials were responsible for management tasks requiring action in schools, such as organising movement of furniture from closing to surviving institutions. DfEE civil servants and senior LEA officials liaised with each other to ensure that proposals lay inside central government parameters.

Fourth, a complex educational change is *differentially impacting* on people involved or affected, contributing to the diversity of management tasks. There will be a *variable shift in practice and learning required* of different individuals and groups according to the novelty of whatever they have to do. The head of Moor First School experienced a steep learning curve. Similarly the LEA initiative was a novel project for many officials, and operating without authority over staff appointments was new for them all. Mounting a campaign to counter LEA proposals was a first-time experience for many community members. Stakeholders elsewhere faced far less disturbance to their existing practice. Many schools expanded or contracted by gaining or losing just one year group of students.

Shifts in practice will have *variable congruence with perceived interests and associated emotive force, altering with time.* The experience of the Newell and Moor communities indicates how the content of reorganisation proposals was aligned with some individuals' perceived interests while diametrically opposed to those of others. Whose interests were being served and whose were being challenged switched to some extent as the change process proceeded. The initial formative proposals suited neither community. The firm proposals suited Newell parents but not those at Moor. The strength of emotion varied with the implications of the change for individuals' interests and with their evolving experience: outrage at Newell over the LEA perceived attempt to 'rip the heart out of local rural communities' became enthusiasm for building a new school in the village. For officials and the diocesan representative, reorganisation was but one part of their job – even if burdensome. The emotive potential of reorganisation hit mainly those who had to run contentious public meetings or endure public protest.

The change will have a *variable reciprocal effect on other ongoing activities.* Reorganisation tasks were a minor concern of some officials and school staff while, for others, managing their part of the reorganisation initiative consumed most working hours over many months. Members of the Newell Steering Committee and the Moor governing body had to make time alongside other commitments to engage in the sustained attempt to meet their shared interests.

There will be *variable awareness of the totality of the change beyond those parts of immediate concern* to particular individuals and groups. Grasp of the change and its parts is likely to be hierarchically distributed. Breadth of knowledge of reorganisation at central and the intermediate LEA level was marked by superficial awareness of community circumstances. Conversely depth of knowledge of the local scene at the peripheral level was marked by superficial awareness of the totality. Senior LEA officials had an overview of the entire reorganisation initiative, though they were shorter on appreciation of the impact of their efforts on particular schools and communities than the people based at this level. Civil servants had an overview of firm proposals and documented responses from school level but few had seen any of the schools. Informants from Newell and Moor had only a summary view of the reorganisation initiative, little knowledge of its impact on schools other than those close by, but detailed awareness of what lay inside their first-hand experience.

Fifth, complex educational change is intrinsically *contextually dependent,* facilitated and constrained by many aspects of the wider political and historical milieu with which it interacts. The change will *interact with an evolving profile of other planned and unplanned changes.* In a climate of central government public sector reform, abundant policy initiatives under way at any time are likely to impinge on each other. All school staff at Newell and Moor had to implement education reforms of the day alongside reorganisation, and were subject to the wider central government imperative of achieving greater efficiency in public sector expenditure.

The *impact of the accretion of past changes affecting resource parameters* for the change may be facilitative or inhibitory. The origin of Newell First and Moor First as church schools founded in the 1840s was an important factor leading to the new school for Newell. The imperative to downsize provision in the LEA was a direct consequence of past expansion during a period of population growth. The legacy of surplus capacity following more recent population decline had contributed to public expenditure at a level that was now deemed excessive in a harsher economic climate of increased global competition.

Managing complexity

These characteristics of complexity exhibited by the LEA reorganisation initiative reveal patterns suggesting that complexity need not imply impenetrability. They are unlikely to be exhaustive for reorganisation and almost certainly do not cover all forms of complex change in large education systems. Yet they appear sufficiently general to have relevance to other complex changes in different situations after allowing for the context-specificity of reorganisation in the UK of the mid-1990s. They point to multiple forms of differentiation between the parts of the complex change as an entity and to intrinsic reciprocal links between this change and the evolving context in which it occurs.

Identifying patterns in complexity is one thing. Managing complex educational change is another. Arguably, the potential capacity to manage complex change is likely to be inherently restricted because there are so many factors beyond any individual's understanding, let alone control. But, while a degree of ambiguity and unpredictability may be endemic, it must still be feasible to maximise such capacity as is possible. Our detailed account of the process of reorganisation in chapters to follow will show how these characteristics of complexity did leave managers with sufficient agency to develop coherent management strategies while imposing very real constraints on its manageability. To focus our analytic effort, a conceptual framework is needed which embraces interactions between the various stakeholders and the structural parameters channelling their course. That is the subject of the next chapter.

3 Complex change in perspective
A free for all (within limits)

It is often said that people make history, though not entirely under conditions of their own choosing. Individuals and groups interact as they pursue their goals according to their reading of the situations in which they find themselves. The outcome of their efforts over time is the flow of enduring or temporary stability and evolutionary or revolutionary change that makes up what we call history. Their reading of situations and ability to do much about them are endemically framed by the social and political context constituting the epoch in which they are located. In this sense history also makes people. There are structural limits to the variety of interpretations that people are likely to make and to their power to get their own way. The past creates unacknowledged conditions of action like the tradition of village schools or the accretion of laws constituting the present national legislative framework. They form parameters bounding assumptions according to which interaction in the present is conducted. Interaction in turn produces a stream of intended and unintended consequences that help to perpetuate these conditions or occasionally to trigger change. Interaction between members of the Newell and Moor communities, diocesan representatives, and officials had sustained their village schools over many years. It took a shift of wider demographic and economic circumstances to stimulate officials and councillors to think the hitherto unthinkable. The initial formative reorganisation proposals were a bombshell for the communities, challenging members' implicit assumptions about their entitlement to a state school in their village and precipitating the sequence of interactions that brought about a change no one had predicted.

Similarly it is people who make educational change complicated, though not entirely under conditions of their own choosing. Individuals and groups are affected who understand different things by the change, want different things from it, have access to different sources of power to realise their goals, are constrained by their current traditions derived from past changes, operate within large multilevel education systems where they routinely interact with others whom they never meet, and are subject to global economic trends. As we argued earlier, there is room for agency to choose different courses of action according to individuals' contrasting interpretations of situations, but only within limits imposed by the expression of agency by other parties to interaction and by deeper structural factors. Reorganisation might be more manageable if financial constraints imposed by central government were relaxed. However the underlying economic conditions generating this stringency are immutable by individual human agency even though they are created and perpetuated by human agency worldwide. Resources will be limited in any economic system. But the bottom line profit motive of capitalism means that the cost to the economy of meeting human needs must be set against the imperative to create wealth. More generous financing of reorganisation would exacerbate the economic problem of high public expenditure in the short term which reorganisation is designed to ameliorate. So LEA officials' and councillors' agency is delimited by economic circumstances: they can ill afford to spend on reorganisation now to save later.

Fullan (2001: 8) has argued that educational change is about individuals making sense of an experience that, by definition, is new:

> The problem of meaning is central to making sense of education change. In order to achieve greater meaning, we must come to understand both the small and the big pictures. The small picture concerns the subjective meaning or lack of meaning for individuals at all levels of the educational system. Neglect of the phenomenology of change – that is, how people actually experience change as distinct from how it might have been intended – is at the heart of the spectacular lack of success of most social reforms. It is also necessary to build and understand the big picture, because educational change after all is a sociopolitical process.

Conceiving complex change as a flow of interaction entailed in meaning-making has the advantage of reducing the tendency otherwise to reify the contributions of individuals and groups based in institutions at particular system levels which lead to collective policy statements. The general term *reification* implies 'apprehension of the products of human activity *as if* they were something other than human products – such as facts of nature' (Berger and Luckmann 1967: 106). Our concern is specifically over treating a collectivity as if it was an entity capable of action independent of those who comprise it, as in metaphors such as the 'self-managing school' (Caldwell and Spinks 1988) or using conceptual shorthand such as: 'a number of LEAs have decided that pursuing the difficult process of planning reorganisations and of gaining political support for them, is now futile' (Ranson 1990: 47). A school does not literally manage itself any more than an LEA decides anything. School staff and governors manage schools. Officials and councillors manage LEAs. We accept that there is a place for concepts such as 'school' or 'LEA' that describe collectivities, and that it can be appropriate to describe the combined actions of their members in summary terms. But fitness for purpose must be the key consideration in deciding when such shorthand obscures more than it illuminates. For our analytical purpose, it is vital to delve beneath the surface of collectivities to examine the interactions within.

To deepen our understanding of complex educational change we need conceptual tools that enable us to track how individuals and groups act and respond to each other according to the meanings their encounters have for them. We should also allow for variable agency: people may have differential access to sources of power to achieve their goals within their interpretation of situations. They may use power not only to express their agency but also to channel and delimit that of others with whom they interact. The aggregate of actions and responses comprises the flow of interaction that makes up the change process. At or between whichever system levels this interaction occurs – during an LEA public consultation meeting, among a group set up to save the school – it forms part of the 'small picture' of subjective meaning exemplified in our account of reorganisation at Newell and Moor.

Equally our tools for analysis must sensitise us to the structural limits of agency: the boundaries circumscribing alternative courses of interaction. Should such limits exist, we would not expect to find interaction stepping beyond them. Rather, where interaction approaches structural limits we would anticipate the constraints they impose on agency increasingly to surface. In Chapter 2 we also portrayed how the economic imperative to reduce public expenditure inhibited LEA officials from proposing a new school for Newell since financial restrictions governing their reorganisation initiative were tight. Members of the parish council found a way round by relinquishing land for the site and selling land to realise capital for paying the diocesan authority's share of building costs. Officials negotiated with ministers to borrow the remaining capital, a cost to be set against the reduction in public expenditure brought by reorganisation. Such economic factors are structural, contributing to the 'big picture' enveloping the myriad small pictures of interaction. Where people are unaware of the big picture it will figure little in their subjective development of meaning. But understanding educational change entails grasping the small and big pictures and their interlinkage, as we attempted to do in contextualising reorganisation at Newell and Moor.

Here we articulate an eclectic conceptual framework encompassing agency and structural limits to guide our exploration of reorganisation as a complex educational change. First, we advocate a pluralist theoretical perspective on agency. Our focus lies on the intricacies of interaction that are the expression of agency while being sensitive to its structural limits through a neo-Marxist orientation. We indicate how characteristics of complex educational change we identified earlier relate to concepts that Hargreaves (1983) put forward for understanding agency and the impact of structural limits on its operation.

Second, we set out tools for exploring how individuals and groups across system levels use whatever agency they have to achieve their interests through interaction, whether face-to-face or indirect. We outline an integrated cultural and political perspective foregrounding the link between actors' beliefs and values and their use of power to realise their interests, the role of power in shaping culture, and the impact of cultural factors on deployment of power. We consider how stakeholders may be conceived as nodes in an evolving network of relationships. No individual had direct contact with more than a modest proportion of the others yet all stakeholders' activity was at some point connected, often through intermediaries. The result was a flow of interaction within and between education system levels towards completion of the reorganisation initiatives even though no individual possessed a comprehensive overview. We typify the change process in each phase of reorganisation as sequential stages, drawing on Fullan's (1991, 2001) conception of single innovations. These stages span the chronology of the change from instigation of the LEA initiatives to adaptation of school staff after reorganisation. Their sequence determines which stakeholders were central to each part of the process. We consider how they might act as change agents, users of the change, or both.

Third, we define concepts addressing how interaction connected with reorganisation is linked elastically with underlying structural conditions, yet inside firm limits. Instruments or means for promoting implementation of policies originating at different levels include financial arrangements linked with the funding of provision in the public sector. Some room for agency remains where the limits are approached but not reached. One indication of agency among policymakers based at the same and different education system levels is the coexistence of policies that impact, by design or by default, on a complex change such as school reorganisation. Several forms of interaction have an inhibitory effect, adding weight to the idea of relative autonomy: the state does not act monolithically but consists of a network of policymakers and their agents who are not necessarily aware of the consequences of their policies for other stakeholders. We will advance the idea of a 'counter-policy' to capture how stakeholders at a more peripheral system level may react against a policy initiated more centrally that does not align with their beliefs and values. They may possess sufficient agency to mediate the policy as envisaged by its instigators.

Finally, we note how a raft of 'managerialist' central government policies is designed to change the power relationship between stakeholders concerned with state education. While not necessarily concerned with reorganisation, they altered the distribution of authority affecting senior LEA officials' orchestration of reorganisation initiatives. Officials achieved their goals in spite of certain central government policies. The amount of agency remaining in the face of these policies designed to narrow its limits derived in significant measure from inconsistencies inside the state reflecting incompatible political values of stakeholders within and around government and its agencies.

Getting to grips with agency and its structural limits

Some years ago Hargreaves (1983) put forward an insightful framework for analysing the complexities of education policy and associated change. He addressed agency and its structural limits, suggesting that complementary aspects of pluralist and Marxist theoretical orientations were reconcilable. Pluralism is strong on describing the workings of agency: the surface interaction between groups of people among whom power is unequally but nevertheless universally distributed. It is weak on identifying underlying structural limits of agency and boundaries inside which distributed power lies. Marxism, at least in its less crudely deterministic neo-Marxist variants, is strong on explaining how agency and the distribution of power are subject to broad but constraining structural limits. It is weak on describing the extent of agency and expression of power inside the limits – and in demonstrating their existence since, by definition, what happens on the surface is interpreted as lying within structural boundaries.

A key to synthesis lies in the neo-Marxist notion that there is *relative autonomy* between major institutions (or patterns of relationships between groups) in society, most relevantly here the state – government and its agencies, including state-funded educational provision – and the capitalist economy. This concept embraces the possibility of diverse practices in so far as institutions are independent, while pointing to the boundaries of variation following from the degree to which they are also mutually dependent. Linkage between state education and the economy is therefore viewed as elastic: agency connected with education may centre on non-economic issues (such as protecting provision of church schools for religious reasons). But the linkage becomes stretched to the limit where it threatens to undermine capital accumulation. Dale (1986) has argued that relative autonomy between the economy and the state enables different groups to impact on education policy although a small number have greatest control over its content. Education policy contributes to creating conditions that are not inimical to capitalism, serve to legitimate capitalism, and in many cases assist in capital accumulation. In recent years UK central government education reforms have been directed towards enhancing wealth creation in the face of global competition.

Hargreaves asserts that variation among education policies and their implementation arises because of *multicausality*: determination of educational change is loose and indirect while activity remains well inside structural limits. To the extent that the state and state education have independence from the economy, there is room for members of a multiplicity of groups to express agency through interaction in alliance or in conflict with each other in pursuing divergent (and often non-economic) educational goals. Second, since the state does not act as a unitary force within and between system levels, variation arises also from *administrative complexity*:

> The multifaceted nature of educational change is complicated still further by the fact that variations in outlook, interpretation and social support occur not only between different localities, but also at different levels of the educational decision-making process, each level having the capacity to generate proposals of its own and to frustrate or obstruct the implementation of proposals framed at other levels.
>
> (Hargeaves 1983: 44)

There is potential for groups to express agency by mediating policies, both between neighbouring institutions and across system levels. Third, variation arises from *historical lags*, the expression of agency among groups retaining commitment to past policies and beliefs in a changing context, so affecting parameters for new policies in the present.

But autonomy between the state, state education, and the economy is only relative:

> there are certain tendencies inherent in capitalism as an economic mode of production which place important though exceptionally broad limits on the options for educational and social reform, both through the logic of resource allocation to social and educational ends in a profit orientated system, and through the boundary affirming assumptions of what changes are desirable, possible and even thinkable in such a system.
>
> (Hargreaves 1983: 40)

Delimitation of the options for education policies is ideological and economic. Boundaries of agency arise, first, from shared, unquestioned *assumptions* about the naturalness and legitimacy of the present economic order. The radical right-wing and centre-left education reforms since the postwar consensus period when Hargreaves was writing have reflected explicit assumptions about improving national performance in a capitalist economy. Increased pressure for economic efficiency brought by international competition, the establishment of new markets following the collapse of communism, technological change, and expansion of the public sector combined to reinforce assumptions about the instrumental role of education in producing the newly skilled and more adaptable workforce needed for prosperity in tomorrow's global marketplace. Second, such assumptions are – unsurprisingly – rooted in the *economic conditions* that restrict agency. These conditions frequently force policymakers into adopting compromise solutions to achieve their goals inside immutable economic constraints, a phenomenon which Hargreaves terms *administrative convenience*. As policymaking moves closer to structural limits, compromises become more common. They indicate the presence of delimiting economic conditions.

In Chapter 2 we suggested that the acceleration in public expenditure more quickly than the level of economic growth needed to sustain it during the second half of the last century brought state education ever closer to the structural limits. The result was a proliferation of policies, including reorganisation, where administrative convenience featured prominently (to be discussed in Chapter 4). Here delimitation of agency was clearly apparent: LEA officials must find compromise solutions within available resources or central government ministers would take over and do the job for them. Administrative convenience is the closest we are likely to come to observable phenomena corroborating Dale's view that education policy cannot be inimical to capitalism. We will not expect to see a refusal to compromise such that education policy oversteps the structural limits imposed by pressure to sustain economic conditions perpetuating a capitalist economy.

Our characteristics of complex educational change with management implications parallel and extend the range of phenomena addressed by Hargreaves's framework. Consequences of the complexity of educational change for his factors explaining the operation and limits of agency are summarised in Table 3.1. Just

Table 3.1 Impact of complex educational change on the operation and limits of agency

Factor linked with expression of agency	Characteristics and constituents of complex educational change	Factor linked with structural limits of agency
Multicausality	1 Large-scale • a multitude of stakeholders with an extensive range of specialist knowledge and priorities • the allegiance of stakeholders to partially incompatible beliefs and values, within limits	Assumptions
Multicausality and administrative complexity	2 Componential • a diversity of sequential and overlapping components affecting different stakeholders at particular times • a multiplicity of differentiated but interrelated management tasks	
Administrative complexity	3 Systemic • a multidirectional flow of direct and mediated interaction within and between system levels • an unequal distribution of power between stakeholders within and between system levels who are nevertheless interdependent • the centrality of cross-level management tasks	
Multicausality and administrative complexity	4 Differentially impacting • a variable shift in practice and learning required • variable congruence with perceived interests and its associated emotive force, altering with time • a variable reciprocal effect on other ongoing activities • variable awareness of the totality beyond those parts of immediate concern	
Administrative complexity Historical lags	5 Contextually dependent • interaction with an evolving profile of other planned and unplanned changes • impact of the accretion of past changes affecting resource parameters	Economic conditions

as the categories of complexity are not entirely distinct from each other, so also they are not tied exclusively with any one factor. We have highlighted only the closest ties.

The process and outcomes of *large-scale* change tend to be multicausal because so many stakeholders from diverse contexts can express agency according to varied beliefs and values framing their educational goals. As we noted in Chapter 2, however, these beliefs and values do lie within limits where the present economic order is unlikely to be questioned. Similarly, the *componential* nature of complex change adds to the number of potential causes contributing to the outcomes: different people perform different management tasks at different times, the earlier activities impacting on those that follow.

The components of complex change contribute also to administrative complexity since the distribution of responsibility for different parts of the whole provides space for mediation through agency. Possibilities for mediation are particularly extensive when the change is *systemic*. Stakeholders must rely on intermediaries through whom they attempt to express agency in affecting activity at system levels other than the one where they are based. So they will probably have restricted awareness of the consequences of their actions. The *differentially impacting* character of complex change on stakeholders possessing variable degrees of agency, coupled with their diverse responses according to the evolutionary meaning it carries for them and the relationship between the change and their other concerns, all contribute to multicausality.

A crucial aspect of the *context-dependent* character of complex change not explicitly addressed by Hargreaves is the interaction that may occur between any change and other changes impinging upon it. Administrative complexity does not only emerge in consequence of the capacity for agency between levels that systemic change allows. It also follows from the probability that the change occurs in the context of other changes, so constraining or enhancing the ability of actors to deal with the change at hand. Hargreaves does attend obliquely to the second aspect of context-dependency through his notion of historical lags. This factor featured in our illustration: diocesan representatives sought to protect provision of church schools in a country where most of the population are no longer practising Christians. But the accretion of past changes has greater significance for complex change than simply the ability of people who hold on to beliefs born of past times to express agency. Constraints on resource parameters for contemporary change following from past change decisions have a major bearing on the search for compromises that is a hallmark of administrative convenience. Complex educational change tests the potential of agency to the structural limit in a context of global competition where change costs threaten to overburden public sector expenditure.

Towards a pluralistic framework for analysis

Pluralism is a useful tool for exploring agency. The 1970s witnessed a series of pluralistic studies of educational policymaking at national and local levels in the

UK (e.g. Saran 1973; Kogan 1975, 1978) focusing on the surface features of interaction connected with decisions embodied in policy changes. The theoretical orientations they adopted share the assumption that power to affect political decisions is distributed, however unevenly (Lindblom 1983), amongst individuals and groups based at the various levels of the education system. Each stakeholder is regarded as possessing sufficient agency to contribute to decisions. Conversely none are viewed as all-powerful. They use whatever resources they can to realise their perceived *interest*: some desired state of affairs contributing to the fulfilment of their purposes. The main groups of stakeholders featuring in our study and their reorganisation-related interests are listed in Table 3.2. Some form part of local or national government, whether elected politicians, their professional staff, or their agents – such as officials from the Funding Agency for Schools concerned with GM school administration. (This agency played a minor part in the county, where GM high schools were due to fill surplus places by taking students at the age of 11 for the first time.) Other groups include voluntary associations such as school staff unions.

Interest groups may exist because of an enduring *sectional* interest in supporting their members. They may have a *promotional* interest in a single issue (O'Donnell 1985), as where senior LEA officials orchestrated the reorganisation initiative. Politicians had both a promotional interest connected with reorganisation and a long-term sectional interest in protecting themselves and their political party. They and their professional staff in national and local government shared a promotional interest in seeing reorganisation initiatives through, but groups at school level had a sectional interest in getting the best for their institution, rather than ensuring the LEA-wide success of reorganisation. If a school came under threat from LEA proposals, a promotional interest might emerge as a local community group coalesced around the search for an alternative outcome, as in the case of the creation of the Newell Steering Committee to save the village school. These groups also vary in the formality of their association, from the informality of the parents' pressure group created to counter proposals to close schools in the south of the county through to professionally staffed organisations such as the Council for the Protection of Rural England, concerned with preserving village schools. Their power base differs (Kogan 1975): *legitimised* interest groups have a statutory or conventional right to be consulted on issues affecting them. The sole *non-legitimised* groups in our study were parents' pressure groups. Legitimation is a matter of degree: even members of such pressure groups were entitled to present their case as parents at the relevant public consultation meeting.

The meanings that participants make of their situations lie at the heart of interaction, affecting their deployment of power. A combined cultural and political perspective links uses of power with meanings and the extent to which they may be shared. It focuses on questions such as 'who has power to shape meanings that are shared in a culture?' and 'how do meanings shared in a culture affect the ways in which power is used to realise interests?'. It is assumed that interaction may be synergistic or conflictual, beliefs and values may or may not be shared with other parties to interaction, and compatible versions of core

Table 3.2 Major interest groups among stakeholders connected with reorganisation

Interest group	Type of interest	Examples of interests connected with reorganisation initiatives
LEA officials (officers)	Promotional and sectional	Managing a successful initiative to reorganise schools across the LEA, avoiding potential loss of authority through GM applications
LEA officials (inspectors)	Promotional and sectional	Improving the quality of education in reorganised schools, avoiding potential loss of authority through GM applications
Councillors in the ruling group	Promotional and sectional	Sponsoring a successful initiative, avoiding potential loss of authority through GM applications or unpopularity in their ward
Diocesan representatives	Promotional	Improving buildings, ensuring sufficient student places, preserving the character of religious education in church schools
Funding Agency for Schools representatives	Promotional	Supporting GM secondary schools in the county due to expand under reorganisation proposals
Headteachers in high schools	Sectional	Overseeing expansion, extending control over schooling with a 'secondary ethos' by accepting younger students
Headteachers in closing schools	Sectional	A variable personal interest including seeking redeployment to another headship, a variable professional interest including seeking autonomy from the LEA through GM status
School staff union representatives	Sectional	Protecting members' conditions of employment, maximising opportunities for redeployment of displaced staff
School governors	Sectional	Protecting and enhancing the quality of provision in the school, supporting the LEA initiative where it supported this interest
Parents' pressure group	Sectional	Countering proposals to close schools, seeking alternative possibilities to preserve schools including the GM route
Members of the Council for the Protection of Rural England	Promotional	Preserving old rural school buildings of architectural merit, preserving the quality of rural life by retaining village schools
Central government ministers	Promotional and sectional	Removing surplus places, reducing LEA powers, promoting parental choice of school, creating the GM schools sector
Central government civil servants	Promotional	Assessing firm proposals, ensuring that LEA procedures complied with legislation, advising ministers on GM and reorganisation approval, administering loans for building
Members of Parliament (MPs)	Promotional and sectional	Supporting voters in their constituency affected by reorganisation, supporting or resisting central government policies depending on their political party
Individual parents	Sectional	Protecting the quality of their children's education, minimising disruption for them caused by reorganisation proposals

concepts may be taken from the two constituent perspectives (Wallace 1999, 2000). Using power to shape a culture is a means of channelling others' agency if they come to believe in the advocated course of action. Officials publicised their rationale to gain acceptance of the principle of reorganisation among members of local communities who might otherwise have organised themselves to resist. Power may also be used to delimit others' agency. Officials monitored local communities in case members resisted LEA proposals for their school by applying for it to become GM, so opting out of LEA control and perpetuating the surplus of student places. Where GM proceedings were started, officials stepped in quickly to dissuade parents and governors from acting against the LEA promotional interest.

A popular definition of organisational *culture* is 'the way we do things around here' (Bower 1966). Culture is largely internalised. The norms (or rules of behaviour) guiding interaction among those who subscribe to a culture rest on shared symbols, beliefs and values. Norms may be explicit, perhaps codified in a formal policy – as in the code of practice for staff redeployment brokered by county officials – or implicit, surfacing only when transgressed. A school staff professional culture encompasses beliefs and values spanning education, management, and interpersonal relationships. Where different groups in a school share a distinctive set of beliefs and values they may form subcultures (Firestone and Louis 1999). In these 'differentiated cultures' (Meyerson and Martin 1987), meanings are shared inside subcultural boundaries but there is disjunction between the beliefs and values of different groups. The discomfort expressed by informants at the behaviour of members of the parents' pressure group from the south of the county LEA reflected incompatible norms to which these informants and pressure group members subscribed about appropriate behaviour when mounting a protest (Chapter 2).

School mergers bring together staff who may initially retain allegiance to the culture in their pre-merger institution, resulting in a period of *cultural fragmentation* where they discover how similar or different their pre-merger cultures were. There follows a period of *cultural transition* as staff learn to work in the new institution (Wallace 1996b). Transition may lead to varied outcomes, from a unified culture and identification with the new school to incompatible subcultures featuring enduring allegiance to the pre-merger cultures. In such cases fragmentation may be replaced by *balkanisation* (Hargreaves 1992), where staff form allegiances in line with their distinctive subcultures and are indifferent or antagonistic towards other groups. The 'way we do things around here' is then to protect the sectional interest of the group with whom individuals identify most strongly. In the UK, headteachers have been identified as significant *cultural leaders* (Nias *et al.* 1989; Southworth 1998) in their schools, promoting shared beliefs through strategies such as stating their educational vision and communicating their expectations of colleagues, as did the headteacher at Newell Primary School.

The definition of *power* allows for synergy and conflict. Following Giddens (1984), power is conceived as 'transformative capacity': the capability to intervene in events so as to alter their course. It is expressed when parties to interaction collaborate and mutually reinforce the ability of each person to make things happen. Members of the Newell Steering Committee achieved synergy in combining their individual use of resources towards realising their shared promotional interest in preserving a school for the village. Alternatively, each protagonist in a conflict situation may employ transformative capacity to realise incompatible interests. LEA initial formative proposals triggered the campaigns at Newell and Moor to counter them, while latterly members of the two groups also competed against each other.

We may distinguish two forms of power (Bacharach and Lawler 1980). *Authority* implies use of resources legitimated by individuals' beliefs and values associated with status, which may include the entitlement to apply sanctions. Central government authority to press for LEA reorganisation initiatives was enshrined in legislation, with the sanction that ministers had authority to bring forward reorganisation proposals if officials and councillors failed to comply. *Influence* refers to informal use of resources without recourse to sanctions connected with authority, though other sanctions may be available (such as the public demonstrations mounted by the parents' pressure group). While access to resources varies, any individual will possess some agency and so have recourse to influence. Power will therefore be distributed both within and between organisations and system levels. Individuals may collaborate in *coalitions* where they share a subculture, using power synergistically to realise their shared interests.

Complex change across a social network

We have highlighted how the scope of complex change contributes to administrative complexity as individuals attempt to impact on the behaviour of others by indirect means, whether through intermediaries or through distance communication. The totality of stakeholders involved may be construed as forming a social *network*, defined by Laumann *et al.* (1978: 458) as 'a set of nodes (e.g., persons, organizations) linked by a set of social relationships (e.g. friendship, transfer of funds, overlapping membership) of a specified type'. Network analysis has been widely applied to the pattern of *formal* and *informal* relationships between individuals in organisations and relationships between organisations (Nohria 1998). The main route for the flow of interaction as the reorganisation initiatives evolved, especially between system levels, was a set of formal pre-existing relationships. It was supplemented by informal links, notably the local 'grapevines' whereby individuals and groups at the peripheral system level exchanged rumour and harder information according to experience in different schools.

We are principally concerned with the flow of interaction generated by a complex change as the process plays out through the activity of stakeholders in contrasting organisational contexts. (The network encompassing the reorganisation initiatives evolved to cover members of all interest groups listed in Table 3.2.) Some stakeholders will be regularly connected already through stable relationships, as through the formal linkages between an LEA and its schools. But the business of managing a complex change entails a series of interactions. They both flow through a network of stakeholders in some established relationship to each other and extend this network by creating new relationships where people are brought into contact for the first time.

The flow of interaction is broadly directional overall, in that instigators of change initiate contact with others whose acquiescence or support is required. But it is also multidirectional, though not uniformly so, in that others respond and trigger further sequences of interaction. It is hierarchical in that individual instigators at a more central system level attempt to channel and delimit the agency of a large number of stakeholders at a more peripheral level to realise their promotional interest through the change they are seeking to introduce. These instigators may become widely known as individuals with key roles connected with the change right across the network of stakeholders spanning all system levels. Members of the Newell and Moor communities knew that the county CEO had been instrumental in launching the reorganisation initiative leading to the proposals for their schools and that the Secretary of State would formally decide whether to approve the LEA firm proposals.

In contrast, stakeholders at more peripheral levels tended to be more concerned with their sectional or promotional interests relating to their organisation alone. Officials shared a promotional interest in reorganisation solely inside their LEA, and a sectional interest in protecting their authority over schooling by pre-empting a possible central government intervention to reorganise their provision. Members of school communities shared a sectional interest in protecting their own school first and foremost. Instigators of complex change will tend to have only very generalised knowledge about the other stakeholders as a totality and minimal knowledge of their detailed individual circumstances, except in rare cases where contact is made.

The significance of contact through intermediaries and one-way mass communication is illustrated in Figure 3.1. Each circle represents an education system level. Their overlap indicates how some stakeholders based at each level, mostly having specialist responsibility connected with reorganisation entailing cross-level liaison, had a regular formal relationship with those at another level. We have seen how LEA officials instigated the reorganisation initiatives under pressure from central government. The directional drift of interaction across the network of stakeholders at the three main system levels is indicated by the heavy arrows, from the centre, through the intermediate level of the LEA to the periphery in schools. The dashed arrows in the reverse direction reflect the fact that interaction was not simply unidirectional, with many opportunities for stakeholders at all levels to initiate interaction or respond to others. The bulk of interaction between centre and periphery therefore takes place through the medium of stakeholders based at LEA level. Only occasionally could cross-level interaction initiated by stakeholders at school level bypass intermediaries. The dotted arrows from school to LEA and to central system level represent this possibility.

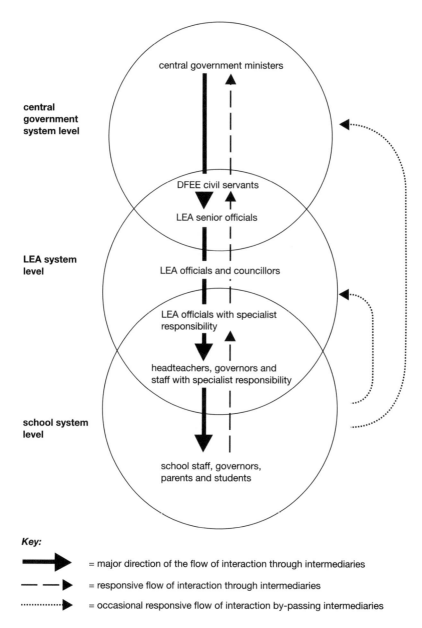

central government ministers

central government system level

DFEE civil servants

LEA senior officials

LEA system level

LEA officials and councillors

LEA officials with specialist responsibility

headteachers, governors and staff with specialist responsibility

school system level

school staff, governors, parents and students

Key:

= major direction of the flow of interaction through intermediaries

= responsive flow of interaction through intermediaries

= occasional responsive flow of interaction by-passing intermediaries

Figure 3.1 The flow of interaction through intermediaries within a multilevel network of stakeholders

When a deputation from members of the pressure group in the county was allowed an audience with a central government minister, civil servants with specialist responsibility for the county proposals attended the meeting. They mediated the interaction through their record of the meeting which informed the eventual decision-making process. The directional flow of interaction was thus achieved through chains of interaction involving intermediaries who could express their agency in facilitating, distorting, or even blocking communication. Small wonder that no one had first-hand knowledge of the county LEA reorganisation initiative in its entirety, and that understanding of reorganisation among stakeholders at school level was mainly confined to the impact of the initiative on their community. We note that there were formal linkages between school and LEA levels through the composition of governing bodies, which included one or more councillors, parents, and school staff. In the borough, the clerk to each governing body was an official.

At the school level there was much informal contact across parts of the network where, say, spouses or friends worked in different schools. There was an instance in the borough of a teacher at Endale Middle School who was also a parent governor for Hillside High. Formal contact also featured extensively, officials facilitating meetings with headteachers, with staff union representatives, and with chairs of governors. In all, contacts at the school level had some mediating effect for particular individuals and institutions. But they did not alter the dominant centre-to-periphery thrust of interaction bringing the reorganisation initiatives through to completion.

Reorganisation initiatives as a change process

The slogan that 'change is a process, not an event' (Fullan 2001: 52) sums up lessons of North American research into the fate of single innovations. Fullan divides this process into a sequence of what we will term *stages* (to distinguish them from the sequential *phases* of the reorganisation initiatives in the present study). *Initiation* is the first stage of the process leading to a decision to proceed with a change. From then, the *implementation* stage covers the experience of attempting to put the change into practice. Finally, the *institutionalisation* stage refers to the way the change becomes built into normal practice and is no longer perceived as anything new. Other outcomes are possible, not least that the implementation effort may be abandoned. Whilst one stage follows another the process is not neatly linear, nor is one stage always totally distinct from the next. It happened that each stage of the reorganisation initiatives relating to the schools in a given phase was sharply delineated. National legislation governing the procedure for approving proposals to reorganise schools and the requirement that reorganisation came into effect on a specified date meant that both the initiation and implementation stages were punctuated by significant events.

The initiation stage entailed officials drafting formative proposals for reorganising schools that were then published – a big event for other stakeholders at school level who learned what reorganisation potentially held in store for their school. Officials consulted stakeholders in each community, and this process culminated in the formal submission of firm proposals to central government for approval. The assessment process there led to the announcement of decisions to approve proposals, an event bringing the end of the initiation stage. The implementation stage involved LEA officials, headteachers, and governors making arrangements for approved proposals to be put into place. They had to be completed by the set date marking the beginning of a school year, an event imposing great pressure for the 'critical path' of implementation activities. The institutionalisation stage was an indeterminate process spanning several years from the reorganisation date where staff in reorganised schools became familiar with working in the new regime.

Many quite specific sub-innovations were undertaken at school level within the reorganisation process. They followed the same sequence of stages as reorganisation as a whole, but not necessarily coinciding with the stage reorganisation had reached. The implementation stage spawned the initiation of many sub-innovations, such as extension of the curriculum to cover a new age range of students. They were not implemented until the institutionalisation stage of reorganisation.

Depending on the part individuals play in the change process, they may be categorised as *change agents*, contributing to bringing about a shift in others' practice related to some component of the change, whether inside or outside the institution or the system level where the change agents are based. (Our definition of the term 'change agent' follows Bolam's (1975) usage, and is broader than that adopted in much North American literature where it may refer solely to professional change facilitators or consultants.) *Users* are individuals whom change agents expect to implement a change in their own practice, entailing some form of learning experience. Since reorganisation took place across system levels, most change agents for some change components were also users of others. Indeed few involved at any level could claim to have had nothing to learn. All struggled to a varying degree to make sense of the reorganisation initiatives. The overlap between experience as change agents and users of aspects of the change rep-resented by the reorganisation initiatives is illustrated in Table 3.3. Components of reorganisation initiatives highlighted will be discussed fully later. The stage or stages of the change process to which each component relates reflects the gradual progression of activity connected with reorganisation initiatives across system levels: initiation was largely a central and local government affair, implementation was the province of LEAs and their schools, institutionalisation was mostly down to school staff and governors.

Inside central government, several civil servants participated under the guidance of senior colleagues in assessing LEA firm proposals for the first time. Ministers set officials and councillors an unprecedented challenge in pushing them to reorganise their schools in the new context where much erstwhile LEA authority had been devolved to the school level. Central government policy-makers had even empowered school staff and governors potentially to avoid reorganisation through the GM route. Civil servants set LEA officials the

Table 3.3 Indicative overlap between change agents and users within and between system
levels

Change agent	System level	Component of reorganisation	Stage of change process	User	System level
Ministers	Central	Assessing firm LEA proposals	Initiation	Civil servants	Central
Ministers	Central	Undertaking reorganisation in the context of the policy promoting the GM sector	Initiation	Senior officials, officials, and councillors	LEA
Civil servants	Central	Developing and submitting proposals in compliance with current legislation	Initiation	Senior officials, officials	LEA
Councillors	LEA	Managing reorganisation in the current political context	Initiation, implementation, institutional-isation	Senior officials, officials	LEA
Senior officials	LEA	Managing public consultation on formative proposals	Initiation	Officials	LEA
Senior officials	LEA	Managing specialised tasks on an unprecedented scale	Implementation	Officials	LEA
Officials	LEA	Managing large-scale reallocation of school staff	Implementation	Headteachers, governors	School
Headteachers	School	Developing the curriculum, and learning and teaching and strategies	Institutional-isation	School teaching staff	School

challenge, on councillors' behalf, of bringing proposals to the point of submission
for central government approval. A few officials had prior experience of
managing large-scale reorganisation. But even the most experienced had to
modify whatever they had done previously because of changes in the context.

The learning curve was perhaps steepest for individuals required to act as a
change agent for others in a new situation in which they were also users. Many
officials who represented the LEA at public consultation meetings on formative
proposals during the initiation stage had never been through this often highly
charged experience before and ruefully acknowledged how much they had had
to learn. Most were also responsible as change agents for the implementation of
some specialised component of reorganisation at school level, such as the
redeployment of staff from closing schools. Such management tasks were to be
achieved through headteachers and governors of surviving institutions who, as
users, were responsible for implementing redeployment through staff selection
procedures. The transfer of authority over staff selection from LEA to schools
meant that the new procedures had not been used before on this scale.

The fresh start for school staffs brought by reorganisation offered many headteachers the chance to act as change agents in stimulating developments in the curriculum and the teaching and learning process (as occurred during institutionalisation of reorganisation in the primary school at Newell). Some of these sub-innovations would have had to be addressed anyway, because central government ministers were iteratively introducing compulsory changes in curriculum and assessment requirements. Most staff, as users, faced having to make multiple changes in their practice. We noted above how Hargreaves did not fully address the issue of coping with multiple changes. In the new era, change agents at all system levels must learn how to manage an evolving profile of innovations and unplanned changes alongside their ongoing work (Wallace 1991b: 200–1):

> The distinctiveness of managing multiple innovations appears to lie in the iterative process of decision-making and planning arrangements for the implementation, adaptation or postponement of this profile of innovations, whose characteristics frequently and unpredictably changed within a wider context which itself frequently and unpredictably changed.

As change agents headteachers and, to a lesser extent, senior officials were presented with the 'metatask' of juggling with their part in managing reorganisation alongside other innovations in the profile confronting them – especially various education reforms.

Policy instruments for promoting change

Parameters for each stage of the reorganisation initiatives were set by central and local government policies. Policymakers employed certain mechanisms or *policy instruments* to promote implementation at a more peripheral system level. McDonnell and Elmore (1991) argue that there is limited choice of policy instruments, determined by policymakers' access to three types of resource – the ability to make rules, to spend money, and to shift the balance of authority between system levels. The instruments are defined in the following terms:

> *mandates* are rules governing the action of individuals and agencies, and are intended to produce compliance;
> *inducements* transfer money to individuals and agencies in return for certain actions;
> *capacity-building* is the transfer of money for the purpose of investment in material, intellectual or human resources; and
> *system-changing* transfers official authority among individuals and agencies in order to alter the system by which public goods and services are delivered.
> (McDonnell and Elmore 1991: 158)

We suggest that these instruments should not be regarded solely as alternatives. They may be employed in combination, both within a policy and where a multiplicity of policies is brought to bear on a perceived problem such as surplus school capacity Also, inducements and capacity-building may operate not only through giving money but also by withholding it unless potential recipients comply with policymakers' requirements – they may constitute an 'offer you dare not refuse' where stakeholders are starved of urgently needed resources which offers of money will ameliorate, even though there may be strings attached (Wallace 1991b).

The instruments operate differently in channelling and delimiting the agency of stakeholders at other system levels. They each tend to produce consequences that may or may not serve policymakers' interests. Mandates are based on securing compliance, so they require surveillance to detect non-compliance and the authority to impose sanctions that will bring change users into line. While they may guarantee minimal compliance, they may also inhibit variation in implementation – including the possibility of unanticipated outcomes that accord with the spirit of the policy change as envisaged by its instigators. Inducements rely on bringing out the latent capability of users to do what is required in exchange for additional money. As with mandates, the less variation allowable to comply with the conditions of an award, the more surveillance is required to delimit users' agency and ensure the money is spent on what policymakers intend. Capacity-building is designed to enhance whatever capability currently exists among users. Its impact will therefore be both long-term and diffuse. This instrument offers considerable room for users' agency, allowing outcomes to be achieved that policymakers never envisaged. Policymakers incur short-term costs for which they may experience difficulty in accounting because capacity-building is unlikely to yield immediate returns. System-changing operates by altering the balance of authority, frequently between system levels. Stakeholders who lose authority may be provoked into a defensive response. Those who gain must learn how to use their new authority, giving rise to the possibility of variation in outcomes and of incurring the cost of providing learning support. All four instruments featured in the reorganisation initiatives, either integrally or as embodied in other policies impinging on them. Table 3.4 indicates how these instruments could be instigated inside central government or an LEA, but each was designed for implementation at a more peripheral system level. We will explore consequences of employing these policy instruments in later chapters.

Slipping through the cracks

Whichever instruments are chosen, implementation of any policy is likely to involve interaction with other policies. We have argued that the context dependency of complex educational change includes planned and unplanned changes. Especially significant are the policy changes that were planned by policymakers but not, it seems, with reorganisation in mind. Our data analysis revealed four types of policy-related factor impinging on reorganisation initiatives. The first pair arises by default, implying unintended consequences of

Table 3.4 Range of policy instruments connected with reorganisation initiatives

Policy instrument	Example connected with reorganisation	System level of policy initiation	System level of policy implementation
Mandate	Statutory requirements for public consultation on formative LEA proposals	Central	LEA
Inducement	Capital borrowing for new building and refurbishment of schools	Central	LEA
	'transition allowance' to schools to support the implementation stage of reorganisation	LEA	School
Capacity-building	Investment of extra money in newly created GM schools	Central	LEA
	reinvestment of revenue savings in reorganised schools	LEA	School
System-changing	Devolution of LEA authority over the allocation of staff to schools	Central	School

policymakers' failure at a more central level to take into account circumstances at a more peripheral level related to reorganisation:

- *Policy vacuum* encompasses situations where there is no policy to frame particular implementation tasks.
- *Policy insensitivity* refers to a gap in the circumstances for which another policy caters that renders it insensitive to the one in question, especially where it imposes requirements that do not suit the situation, leading to uncertainty over what should be done.

The second pair describes opposing forms of interaction between the planned requirements of other policies and the one being implemented:

- *Policy congruence* covers situations where one or more other policies facilitate implementation of the one at hand.
- *Policy contradiction* refers to circumstances where practices associated with one or more other policies run counter to the policy in focus, inhibiting its implementation.

Here the positive or negative interaction between policies is a product of policymakers' design rather than lack of planning, though the undermining effect of contradictory policies can hardly be intentional. Most instances of these positive and negative forms of interaction occurred between central and LEA levels. But ironically the deepest contradiction lay between central government policies, indicative of divisions at the heart of the state. Table 3.5 gives examples of these types of factor and their impact on the reorganisation initiatives and schools.

Most of these factors featured in Chapter 2. Lack of a central government policy providing for the extra work to manage reorganisation contributed to the stress felt by the headteacher-designate of the new Newell Primary School when preparing for reorganisation, and to the complaint of some staff that they received little proactive LEA support – officials were too busy coping with other tasks. We saw how the new building was not completed in time, adding to the work-

Table 3.5 Types of policy-related factor impinging on the reorganisation initiatives

Type of policy-related factor	System level of origin	Instance	Impact on LEA reorganisation initiatives	Impact on schools undergoing reorganisation
Policy vacuum	Central	No central government provision for work to manage reorganisation in LEAs	An extra workload for LEA officials over several years	An extra workload for governors, headteachers and senior staff over several years
Policy insensitivity	Central	Finance for building work available only in the financial year when building was to be completed	Short-term LEA saving was constrained and the start of building work had to be delayed	LEA financial support with implementing reorganisation was restricted, completion of some building work was delayed until after the reorganisation date
Policy congruence	Central and LEA	Reducing surplus places and the LEA effort to improve schools	Officials able to plan improvements in provision (e.g. in building stock)	A new start in reorganised schools, improvement in buildings for some of them
Policy contra-diction	Central versus LEA	Removal of LEA authority over school staff allocation versus the requirement that senior LEA officials orchestrate redeployment of staff from closing schools	Officials engaged in lengthy negotiations with each governing body of surviving schools with staff vacancies	Prolonged uncertainty and stress for staff from closing schools who faced redeployment
	Central versus central	Expansion of the GM schools sector versus removal of surplus places	Officials and councillors campaigned to prevent schools becoming GM, some loss of savings from planned school reorganisations	An increase in the number of GM schools which shored up surplus places and led to competition against LEA schools for students

load of staff. They had to open the new school in the old building and then move in the middle of the term. A contributing factor was the central government rule that capital for building could be released only in the financial year when building would be completed: LEA officials received funds in early April for schools reorganising in September of the same year. This capital borrowing policy was insensitive to the need in LEAs and schools to start building work far enough ahead of the scheduled reorganisation date to allow for unforeseeable delays.

Congruence between central government and LEA policies could produce synergy. At Newell, responding to the inducement to borrow capital for the construction of a new school building represented a tangible improvement in educational provision for the LEA and the local community. Contradiction between policies on the other hand spelled problems for aspects of reorganisation affected. System-changing by central government to reduce LEA powers meant that officials had forfeited authority over school staff appointments yet were still expected to deal with the surplus of staff during the implementation stage of reorganisation. The consequence was additional work, brokering the voluntary agreement with governors in schools across the LEA to consider displaced staff first when filling vacancies and negotiating with individual governing bodies. Even more pronounced during the initiation stage was the contradiction between the central government education policies of removing surplus places and promoting the GM sector by allowing schools to avoid closure or merger under LEA proposals.

Opening up an implementation gap through a 'counter-policy'

Complex educational change is typically systemic, planned at a more central system level for implementation at a more peripheral level. Central government and LEA policies express their instigators' political and educational values, which commonly conflict with those of stakeholders who are expected to implement such policies. Stakeholders at a more peripheral level may express agency by organising themselves to counter externally initiated policies of which they disapprove. (Their 'self-organisation' here is a far cry from Stacey's conception that we challenged in Chapter 1. He assumed that offering stakeholders agency would result in them using their discretion in support of managers' goals.) Such concerted blocking tactics may be conceived as a local *counter-policy*, a heuristic device for analysing aspects of the implementation gap that is commonly found where policies originating at one level are to be put into practice at another. While there may sometimes be a policy vacuum where there is room for a policy as we claimed above, no policy is ever introduced into a vacuum of practice. Where a new policy has been designed to bring about change, it will probably transgress the cultural beliefs and values of stakeholders with a vested interest in maintaining the status quo. They are likely to direct such agency as they possess towards protecting whatever they currently value. A counter-policy may be defined as:

a proactive response by powerful actors in a locality to a policy initiated elsewhere that they perceive to threaten their beliefs and values, where they harness their institutional resources in a co-ordinated manner to mediate implementation of this external policy in ways that challenge or subvert its initiators' stated aims.

(Wallace 1998b: 198)

It may vary between the formal and explicit, expressed through public statements, and the informal and implicit, articulated only in private conversation. A counter-policy may be oriented primarily towards *active resistance* to the external policy, especially when it is first launched, by persisting with present practice expressing existing values in the face of external pressure for change (Figure 3.2). It may become more subversive through *co-optation*, hijacking the external policy by adapting its implementation to express contradictory values. Where sufficient agency is found, resistance may lead to *rejection* of the policy. When external policies contradict each other, as with removal of surplus places versus promoting the GM schools sector, we shall see how it is even possible to play one off against the other.

Where stakeholders' agency is tightly delimited through mandates, they may become resigned to complying with the letter of the new requirements sufficiently to get past accompanying surveillance and accountability measures. Then stakeholders whose culture remains antithetical to the new order may use whatever agency is left to them in offering continued *passive resistance* where compliance remains minimal. Equally the synergistic effort put into a counter-policy may dissipate, replaced by gradual *acceptance* of the policy where stakeholders' beliefs and values change in its favour. Where what is proposed is congruent with local stakeholders' beliefs and values, they may either accept it or more enthusiastically give it their *endorsement* and contribute actively to its implementation.

We related in the last chapter how members of both the Newell and Moor communities mobilised themselves to counter the formative LEA proposal to ward off the threat to their respective village schools. They used agency to resist, developing the strongest possible argument for retaining a state funded school in their village. As the situation unfolded, members of the Newell Steering Committee shifted ground by seeking to maximise the possibility of realising their interest while also realising those of officials, councillors, and diocesan representatives. Once the decision on the firm proposal was made in their favour they actively endorsed implementation of the policy. At Moor, agency was successfully directed towards finding an alternative to state funded education in the village, using the very buildings that had been closed to remove surplus capacity. The surplus remained, now outside the state and in competition with state provision at Newell. Parents sending their children to the Moor independent school instead of Newell Primary School helped to perpetuate some surplus capacity in nearby state schools. Their action marginally reduced the LEA savings that could otherwise have been made.

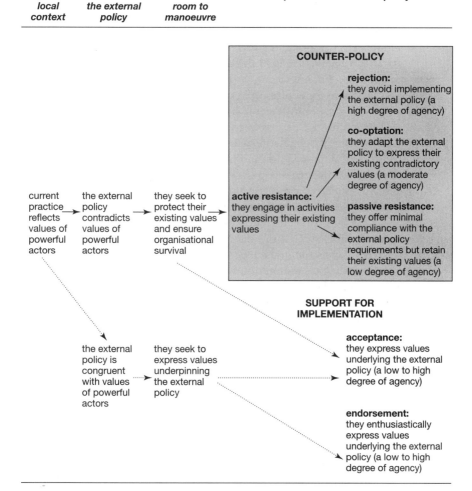

The initial local context	Introduction of the external policy	The search for room to manoeuvre	Response to the external policy

COUNTER-POLICY

rejection:
they avoid implementing the external policy (a high degree of agency)

co-optation:
they adapt the external policy to express their existing contradictory values (a moderate degree of agency)

current practice reflects values of powerful actors → the external policy contradicts values of powerful actors → they seek to protect their existing values and ensure organisational survival →

active resistance: they engage in activities expressing their existing values

passive resistance: they offer minimal compliance with the external policy requirements but retain their existing values (a low degree of agency)

SUPPORT FOR IMPLEMENTATION

the external policy is congruent with values of powerful actors → they seek to express values underpinning the external policy

acceptance:
they express values underlying the external policy (a low to high degree of agency)

endorsement:
they enthusiastically express values underlying the external policy (a low to high degree of agency)

Figure 3.2 Responses to an externally initiated policy at the sites of implementation

Managerialism: an ideology for keeping agency within structural limits

We earlier pointed to economic conditions that pushed central government ministers into pressuring LEA officials to undertake reorganisation initiatives. The structural limits to agency represented by these forces have surfaced in many western countries as the relative degree of autonomy between the state and state education and the economy has approached its elastic limit. The central government imperative behind reorganisation was to reduce the contribution that maintaining surplus student places was making to an expanding level of public expenditure which, in turn, contributed to compromising the nation's economic profitability. Simultaneously, education reforms were designed to safeguard national prosperity by raising standards of state education to create a more highly skilled and flexible workforce required for successful competition in the global marketplace. Reorganisation held the dual attraction for ministers of enabling them to cut back on unproductive public spending while creating more propitious conditions for education in surviving schools.

The means of reforming the public sector, of which reorganisation and education reforms are a part, has been widely conceived as *managerialism*: the belief that all aspects of organisational life can and should be managed according to rational structures, procedures, and modes of accountability in the pursuit of goals defined by policymakers and senior managers. The assumption that management has such potential to channel and delimit others' agency on behalf of policymakers originated in the private sector. It has been translated to the public sector to improve efficiency as a contribution to better economic performance (Pollitt 1993; Clarke and Newman 1997). Building on the earlier analysis of agency and structural limits, we interpret managerialism as a product of its time, an ideological assumption surfacing when capital accumulation has come under strain. Managerialism complements economic conditions in reinforcing the structural limits of agency by promoting a more efficient and effective public sector that will assist in capital accumulation. Pollitt's account of the logic underpinning this assumption demonstrates the alignment between ideology and economic conditions:

- social progress requires continuing increases in economic productivity;
- productivity increases come from applying ever more sophisticated technologies to produce material goods, plus information and organisational technologies;
- application of these technologies can be achieved only through a workforce disciplined to accept the drive to increase productivity;
- management is a discrete organisational function crucial to planning, implementing and measuring necessary productivity improvements;
- to perform this function, managers must be empowered by giving them sufficient room to manoeuvre – the 'right to manage'.

(Pollitt 1993: 2–3)

Managerialism implies the belief that the agency of those through whom central policies are implemented can and should be channelled within limits specified by central policymakers or managers (such as officials and headteachers) acting for them. Policymakers wield extensive control over managers' agency, while managers express their right to manage (actually as delimited by policymakers) through wielding extensive control over the agency of the managed. Managers and those they manage are empowered to express agency within the centrally specified direction. They may be encouraged to believe in policymakers' goals and become committed to them through acculturation. They may be monitored to inform policymakers whether they stray off-limits. If so, they may be disciplined, disempowering them until they step back into line. Managerialism promotes the unequal distribution of power between interest groups by privileging policymakers and managers who conform to their requirements over the managed and any obdurate managers who fail to conform.

However the content of managerialism belies precise definition because it refers to an assemblage of partially incompatible beliefs and values, only some of which may be emphasised by particular groups. A crucial difference between managerialist policy initiatives lies in the choice of instruments for channelling and delimiting others' agency to achieve the goal of increasing managerial control. The three versions of managerialism identified here are 'ideal types', commonly expressed in some combination (Table 3.6).

Neo-Taylorism, exemplified in the UK by the central government initiative to create the National Curriculum, opts for channelling agency and delimiting its boundaries through the overt directive control of mandates, often reinforced through resource starvation plus inducements that are contingent on detailed requirements for compliance. It may entail system-changing where authority to enforce mandates is initially lacking. Power is concentrated in the hands of policymakers and managers acting on their behalf. It operates through detailed specification of who is to do what to achieve identified targets, backed by narrowly focused training, surveillance, and accountability measures to ensure tight discipline. The bottom line is securing behavioural compliance: school staff – including managers – may not agree with policy directives but they must carry out specified tasks or face disempowering disciplinary measures.

Entrepreneurship has been expressed in marketisation reforms across the public sector within the 'new public management' (Dunleavy and Hood 1994; Foster and Plowden 1996). This variant opts for the covert, indirect control offered by capacity-building, backed by more overt system-changing where necessary to devolve authority inside predefined limits over selected areas of management decision-making. It is a strategy of 'steering at a distance' (Whitty *et al.* 1998) with the 'hidden hand' of the market at the wheel. Agency is channelled and delimited through creating conditions promoting competition for institutional survival. The operation of the market maximises efficiency through the aggregate of stakeholders' self-interested activity, ensuring that consumers receive value for money. The bottom line is securing behavioural compliance, this time through consumer demand which shapes and disciplines the response of producers (in our case school staff).

Culture management opts for indirect control through overt and covert mechanisms designed to align the beliefs and values of managers and those they manage with the beliefs and values of policymakers. Capacity-building may be employed to encourage target groups to contribute towards a shared vision, the choice of official goals, and the development of strategies for their realisation. System-changing may empower them to do so as long as they express beliefs and values inside limits specified by policymakers. Mandates may make them go

Table 3.6 Comparison between ideal types of managerialism

Characteristic of managerialism	Ideal type of managerialism		
	Neo-Taylorism	Entrepreneurship	Culture management
Form of control centre–periphery power shift	Direct centralising	Indirect decentralising	Indirect centralising
Control mechanisms	Overt	Covert	Overt and covert
Bottom line for control strategy	Behavioural compliance	behavioural compliance	beliefs and values governing behaviour
Policymaker user relationship	Low trust	Low trust	high trust
Policy instruments commonly employed	Mandates, inducements	Capacity-building, system-changing	Mandates, capacity-building, system-changing
Examples of policies which channel agency within the UK reform of state-funded schooling	Publication of National Curriculum documents, target-setting for teachers	The school operating budget based on student numbers, creating the GM schools sector	The requirement that a school brochure must contain a statement of aims, school development planning
Examples of policies which delimit boundaries of agency within the UK reform of state schooling	National tests for students, staff appraisal, regular external inspection of schools	Publication of league tables of national test results, reduction in the school budget where student numbers fall, empowerment of parents to express a preference for a school	Identification of any lack of commitment by surveillance of teaching and management through regular inspection

through the behavioural motions, minimally, of vision-building and planning for development in compliance with policymakers' requirements. Eventually, as Fullan (2001) suggests, change in belief may follow the enforced change in practice. For policymakers, the long-term aim is to transform compliance into enthusiastic commitment where others' beliefs and values align ever more closely with their own. The bottom line here is to 'win hearts and minds', so that managers and the managed come to trust those who set goals on their behalf and embrace the desired culture. They will be motivated voluntarily to channel their agency along the required lines with commitment to the spirit of the enterprise, delimiting the boundaries of agency themselves through self-discipline because they believe in achieving official goals.

Whilst these ideal types of managerialism involve different approaches to channelling and delimiting agency, the three complement each other in providing a comprehensive set of control mechanisms: direct and indirect, centralising and decentralising, explicit and subliminal. Policy initiatives of a public-sector reform programme may reflect all three ideal types of managerialism where policymakers seek to maximise their degree of control. The Conservative central government education reform strategy at the period of our study included a strong element of neo-Taylorism impacting on reorganisation as part of the profile of innovations to be managed alongside it. Mandates imposed the National Curriculum and national testing on schools. They were accompanied by system-changing to remove the vestiges of curriculum control from LEAs, and to introduce the school surveillance and accountability system of regular school inspections with public reporting of findings. Neo-Taylorism also featured directly: we noted above how system-changing legislation was brought in empowering ministers to mount reorganisation initiatives if LEA officials failed to respond to pressure. Officials would then be subject to directive control through a contingent mandate designed expressly to exclude them.

Entrepreneurship was promoted through system-changing to give head-teachers and governors the 'right to manage' by devolving LEA authority over school management, including the inducement of managing the institutional operating budget. This shift included devolving authority over decisions on staffing which was so deeply to affect reorganisation. At the same time conditions were created to foster marketplace competition between schools. These condition-setting arrangements included publication of league tables of National Curriculum test results to inform parental choice. Once established through system-changing legislation, the GM sector was promoted through capacity-building which also acted as an inducement for parents and staff to opt out of LEA control. GM schools were financed at a more generous level than LEA schools (Bush *et al.* 1993). The GM sector was designed to offer parents more choice between types of school. But this policy undermined reorganisation initiatives through the escape route it provided.

A genuflection towards culture management was embodied in central government policies such as the promotion of school development planning, involving exercises to articulate school aims, and directions for development (Wallace and McMahon 1994). Policymakers' desire to break the mould of the postwar educational consensus, together with their faith in applying market principles to education, appears to have attracted them towards ideal types of managerialism promising the most rapid and predictable results as they require only behavioural compliance, not a change in belief.

Central government system-changing to create conditions for a centralised National Curriculum and a marketplace at school level left LEA officials with a form of culture management as their sole feasible approach to reorganisation. Proposals at the initiation stage may have had the status of provisional mandates, but they were subject to community response and central government decision that would be sensitive to local feedback. They would become firm mandates only if they were approved. Then they would give senior officials authority to orchestrate implementation – without authority over the reallocation of staff.

LEA reorganisation initiatives became a high-risk enterprise for officials and councillors owing to the strong chance of triggering a 'nimbyist' negative response to closure or merger proposals, coupled with the possibility of losing schools through GM applications. Councillors could easily withdraw their commitment if there was strong community resistance. Past experience of failed reorganisation attempts (Ranson 1990) in the days of greater LEA authority suggested that the present initiatives might never get past the initiation stage.

As we shall see, officials' strategy during this stage was to seek cultural hegemony by engendering the belief amongst councillors and community members alike that reorganisation was in their interest. Acquiescence was essential if proposals were to win central government approval. During implementation, officials would be dependent on the co-operation of school staff and governors with sole authority over staffing. Officials relied on a widespread belief in their impartiality and professionalism to gain acceptance for their proposals. They also employed the instrument of capacity-building. They promoted higher-quality educational provision across the LEA through capital borrowing for building and refurbishment, reinvesting savings in surviving schools, and supporting the new start for staff as a school improvement effort.

Pluralism and the rolling out of the state

In the public sector, government pursuit of managerialism has been viewed as an attempt to reconstruct the state by 'rolling out' state power between central government and organisations at the periphery (Clarke and Newman 1997). In the case of state education in Britain, the system-changing combination of centralisation and devolution is designed to squeeze out LEA authority. Yet the complexity of such a change reduces the likelihood that any group can channel and delimit the agency of other groups such that a predictable outcome is guaranteed. The size of the education system and the distribution of power across a vast network of stakeholders based at different system levels leave significant room for agency to mediate the central government policy thrust. Clarke and Newman argue that:

> The contradictory consequence of dispersal is that while it aims at the breaking up of the institutionalised centres of power characteristic of the old state form, it also multiplies new sites of potential resistance by increasing the number of decision making nodal points. Although these are dispersed by contrast with the centralised power exercised at the heart of the state, they are nevertheless open to potential co-option by localised interests and alliances.
>
> (Clarke and Newman 1997: 31)

In the coming chapters we shall discuss how ministers actually depended on the same officials whose authority they had dispersed to realise their interest in large-scale reorganisation. When our study was undertaken, expression of agency at LEA level in managing reorganisation represented an enduring 'lump' in the state that ministers could not afford to roll out – despite their rhetoric. A pluralistic framework for analysis will help us to explore how agency was expressed in managing reorganisation within and between system levels and inside the structural limits. We begin by focusing on the context of this complex educational change as an entity of many parts.

4 Reorganisation initiatives
Origins and outline

During the 1980s, senior officials in our case-study LEAs became engaged in an ambitious, risky, and stressful attempt to achieve a lasting solution to the problem of maintaining extensive surplus student capacity in the schools for which they were responsible. The reorganisation initiative on which they embarked was to dominate their professional lives for the best part of a decade. They had no guarantee of success as the managerialist orientation of system-changing national policies put them in a potentially 'no-win' situation, pushing them to take decisive LEA-wide action while reducing their authority to ensure implementation. Officials would not be popular with members of local communities, who stood to discover what they might lose long before they could experience what they might gain. Why and how were the initiatives launched and to what effect? In developing a summary answer to this question we employ the pluralistic perspective to interpret the process of complex educational change exemplified by the LEA reorganisation initiatives.

The first task of the present chapter is to explore the origins of the initiatives, since context-dependency was such a prominent characteristic of their complexity. External pressure to reorganise provision driven by structural factors was complemented by a unique mix of past and present policies and unplanned changes. Together they channelled and delimited the agency of the instigators of reorganisation initiatives. The second task is to summarise the initiatives as a whole, since their componential nature contributed equally to their complexity. They consisted of several overlapping phases, each breaking down into the same sequence of stages. We note how officials organised themselves to manage the initiatives in their entirety. The final task is to document outcomes of the reorganisation initiatives for provision in reorganised schools. We consider briefly the extent to which these outcomes reflected the promotional interest of officials and central government ministers in streamlining and improving the quality of provision. We also consider how far diocesan representatives achieved their promotional interest in reorganising church school provision. This account sets the scene for our further exploration of each stage in the change process for any phase of reorganisation.

Context-dependence: past changes, present problem

The Conservative central government's White Paper setting out its education policy agenda for the mid-1990s concluded that:

> both locally and nationally it is educationally undesirable as well as poor stewardship of taxpayers' money to waste it on surplus places. One of the most important tasks for the rest of this decade is to eliminate surplus places while at the same time ensuring high quality provision of new schools in areas where this is necessary.
>
> (DFE 1992: 12)

No one had planned to generate the high proportion of surplus student places that was the object of government criticism. How had the borough and county LEAs arrived at a situation before reorganisation where both contained a substantial surplus, unevenly spread across a mixture of school systems, and occupying school buildings ranging from a few years to one and a half centuries old? This predicament was the product of iterative decisions for planning education provision, a duty falling to LEAs but also a legacy of religious community decisions before state involvement in mass education when many church schools were founded. It was equally the product of unplanned population changes affected by diverse national policies such as the raising of the school leaving age, local policies including those determining new areas for housing development, and economic trends determining the nature of the local labour market. It was also related to councillors' diffidence born of their failed piecemeal attempts to reorganise schools.

The surplus in the two LEAs reflected the national picture of a declining school age population since its peak in the 1970s. But variation among population movements in different areas meant that the distribution of surplus capacity did not necessarily match the shifting demand for school places, especially in areas of population growth with a high proportion of young families. Schools that were popular with parents could be full while unpopular schools nearby remained half-empty.

It is hardly surprising, therefore, that the reorganisation initiatives to reduce the high level of surplus student capacity were deeply affected by their context. Table 4.1 summarises the pre-reorganisation situation in both LEAs and key contextual factors contributing to it. The demography of the borough and the county differed markedly. But both contained a mixture of urban and suburban areas where most large and more recently built schools were located, and outlying rural districts containing the majority of small primary sector schools. The central government policy of promoting entrepreneurship through the GM sector had so far proved attractive to a few secondary or high school communities. However, one effect of system-changing here had been to encourage governors in two GM 12–18 high schools in the county to use their new authority over admissions. They had notified officials of their intention to seek central government approval to fill their surplus

Table 4.1 LEA contexts and contributing factors before reorganisation

Factor	Borough LEA	County LEA
Demography	Industrialised area containing a large town and surrounding rural district	Large area containing several market towns and an extensive rural 'commuter belt' district
Number of state-funded schools in primary and secondary sectors	161 (including 1 GM secondary school)	282 (including 8 GM secondary or high schools)
Number of surplus student places	15,000	19,000
Surplus student places as a percentage of schools' capacity	25%	19%
Distribution of surplus student places across school sectors	Two-thirds primary sector, one-third secondary sector	Two-thirds primary sector, one-third secondary sector
Administrative divisions	17 'pyramids' based on each secondary or high school and its feeder schools	5 areas – northern, north-eastern, eastern, central, southern, each with several secondary or high schools and their feeder schools
Political allegiance of the local council	Labour, with a large majority of seats	Conservative, with a small majority of seats (becoming a 'hung' council in the 1993 local election, controlled by Labour with Liberal Democrat support)
Establishment of the LEA	Created through a national policy to reorganise local government in 1974 from parts of three LEAs, each with a different school system	Created through a national policy to establish LEAs in 1944
School systems	Primary-secondary, first-8–12 middle-high, first-9–13 middle-high	Primary-secondary, first-8–12 middle-high
Origin of these school systems	The legacy of different policies in the three LEAs from which the borough was created in 1974	The first-middle-high school system was introduced 1973–6 in all areas except the southern area where it was impracticable as school sites were dispersed across a rural district
Reorganisation of schools since the mid-1970s	Removal of surplus capacity in 1978–83 by extending the first-9–13 middle-high school system	None

student capacity by accepting 11–12-year-old students. If approval were given, the GM schools would fill their surplus capacity at the expense of nearby LEA middle schools currently catering for this age group. Such a possibility contributed to the pressure on officials to contemplate reorganisation sooner rather than later.

Senior officials in both LEAs perceived that the level of surplus student capacity was unacceptably high, and certainly well above that needed for flexibility in dealing with fluctuations in population. The central government policy promoting entrepreneurship by enabling parents to express a preference for their children's school required some surplus capacity as a platform for parental choice. Officials in the borough estimated that this surplus should not exceed about 10 per cent. Moreover, it was unevenly distributed, both between schools catering for younger and older students and demographically. The mismatch between the supply of surplus capacity and parental demand for student places was especially stark in the affluent and predominantly rural southern area of the county. An educational market now existed where a significant proportion of middle-class parents expressed their preference for a village school. Many transported their children by car to their chosen school on their way to work in urban areas, creating the phenomenon of rural 'commuter schools'.

The political complexion of the local council (of which the LEA was part) followed the national picture for local government areas with similar demography. The industrial heritage of the borough and its mainly urban population had been reflected in solid support for the Labour Party over the past decade. The more affluent and mixed rural and commercial demography of the county was reflected in a less clear-cut balance of power between political parties. It was a 'pendulum authority', the political party in power tending to switch every four years when local elections were held. The 1990s opened with the Conservative Party holding sway in the county council until the local government elections of May 1993, when the reorganisation initiative was already under way. A swing away from the Conservatives resulted in a 'hung' council, with Labour obtaining most seats but failing to win an overall majority. Consequently, Labour councillors formed a coalition with their Liberal Democrat counterparts and took the reorganisation initiative forward.

An aspect of the historical legacy of the borough with great significance for reorganisation was its creation in the 1974 nationwide reorganisation of local government. Comprehensivisation in two parts of three adjacent local authority areas from which the borough was formed had earlier produced different first-middle-high school systems. In a reorganisation exercise at the turn of the 1980s one of these systems was extended to part of the borough that in its pre-borough local authority existence had not gone fully comprehensive. The upshot was an inheritance of three school systems. The situation in the county was only slightly less complicated. Here comprehensivisation had entailed creating a first-middle-high school system everywhere except the southern local authority area. Primary sector schools were thinly spread across this rural district, precluding establishment of larger first schools and middle schools because of the long distances many young students would then have had to travel.

Administration of a mixture of school systems was difficult. Parents could be confused because students transferred between schools at different ages (see Figure 4.1). The longest established primary-secondary school system involved transfer at the age of 11 for all students. The primary sector also featured separate infant and junior schools with an additional transfer at the age of 7, mainly in urban areas with high population density. The 'first-8–12 middle-high school' system entailed transfer at the age of 12 for all students and at the age of 8 for those in separate first schools. First and middle combined schools were often created in districts with a low population density. The 'first- 9–13 middle-high school' system embodied two transfers for all students, at the ages of 9 and 13. During their school career students in different parts of the borough might transfer between schools at the ages of 7, 8, 9, 11, 12 or 13. Not all secondary or high schools in either LEA had a sixth form for older students, so those wishing to continue their formal education might also have to transfer at the age of 16 to a school sixth form or other form of post-16 provision. Equally not all primary, infant, or first schools in either LEA had a nursery. Where they did, students would attend from the age of 3. Where they did not, students would start school at the age of 4.

From 1988 a further administrative and educational complication arose with the advent of the neo-Taylorist central government reform mandating all state

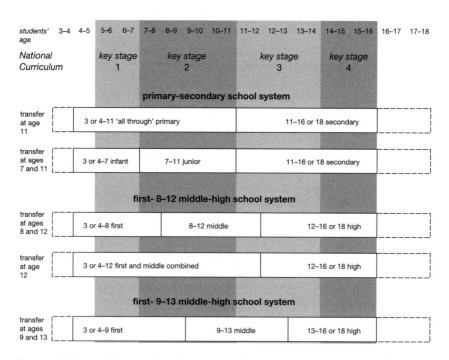

Figure 4.1 National Curriculum key stages and age of student transfer in different school systems

schools to follow the National Curriculum. It was divided into four 'key stages', covering the years of compulsory education. The transition between key stage 2 and 3 at the age of 11 coincided with the traditional transfer point for all students in the primary-secondary school system. The transition between key stage 1 and 2 occurred at the age of 7, the infant–junior school divide for many students in that system. Students' transfer under both first-middle-high school systems came during a key stage, so teachers' responsibility for it was split between staff of different schools. A consequence of implementing the National Curriculum policy in both LEAs was to heighten the significance for officials of questioning the relative educational merits of the different school systems.

A review in the mid-1980s of the age of transfer in the borough had concluded that 'on purely educational grounds, it is doubtful whether there is a clear balance of advantage in operating transfer at 11+ or 12+'. When officials in the county first surveyed parental opinion about the possibility of changing the first-middle-high school system in four administrative areas back to the primary-secondary still operating in the fifth, only a small majority favoured transfer at the age of 11 rather than 12. Yet in both LEAs educational arguments were to become central to initiatives designed to revert to a unified primary-secondary school system. Some were connected with the lack of alignment between the first-middle-high school systems and the National Curriculum key stages. The educational ideology widely shared among senior officials included the belief that students at key stage 3 in middle schools reached a lower standard of education than their secondary school peers. As one put it: 'There was often a plateau, if not a falling away, between the top years of the middle school and the bottom of the secondary school.' Evidence supporting this view appeared largely impressionistic.

In the borough the argument was advanced in a public consultation document on reorganisation that the introduction of the National Curriculum had strengthened the case for students to transfer at the age of 11. Standardised assessments of students' achievement would be mandatory at the end of each key stage alongside continuous assessment yet, under both the first-middle-high school systems, 'there would be *divided responsibility* for the delivery of National Curriculum programmes, and breaks in what should be a continuous system of assessment' (italics in original). A county public consultation document referred to other educational advantages, notably: 'enabling eleven year olds to start key stage 3 in secondary schools, which are more likely to have the specialist teachers, accommodation and equipment the programmes of study require', and 'making it clearer to parents which school was responsible for their children's progress during each key stage'. As we shall see, the LEA connection between abolishing first-middle-high school systems and alignment with National Curriculum key stages is open to interpretation as an instance – at least in part – of administrative convenience. Economic pressures imposed narrowing structural limits on agency at LEA level. Abolishing the first-middle-high school systems offered a solution to financial and practical restructuring difficulties as well as to perceived educational drawbacks.

Approaching structural limits: the capitalist economy drive

The borough and county did not reflect national trends only in respect of the declining birth rate. They also reflected economic constraints imposed by the central government thrust to increase the efficiency of the public sector. Rising public expenditure was perhaps in danger of becoming inimical to capitalism, and the tightening grip of central government over local government spending suggests that agency at the local level of the education system had come too close to structural limits for central government ministers' comfort. Their policy thrust indicates how autonomy between the economy and state education can be only relative. Congruence amongst a cluster of interacting central government policies operated to channel the agency of LEA officials and councillors in the direction of reorganisation initiatives. They narrowly circumscribed the resource parameters for local education provision while providing inducements that increasingly amounted to 'offers you dare not refuse'. Table 4.2 indicates how economic factors apparently had more immediate impact than educational considerations on the urgency of reorganising schools on a grand scale.

First, the annual cost of maintaining each surplus student place was estimated to be substantial, especially in secondary sector schools, and was rising each year. The total drain on the LEA revenue budget of such a high proportion of surplus capacity ran into millions of pounds of local taxpayers' money each year. Further, the central government Department of the Environment (DoE) was responsible for contributing to the funding of local government (including school provision) through its annual 'revenue support grant'. The grant was awarded in the light of a 'standard spending assessment' each year of each local authority making up local government, which included the LEA. The assessment took no account of revenue expenditure due to surplus capacity (Ranson 1990). LEAs with the highest proportion of surplus places received proportionately the least central government support for maintaining them.

Second, against this unproductive ongoing expenditure had to be set the central government 'starvation tactic' of excluding LEAs from the opportunity to benefit from the only route open to officials and councillors for borrowing large amounts of additional capital needed to repair, maintain, or improve their stock of school buildings. Throughout the early 1990s the overall level of annual central government expenditure by the Department for Education and Employment on LEA capital projects declined slightly (Audit Commission 1996). Central government priority was increasingly given to 'basic need' for new schools in areas of rising school population, and to 'exceptional basic need' – replacing accommodation condemned as inadequate, unsafe, or structurally unsound. Very little money was left for unexceptional expenditure of the kind needed in the borough and the county where the school population was falling, as reflected in the low annual level of capital borrowing they were allowed. By 1994 the backlog of capital building maintenance and repair work needed in the county was estimated to be at least £36 million. The one remaining category under which LEA bids for

Table 4.2 Economic factors affecting the LEAs before reorganisation

Economic factor	Borough LEA	County LEA
Estimated annual maintenance cost per surplus student place in primary sector schools	£145	£140
Estimated annual maintenance cost per surplus student place in secondary sector schools	£240	£230
The annual cost of maintaining surplus places LEA-wide, not reflected in the central government (DoE) Contribution to funding school provision through the 'revenue support grant' to local authorities	£2.25 million	£4 million
Low annual LEA capital borrowing allowed by central government (DfEE)	£0.5 million	£2 million
Imposition of central government (DoE) 'cap' prohibiting local authorities from raising more revenue through increased local taxation and precluding any increase in the revenue support grant	No	Yes
Number of primary sector schools with fewer than 90 students (where the annual cost of providing each student place is greater than for larger schools)	9	46
High annual revenue cost as the central government (DoE) contribution to funding provision for the oldest students in middle schools through the revenue support grant is less than the equivalent for funding students of the same age in secondary schools	First-middle-high school systems with 8–12 and with 9–13 middle schools	First-8–12 middle-high school system in four out of five areas

additional capital borrowing might be approved was for removal of surplus student places. It was a very powerful inducement in a context of LEA dependence on central government resources that were increasingly hard to come by. The amount of money for which bids could be made related to the number of surplus places removed. Contributing to this inducement was the possibility for most LEAs that the debt charges levied by the DfEE for capital borrowing would effectively be cancelled out by a proportionate increase in the revenue support grant made as a result of the DoE standard spending assessment. Calculation of the revenue support grant would take the debt charges into account.

Third, councillors in the county were precluded from increasing their taxation of residents as an alternative source of revenue beyond a limit imposed by the DoE. The central government policy of 'capping' local government to keep down public expenditure made a major impact on the county from the early 1990s. The cap was, ironically, imposed by a Conservative central government on a local government where the majority of councillors held allegiance to the same political party. Capping was amongst the raft of managerialist central government system-changing policies designed to reduce local government authority in the public sector. Conservative ministers had originally heralded them as means of curbing the alleged profligacy of high-spending Labour-Party-controlled local councils. Equally ironic was the contrast with the borough, where the Labour majority controlling the council ensured that taxation was kept below the level where it might be capped. The implication of capping for the county LEA was that the DoE revenue support grant would not be increased as the standard spending assessment would exclude the debt charges incurred by capital borrowing connected with reorganisation.

Senior officials in the county lobbied ministers from both the DoE and DfEE intensely over several years to persuade those from the DoE to remove the cap, without success. Pursuit by one central government department (DfEE) of the capital borrowing policy as an inducement to councillors and officials to remove surplus capacity in schools was all but negated by the impact of the capping policy in another department (DoE). Here was a clear instance of policy contradiction indicative of a schism between activities in two departments of the central state whose unintended consequence was mutually to inhibit each other.

Fourth, the per capita cost of educational provision in small primary sector schools, most prevalent in rural districts, increases rapidly as the number of students decreases below about ninety (Audit Commission 1996). Most small institutions in both LEAs were church schools in rural districts, typified by the schools at Newell and Moor. The proportion of small schools was particularly high in the county, representing a significant LEA financial burden which closures or mergers could reduce.

Fifth, we have seen how older students in middle schools were judged to fare less well educationally than those of the same age in secondary schools. There was stronger quantifiable evidence of relative economic disadvantage. The level of central government support through the revenue support grant for middle schools catering for students beyond the age of 11 was less than that for equivalent provision in secondary schools. Consequently, the annual revenue cost of retaining first-middle-high school systems was greater than would be the case if they were reorganised to a primary-secondary system. For areas of the curriculum requiring specialist facilities and equipment such as science, technology, or physical education it was particularly difficult to make provision in the upper years of middle schools of an equivalent quality to that found in most secondary schools. It is understandable that officials came to regard abolishing their first-middle-high school systems as a key to removing surplus capacity, given their educational misgivings about middle schools, the new demands of the National Curriculum at key stage 3 and the financial burden these schools represented. Yet the absence of hard evidence about the relative merit of the different systems suggests that the ideology of abolition came to the fore because it was expedient. Educational justification was offered for a compromise solution to the problem of how to alleviate economic constraints through reorganisation.

The enduring economic squeeze

Economic factors continued to be critically important (Table 4.3). First, compared with the minimal amount of capital borrowing allowed by the DfEE hitherto, the allowance for building and refurbishment connected with reorganisation was without precedent in living memory. For councillors, officials, and diocesan representatives alike the prospect of capital borrowing on such a scale after years of inability to deal with the poor repair of much of their building stock was the greatest incentive for persevering with reorganisation. The county continued to suffer greater financial stringencies than the borough because of the DoE cap on raising revenue through local taxation. The debt charges for capital borrowing had largely to be met through the annual revenue savings accruing from the removal of surplus capacity. Unlike their counterparts in the borough, councillors and officials in the county were precluded from reinvesting these revenue savings in improving the quality of education inside all schools. The savings merely paid off the loan for a minority of schools where new building and refurbishment was required. By 1996 the effect of the cap and the overall reduction in central government funding of state schools was so severe that councillors had to dip into the council's financial reserves to meet the shortfall in revenue for educational provision while simultaneously completing their reorganisation initiative.

Second, there was a central government shift of policy in 1994 on capital borrowing to remove surplus places when county officials were planning the major part of reorganisation. Its effect was to tighten further the economic constraints dictating the administratively convenient compromise they sought. The threshold for capital borrowing was raised. Formerly, the minimum annual rate of LEA revenue savings from ceasing to maintain surplus capacity had to be 6 per cent. Now the minimum rate of savings had to be 8 per cent. Officials had worked on the assumption that reorganisation must bring revenue savings of at least 6 per cent in developing the reorganisation proposals that had already gone out to public consultation. They now had to revise upwards the scale of surplus place removal to be achieved if the necessary capital borrowing was to be permitted. It became imperative that reorganisation should include the southern area where there were surplus places but no first-middle-high school system to be dismantled. We shall see in the next chapter how officials had greater difficulty convincing parents whose children attended schools in this area that closures and mergers were necessary, given that a major element of the public rationale for the rest of the LEA was to abolish the first-middle-high school system. Officials put forward the economic argument that some surplus places to be removed were in communities where demand was unlikely to rise anyway, alongside the educational arguments they advanced for reorganisation in all areas.

Third, both LEAs were hit by a different central government policy shift that contradicted the educational thrust of their reorganisation initiatives. A year-on-year cut in central government funding of school provision during the early 1990s inhibited councillors and officials still further from demonstrably delivering

Table 4.3 Economic factors affecting the LEAs during and after reorganisation

Economic factor	Borough LEA	County LEA
LEA capital borrowing approved by central government for reorganisation	£20 million	£23 million
Capital borrowing on behalf of the church diocese approved by central government for reorganisation	£5 million	£7 million
The central government debt charge for LEA capital borrowing offset by an increase in central government contribution to funding school provision	Yes	No, as 'capped' (see below)
Continued imposition of the central government 'cap' prohibiting any planned increase in local taxation as a source of income for the LEA and any increase in central government contribution to funding school provision	No	Yes (removed in 1997 by Labour central government)
Impact of central government raising the threshold of annual revenue savings required for capital borrowing to remove surplus student places from 6% to 8% in 1994	Minor	Major – had to include the southern area where there were no middle schools
Cut in the central government contribution to funding of school provision reduced by reinvestment of savings accruing from reorganisation	Yes	No, as 'capped'
Impact of central government decisions to enable schools proposed for closure to become GM, so retaining surplus capacity and competing with neighbouring LEA schools	N/A	Minor – those becoming GM were small primary sector schools
One-off transitional costs for supporting staff and curriculum development during implementation in schools	£0.7 million	£1.5 million
Total cost of offering a voluntary premature retirement package to eligible school staff	£4 million	£1.3 million
Increase in the annual cost of providing school transport	Minimal	£0.2 million
Annual revenue savings accruing from reorganisation	£1 million	£1.7 million
Number of headteachers' salaries saved owing to the reduction in number of schools	31	42
Number of primary sector schools with fewer than 90 students (where the cost of providing each Student place is greater than for larger schools)	2	12 (+ 3 GM)
Removal of temporary classrooms which were expensive to operate and maintain	Yes	Yes
Capital raised from disposal of redundant school sites (50% to be spent on reducing debt charges for capital borrowing, the remainder might be spent on any local government area)	Yes	Yes
Annual savings from a reduction in the number of students residing in the LEA being educated in an adjacent LEA	Minimal	£0.1 million

their publicly stated promise to reinvest revenue savings in improving educational provision. It was possible in the borough to make up the shortfall in the revenue support grant from the revenue savings available from reorganisation. But the additional amount that school governors and staff in the primary sector had expected to see as a result of reorganisation was reduced. In the county this option was not feasible because the DoE cap meant that revenue savings were already fully committed to paying the debt charges for capital borrowing. Here the only ways of ameliorating the cuts were to reduce expenditure on other local authority services such as public libraries and, as mentioned above, to use local authority financial reserves for this purpose.

Fourth, both LEAs could have been much harder hit than they were by the contradictory central government policy of promoting the GM schools sector. Nationally, during the period of the reorganisation initiatives the Secretary of State approved some 40 per cent of applications for GM status to escape LEA reorganisation proposals (Audit Commission, 1996). In the event, no such applications in the borough succeeded, and only five in the county did. Since they were mostly small primary sector schools, their impact in competing for students with neighbouring LEA schools was minor, and they made only a modest dent in the level of revenue savings achieved overall.

Fifth, there were significant but one-off or time-limited costs for the LEAs to facilitate the implementation of reorganisation. They included transitional funding allocated to schools according to an assessment of need for up to two years to facilitate the implementation of changes connected with approved LEA reorganisation proposals. This money was used for diverse activities to help staff make the transition to their post-reorganisation situation. They included enabling teachers from closing middle schools to visit nearby primary or secondary schools when considering to which of these school sectors they should go as the next step in their professional career. Funding of voluntary premature retirement (VPR) packages entailed a redundancy payment plus, in the borough, pension enhancement. But here the overall cost would be spread over more than a decade, so the annual claim on the revenue budget was moderate. Pension enhancement had to be curtailed in the county because the greater financial constraints obtaining there precluded offering it to all school staff wishing to take up the offer of early retirement. A major contribution to the cost of these packages came from a national pooling arrangement for all local authorities. Other longer-term but minimal costs included providing transport where reorganisation necessitated children travelling further to and from school.

Finally, the annual revenue savings in both LEAs derived from a range of sources connected with reducing the building, staffing, maintenance, and running costs of surplus capacity. They included a reduction in the staff salary bill as a whole, but especially in the number of headteachers' and deputy headteachers' salaries because of the drop in the number of schools in each LEA; a drastic reduction in the number of small schools, especially in the county, which were so expensive to run; the extensive removal of temporary classrooms – poorly insulated and so costly to heat; and, in time, a small proportion of the capital received from the sale of some redundant school sites. Central government regulations stipulated that up to 50 per cent of the sale proceeds could be used for local government expenditure, so potentially for education, while the remainder must be used to pay the debt charges that local government borrowing incurred.

Overall, achieving the best compromise in straitened economic circumstances was central to both LEA reorganisation initiatives. Educational ideology did play a part in the demise of the first-middle-high school systems. But it was intimately linked to the economic conditions which, through a combination of central government policies, constrained councillors and officials from spending as they would have wished on improving the quality of school buildings and equipment and promoting improvement in the quality of teaching and learning. Filling surplus capacity in secondary schools while removing capacity in other school sectors by lowering the age of transfer to 11 where middle school systems existed was actually the most economical way of removing surplus capacity. As a borough LEA consultation document stated:

> Firstly, the scope for the elimination of surplus places is greater in the primary rather than in the secondary sector. Thus, it would be difficult to envisage the closure of secondary schools in an Authority such as [the borough] with its relatively widely separated communities since in most cases major travel problems would be created . . .
>
> A second consideration turns upon the comparative size of primary and secondary schools. It is obviously easier to reaccommodate a number of smaller groups of pupils, for whom there may be more than one alternative, than it is to reaccommodate a single large group, for whom there may be only a single alternative.
>
> A third consideration turns upon the comparative costs of maintaining surplus places in the primary and secondary sectors . . . the cost in the secondary sector is considerably greater than the cost in the primary sector.

The county LEA was bordered by nine LEAs, whereas the borough was bordered by only four. A county consultation document added yet another economic consideration related to the regional context:

> Almost all the areas surrounding [the county] now transfer children to secondary school at eleven and most of the primary schools are for four to eleven year olds . . .
>
> [The county] 'loses' more eleven to eighteen year old children to schools in neighbouring LEAs than it gains from them. [The county's] secondary [i.e. 12–16 and 12–18 high] schools believe that transfer at eleven could reduce the number of pupils going elsewhere and give them a better chance of educating such local [county] pupils. This would benefit all schools educationally, as well as financially.

Each LEA was charged a levy where students of parents residing within its boundaries were educated in a neighbouring LEA. The county LEA gained some income from students living beyond its boundaries who were educated inside the county. But it was a net loser of students to adjacent LEAs because many parents wished their children to enter a secondary school at 11 rather than stay on in a middle school until they were 12, so contributing to the county's surplus capacity in middle schools. Reorganisation brought a significant saving here, too.

In sum it appears that administrative convenience may have featured as prominently in the demise of at least some first-middle-high schools systems as it did in their emergence as an economic means of comprehensivisation (Chapter 1). Administrative convenience figured equally large in the ideologies combining economic with educational aims in both LEA reorganisation initiatives. Their assumptions left the legitimacy of the increasingly harsh economic order unchallenged and so assisted in delimiting the agency of officials and councillors.

Educational improvement out of economic necessity

The chief education officers (CEOs) were prime movers of the LEA reorganisation initiatives, instigating discussions with their senior colleagues and key councillors that prompted the reorganisation initiatives. The rationale and aims these stakeholders espoused at interview were entirely consistent with those stated in their public consultation documents. Most school staff and governors we interviewed corroborated the official account, suggesting that the LEA message to stakeholders at the school level had been widely received.

First and foremost, they were to reduce surplus capacity. The borough target was to take out half the surplus, some 7,500 places. The county target was to take out 30 per cent across all administrative areas, 5,700 places in all. But senior officials also wished to seize the opportunity to direct the central government economic imperative towards educational improvement. They were able to express sufficient agency to mediate central government pressure within the narrow limits imposed by the pincer movement of central government economically driven policies. Their success in persuading councillors to support the reorganisation initiatives for educational reasons is indicated by the 'key task' members of the county education committee set themselves: 'To eliminate surplus places where this would maintain and promote educational opportunities and quality.' Whether to undertake the initiatives may not have been realistically an option. But there was greater leeway over how they were to be undertaken and for what purposes beyond downsizing. Construing reorganisation as a means of serving valued educational ends represents an assumption which enabled officials to square the economic imperative with their existing educational ideology as they bowed to the structural economic conditions delimiting their agency.

Second, this reduction was to be achieved by reverting to a primary-secondary system throughout both LEAs. There should be all-through primary schools wherever possible so that most students would transfer between schools once only at the age of 11. As a senior official in the county expressed it: 'A firm conviction on my part [was] that an all-through primary school was preferable to having a break at age eight . . . the aim was to reduce the number of times a child and parents have to change schools.'

The strategy of abolishing the first–middle–high school systems was presented as an economic means towards educational ends. Officials' discourse implied the assumption that maximising the recouping of financial resources and the revamping of physical resources would maximise students' educational benefit. We discussed earlier the arguments advanced in both LEAs about improving access to specialist facilities at key stage 3 of the National Curriculum and about the benefit of students transferring between schools at the end of key stages. Revenue savings in the borough were to be reinvested in the primary sector. The relative weighting between primary and secondary sector school operating budgets would be adjusted by about 2.5 per cent in favour of primary sector schools. The rationalisation of provision was couched in a public consultation document in terms of the educational entitlement of all children of primary school age: 'The pattern of schooling must promote an equitable and consistent allocation of resources within the framework of the Local Authority's policies.' In the county the aspiration was expressed in an equivalent document to use revenue savings for the benefit of students in both primary and secondary sectors: 'The overall aim is to make sure the total resources available to [county] schools are being used to secure the best education for children. The intention is, therefore, to invest the money saved by reorganisation back into [county] schools.' (But as noted above the central government capping policy prevented this aspiration being realised.)

Third, the unprecedented chance to borrow capital that removing surplus capacity allowed was heralded as a benefit for school provision in the LEA as a whole. A significant constraint was imposed by the necessity of building work being connected with making provision for students from closing or merging schools. As one senior official observed:

> What determined where the investment could be was really a numerical issue about where places were and what facilities were needed, not about provision of buildings. And so you get the iniquity where one site will be added to and refurbished which was already in reasonable condition, and a bit further down the road is a school crying out for some investment that didn't happen to be caught up in the numbers game.

Fourth, wherever feasible, small schools were to be closed or merged to form larger institutions for both educational and economic reasons. A county consultation document contained the proposal to 'plan for primary schools to be large enough to offer a well-resourced and broadly based education to all pupils, but not so large that they become impersonal. (Guideline: minimum of 90 pupils, maximum of 420.)'. The higher figure was based on the capacity of a two-class-entry 4–11 primary school (i.e. two classes of thirty students in seven year groups). Officials in both LEAs perceived that the expertise and material resources now required for each subject in the National Curriculum to be taught to a high standard made it difficult for staff in the smallest schools to offer students their full entitlement. Likewise poor-quality buildings, including temporary classrooms, were to be taken out of use where possible to improve the quality of educational provision as well as to reduce expenditure.

Fifth, once the LEA reorganisation initiatives were set in train, representatives of the relevant diocesan authorities partially responsible for church schools expressed their sectional interest in sustaining or even enhancing the provision of church school places. Mutual dependence between diocesan authorities and the LEA over reorganising church schools led to a partnership between the LEA and the diocesan authority being forged in both LEAs. Stakeholders from both sides of the partnership sought a confluence between their respective interests. We saw in Chapter 2 how the representative of the CE Diocesan Board of Education aimed to improve the countywide distribution and viability of church schools. It was essential for officials and councillors to work synergistically with such representatives, since they possessed sufficient authority to block proposals for individual institutions or even bring down an entire LEA reorganisation initiative. They served on the local council and had full voting rights, so could contribute to local council decisions on all reorganisation proposals, whether a particular proposal concerned church schools or not. This source of power was especially significant in the county because at no time did the council have a large majority of councillors from one political party. Diocesan representatives could find themselves with the casting vote on proposals where the voting between councillors from the different political parties was even. Should members of the diocesan authorities oppose the LEA initiative it was plausible that they might encourage governors of their church schools to try and avoid reorganisation by applying for GM status. The threat of mass opting out among church schools would almost certainly have prompted local councillors to withdraw their support for the LEA reorganisation initiatives.

Conversely the situation at Newell showed how economic benefit could accrue to the LEA where there was a change from voluntary controlled to voluntary aided church school status. It was in the LEA and diocesan authority interests to increase the proportion of student places in voluntary aided schools relative to the proportion in voluntary controlled schools. This shift of status increased the extent of diocesan authority over the religious character of educational provision in a school. It also enabled councillors to avoid capital borrowing for building work. Most could now be funded through a central government grant, the remainder by the CE Diocesan Board of Education. Had the school remained voluntary controlled, the LEA would have been responsible for borrowing the necessary capital. Officials and councillors were ready to support the diocesan authorities' aims in both LEAs: to reconfigure the distribution and status of church schools so that sufficient student places remained to meet likely parental demand; to ensure that the institutions were large enough to be economically viable; to increase the proportion that were voluntary aided; and to group them so that church primary schools for younger students fed into nearby church secondary schools.

Sixth, another spin-off from reorganisation in both the borough and the county perceived privately by some stakeholders at LEA and school levels concerned the possibility of improving the quality of human resources as a result of the reduction in staffing. Public discourse was confined to finding jobs for present employees wishing to continue in post. Yet, as we explore later, judgements of individuals' competence were made whenever school governors and, where appropriate, headteachers in expanding schools were in a position to select from a field of candidates who were seeking redeployment. We noted above the economic gain flowing from a reduction in the number of headteachers because there would be fewer schools. There could also be an educational gain. Any headteachers seeking redeployment were vulnerable to exposure if they had a poor reputation among school governors in the locality. Similarly, 'natural wastage' (the normal loss of staff moving to posts outside the LEA or retiring) together with the number of teachers taking early retirement in the borough enabled 'new blood' with enthusiasm and new ideas to be brought into the LEA's schools. A hundred or so young teachers were recruited into the borough each year despite the staff reduction exercise necessitated by reorganisation.

Overall it is clear that both LEA reorganisation initiatives were undertaken for intimately linked economic and educational reasons, framed by the structural limits imposing an economic imperative on central government to reduce public expenditure and the unquestioned assumption that local reorganisation to downsize state educational provision was a legitimate response.

Componential change: parts and the whole

Agency within these limits was expressed in the design and execution of the initiatives. The profile of components constituting them evolved incrementally as key events took place that punctuated the change process. The initiatives remained deeply context-dependent, interacting with a variety of other policies. They were systemic in conception, designed at LEA level for implementation in schools. The strategies adopted by senior officials reflected their dependence on the support of the politicians whose professional servants they were: councillors in the party forming the majority in the local council. Councillors' support, in turn, was contingent on the support of parents amongst the local council electorate, both in their individual wards and as a group across the borough or county. If the LEA proposals produced strong protest, councillors' support could evaporate and the initiatives might founder. In such conditions of uncertainty where officials lacked authority to push reorganisation through in the face of resistance from councillors or the voting public, planning of the early components of the initiatives was incremental and tentative. It remained even more incremental in the county than the borough because more unpredicted circumstances requiring a response arose during the initiation stage for all phases. The balance of political power was less decisively weighted in favour of any political party and, as noted earlier, shifted dramatically after the initiative had been launched. An element of incrementalism continued to feature in detailed planning for the evolving sequence of components for both initiatives.

The componential character of the initiatives was expressed through their division into several phases, each covering particular pyramids of schools in the borough and one or more administrative areas in the county. Phasing reflected senior officials' practical interest in keeping such a large-scale change within manageable bounds, given the small number of officials available to manage the initiatives and the uncertainty of success in the early days. The CEO in the borough had learned from failed attempts to reorganise schools on a much smaller scale in the 1980s:

> [The initiative] had been lost on local lobbying, local elected members [councillors], local MPs [members of parliament] all going against closures . . . based on the philosophy 'not in my back yard' . . . If it's been aborted, it's usually either because they've gone for too big a bite to start with, they've not got the momentum going, or they've not tied in a sufficient number of the elected members to make sure they can get it through the Labour group [the majority political party in the borough council].

The CEO in the county had similarly learned from past failure where officials had 'tried to pick off schools individually', and had been instrumental in appointing a deputy with successful experience of reorganising schools on a large scale elsewhere. This person was able to advise on the development of LEA strategy, eventually becoming CEO and taking charge of reorganisation.

Development of the borough initiative

At the heart of the CEO's strategy was an attempt at culture management, perceived as building a 'climate for change' by adopting an LEA-wide approach to promoting a culture of acceptance and support amongst local councillors and parents. Aware of the differential impact proposals were likely to have on other stakeholders' sectional interests, the CEO decided to tackle non-controversial proposals first:

> The early phases we deliberately arranged to be the relatively easy ones, so that gradually you're pulling in more and more of the members [councillors] who had bitten the bullet, and who said: 'Well, *we've* had it, how about you?' By the time we got to the hard ones the momentum was such that local members didn't dare to oppose it.

The first phase entailed removal of temporary classrooms, a few mergers, but no closures and only minimal capital borrowing. The final phase involved extensive closures, mergers, and building work. The only attempts within school communities to escape LEA proposals by seeking GM status occurred in phase 3. In four cases the Secretary of State rejected the application. In the fifth case the statutory ballot of parents, part of the application procedure, failed to return a majority in favour. So this attempt did not get as far as a formal application.

Members of the LEA 'management team' orchestrated the initiative as a whole. This group included the CEO and other senior officials whose responsibilities spanned all aspects of reorganisation. A senior official was given the full-time role of developing reorganisation proposals. The CEO intended to plan one phase at a time, but local councillors in the ruling group (members of the Labour Party) asked for a 'master plan' to be drawn up so that they could see what the entire initiative would involve. A resulting plan for reorganising schools, pyramid by pyramid in five sequential annual phases, was drafted within three months. It was eventually adopted and implemented with minor alterations (see Figure 4.2). A similar sequence of processes and events covering the initiation, implementation, and institutionalisation stages of reorganisation was then followed for each phase. Formative LEA proposals were published after discussions within the borough council, negotiations with diocesan representatives where necessary, and the establishment of a forum for negotiation with representatives of school staff unions. A single round of public consultation was conducted where alternative options were presented and officials' preference for one of them was spelled out and justified. Firm proposals were drawn up in the light of feedback. They were presented to councillors in the ruling group, then more formally to the reorganisation subcommittee of the education committee, then to the full education committee, and finally to the council for ratification. Statutory notices of each proposal were published and a copy of all firm proposals sent to the DfEE for the Secretary of State's approval. The implementation period was contingent on the speed of the approval process, generally leaving less than six months for implementation.

Figure 4.2 indicates how complex the articulation between components was to become as the scale of the initiative expanded. For five years at least two phases of reorganisation were at different stages. Officials were responsible for managing an increasing diversity of components. They had simultaneously to handle different tasks in the sequence implied by the change process across the various phases, cope with the impact of earlier phases on later ones, and monitor progress with all components. The multiplicity of simultaneous tasks peaked during 1994–5 when phase 1 schools had been reorganised and were at the institutionalisation stage, needing LEA aftercare. Phases 2 and 3 were at the implementation stage, so preparatory tasks such as reallocating staff and arranging building work were in full swing. Meanwhile public consultation and preparation for submission of firm proposals were under way for phases 4 and 5. Officials had to cope with multiple changes alongside their other ongoing work. Not only did reorganisation take place alongside routine tasks, but the management structure of the LEA itself was also reorganised in 1995 and their responsibilities adjusted accordingly.

Figure 4.2 Phasing of reorganisation in the borough LEA

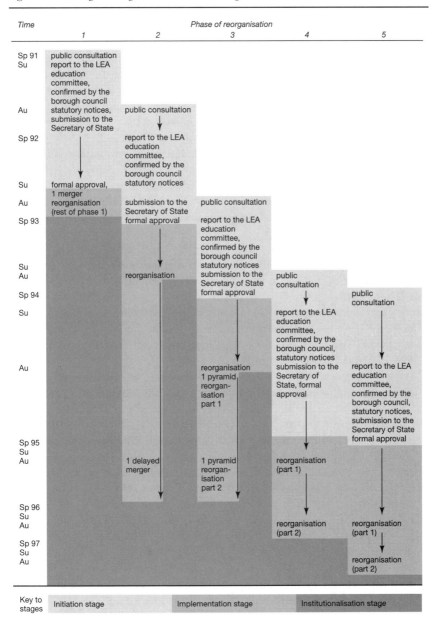

| Time | Phase of reorganisation | | | | |
	1	2	3	4	5
Sp 91 Su	public consultation report to the LEA education committee, confirmed by the borough council				
Au	statutory notices, submission to the Secretary of State	public consultation			
Sp 92		report to the LEA education committee, confirmed by the borough council			
Su	formal approval, 1 merger	statutory notices			
Au	reorganisation (rest of phase 1)	submission to the Secretary of State	public consultation		
Sp 93		formal approval	report to the LEA education committee, confirmed by the borough council		
Su Au		reorganisation	statutory notices submission to the Secretary of State	public consultation	
Sp 94			formal approval		public consultation
Su				report to the LEA education committee, confirmed by the borough council, statutory notices	
Au			reorganisation 1 pyramid reorgan- isation part 1	submission to the Secretary of State, formal approval	report to the LEA education committee, confirmed by the borough council, statutory notices, submission to the Secretary of State formal approval
Sp 95 Su Au		1 delayed merger	1 pyramid reorgan- isation part 2	reorganisation (part 1)	
Sp 96 Su Au				reorganisation (part 2)	reorganisation (part 1)
Sp 97 Su Au					reorganisation (part 2)

| Key to stages | Initiation stage | Implementation stage | Institutionalisation stage |

Phases varied in their managerial complexity. Phases 3–5 included pyramids with the first-9–13 middle-high school system where reorganisation was implemented in two parts at the beginning of two academic years. Most of these pyramids were reorganised by removing the youngest and oldest year group from the middle school in Part 1, then removing the remainder and closing the middle schools in Part 2. The 3–9 first schools (scheduled to be all-through primary schools) retained the oldest year group of students, becoming 3–10 first schools for one year. The 13–18 high schools (scheduled to become 11–18 secondary schools) took two year groups from the middle schools simultaneously, becoming 12–18 schools for one year. For their final year of existence the 'dying' middle schools catered for 10–12-year-old students only. In Part 2 the 3–10 schools retained the oldest students for another year, becoming all-through 3–11 primary schools. The 12–18 schools took two year groups from the middle schools at the same time, becoming 11–18 secondary schools (see Figure 4.3).

An alternative arrangement was made in one phase 5 pyramid involving our four case-study schools. Headteachers of the closing middle schools had expressed concern about the negative effect on staff morale and on staffing the full range of curriculum provision for the students in the final year if only half the students remained. Instead the youngest year group alone was removed in Part 1 and the remaining three year groups in Part 2. The 3–9 and 4–9 first schools retained the oldest year group of students for a year in Part 1, as in the more typical arrangement described above. But the 13–18 high schools took only one year group so that three remained in what became 10–13 middle schools for their final year. Then, in Part 2, the 3–10 and 4–10 first schools retained the oldest year group of students, becoming 3–11 or 4–11 primary schools while the high schools took three year groups from the closing middle schools to become 11–18 high schools. The main transfer of students, and therefore the movement of middle school staff, took place in Part 2.

Cumulative effects of earlier phases on later ones affected officials' management tasks. The generally negative emotive force of the early reorganisation proposals was reversed as benefits of the earlier phases became apparent. Many school staff and governors came to perceive that reorganisation would serve their sectional interests. So successful was the endeavour of senior officials to generate a climate for change that governors and headteachers who had yet to go through reorganisation exhorted officials to speed up the reorganisation process. Another type of cumulative effect was linked with the reallocation of school staff displaced by reorganisation. In each phase till the last, some displaced staff seeking redeployment did not succeed in securing an appointment to expanding schools in the same phase or to schools in other phases. They could be found a temporary supernumerary post funded by the LEA for a year until the next phase of reorganisation was implemented and more staff appointments came up. This way of absorbing unplaced staff could be extended until the final phase when, as we shall see in Chapter 7, a permanent solution had to be found.

Development of the county initiative

The county initiative developed more incrementally, public commitment to an LEA-wide reorganisation being made some time after the pilot first phase was under way. It turned out that reorganisation was implemented in just two phases

The most common arrangement in Phase 3, 4, and 5

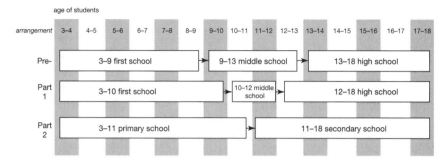

The alternative arrangement affecting the pyramid on Phase 5 which included case-study schools

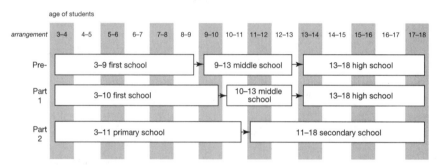

Figure 4.3 Two-part arrangement for reorganising the borough LEA first-9–13 middle-high school system

a couple of years apart. The combination of contextual factors applying in the county was different. We have noted how the less settled balance of political power meant that lasting commitment of councillors and parents to an LEA-wide approach could prove difficult to achieve. This balance varied in different administrative areas, with Labour Party representation strong in the more industrialised north of the county and Conservative Party representation dominant in the rural and affluent south.

The CEO in the county was concerned to make a positive start and to generate widespread acceptance of the need for reorganisation. The politically sensitive nature of the initiative was indicated early on. One stakeholder participating in informal deliberations on the possibility of LEA-wide reorganisation between senior officials, councillors, and teacher union representatives used influence to resist the idea by going to the press. The resulting publicity led senior officials to rethink their approach. They adopted a culture management strategy to gain wider acceptance. They mounted a public consultation exercise on the principle of reorganisation late in 1991 (Figure 4.4). A consultation document and questionnaire were sent to the main interest groups: all parents, school staff and governors, and diocesan and school staff union representatives across the LEA (yielding 11,000 returns). Public meetings were held (attended by 1,500 people altogether) and focus groups were convened. The document set out the case for moving to a primary–secondary system with all-through primary schools where feasible, and suggested that a second phase of consultation might be undertaken on more detailed proposals. It also highlighted 'difficult practical issues' including, 'whether some schools would try to "opt out" [become GM] rather than be a part of a reorganisation'. The outcome of this exercise was reported to the county council's education committee and a summary was sent to schools. The majority response reflected sectional interests in enhancing provision for each community.

Figure 4.4 Phasing of reorganisation in the county LEA

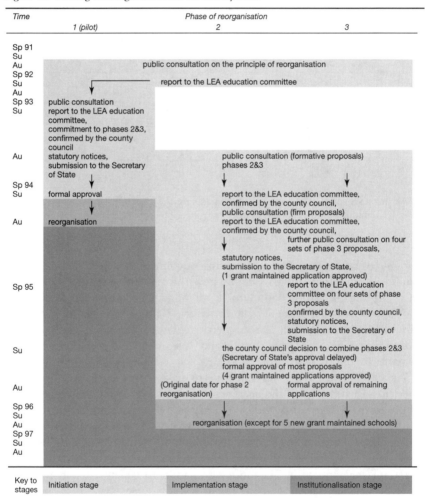

Time	Phase of reorganisation		
	1 (pilot)	2	3
Sp 91 Su Au Sp 92 Su Au		public consultation on the principle of reorganisation report to the LEA education committee	
Sp 93 Su	public consultation report to the LEA education committee, commitment to phases 2&3, confirmed by the county council		
Au	statutory notices, submission to the Secretary of State	public consultation (formative proposals) phases 2&3	
Sp 94 Su	formal approval	report to the LEA education committee, confirmed by the county council, public consultation (firm proposals)	
Au	reorganisation	report to the LEA education committee, confirmed by the county council, statutory notices, submission to the Secretary of State, (1 grant maintained application approved)	further public consultation on four sets of phase 3 proposals,
Sp 95			report to the LEA education committee on four sets of phase 3 proposals confirmed by the county council, statutory notices, submission to the Secretary of State
Su		the county council decision to combine phases 2&3 (Secretary of State's approval delayed) formal approval of most proposals (4 grant maintained applications approved)	
Au		(Original date for phase 2 reorganisation)	formal approval of remaining applications
Sp 96 Su Au Sp 97 Su Au		reorganisation (except for 5 new grant maintained schools)	

Key to stages	Initiation stage	Implementation stage	Institutionalisation stage

A senior official commented:

> Parents and governors were coming through with the desirability of all-through [primary] schools; also, having a school as close to home as possible; and how disgusted they were with some of the physical conditions their kids had to put up with.

But most respondents were against creating all-through primary schools if it meant closures because of their overriding belief that younger children should be educated close to home. Any major reduction in surplus capacity would probably transgress this belief and might stimulate resistance.

The LEA estimate of surplus capacity was broadly confirmed in calculations made by the county's auditors in 1992, lending weight to the LEA decision early in 1993 to undertake a first phase of reorganisation in the northern administrative area. This phase was conceived as a 'pilot', although very much the real thing, LEA commitment to reorganisation at this point being confined to the one area. The CEO adopted this strategy so as 'to put a toe in the water' and 'to learn lessons' which might inform any subsequent extension of the initiative. The northern area was selected on economic grounds. But as in the borough the strategy was to start with an area where there was the strongest chance of early success, paving the way for a future extension to other areas. Detailed reasons behind this choice included:

- a particularly high proportion of surplus student places in the northern area;
- the first-8–12 middle-high school system here providing a means of removing surplus capacity by filling the empty space in the high schools while creating all-through primary schools wherever possible
- the relatively self-contained nature of the population, with less transfer of students into or out of this area during their school career than elsewhere
- the small number of LEA high schools in the area (three) requiring only a small building programme. The ease of completing this modest construction work could have symbolic importance in fostering a climate for change in other areas by demonstrating that building required for reorganisation would be delivered
- the rural location of a moderate proportion of the schools, offering officials valuable lessons as they predicted that such institutions would be most difficult to close or merge because of the strength of local belief in retaining village schools
- the Labour majority among councillors representing this area, whereas the county council was Conservative-controlled at this point. Members of the Conservative ruling group who made up the majority of the county council could outvote Labour councillors who attempted to resist a potentially vote-losing initiative in their wards.

Formative proposals were drawn up and public consultation, revision, and submission of formal proposals followed a similar sequence to that for each phase in the borough. However for most schools two options were presented, one involving reversion to a primary-secondary school system, the other retaining the first-8–12 middle-high school system. The LEA preference for the former option was elaborated and justified. Extensive negotiations were undertaken with diocesan and school staff union representatives.

Significantly, a minority of Labour councillors representing the northern area became the sole group of stakeholders to question the economic assumptions on which reorganisation was built. They argued for what they regarded as the socialist principle that every community was entitled to a state-funded school, however few children of school age it contained. School closure should not even be considered. This was the only time an ideology was expressed whose underlying socialist economic assumption challenged the pro-capitalist beliefs to which all other stakeholders subscribed. If it were to be widely followed, expression of agency in the county would become more inimical to capitalism. Other stakeholders used their greater authority and influence to ensure that the socialist voice was not heeded, helping to keep the expression of agency inside structural limits imposed by the prevailing economic order.

Another local contextual factor impacting on the course of the county reorganisation initiative was the local election of May 1993, mentioned earlier. It occurred immediately after the close of the public consultation period on the pilot first phase. Now, with more Labour councillors than those from any other political party, members of the new Labour–Liberal Democrat coalition ruling group inherited a Conservative local policy directed towards closing and merging schools in the Labour heartland. Officials' extensive lobbying helped to persuade members of the new ruling group of councillors to continue with the initiative and commit themselves to extending it throughout the county. The Conservative heartland in the administrative area of the south duly entered the frame for reorganisation. Conservative councillors had been willing to launch the pilot phase in a Labour area but they had not until now faced the possibility of unpopularity in their own wards.

The LEA strategy was to undertake a more comprehensive two-part public consultation exercise for the remaining four administrative areas, starting just before the firm proposals for the pilot phase were finalised. Public consultation took place on formative proposals, only a minority of which contained options. It is notable that the sole attempt to close a small secondary school aroused vociferous community resistance to the formative proposal and raised the spectre for senior officials of a concerted move towards seeking GM status. They withdrew the proposal. Closures and mergers in both LEAs were therefore confined entirely to primary sector and middle schools.

Revised formative proposals were drawn up in response to feedback and presented to the education committee, followed by a further round of consultation. The finalised set of firm proposals was presented to the education committee for approval and ratified in the full council. For the most complex, including the four case-study schools in one valley in the eastern area (see Table 1.3) and the schools at Newell and Moor, there were one or even two further rounds of consultation. The planned timetable for implementation was for the second phase covering the southern area to be reorganised at the beginning of the autumn term in 1995. The third phase covering the remaining three areas was to be reorganised a year later. Accordingly, statutory notices were published and a copy of 175 proposals where further consultation had not been required was sent to the Secretary of State in the autumn of 1994. By this time governors and the headteacher in one primary school subject to a formative proposal for closure had successfully applied to the Secretary of State for the school to be given GM status. Their counterparts in a further eight schools, also subject to firm proposals for closure or merger, had gained a sufficient majority in the statutory ballot of parents to apply to the Secretary of State for GM status. The submission process was completed for the proposals entailing additional consultation in the spring of 1995.

A feature of the systemic character of reorganisation was the dependence of change agents at the local system level on stakeholders at the centre. Ministers had authority to approve or reject firm proposals or to delay the decision required for implementation of the second and third phases. Despite a central government commitment aiming to reach a decision on reorganisation proposals within five months (DFE 1994), the Secretary of State's decision on the large number of schools involved took eight months. The delay was due in part to an unanticipated legal challenge to the procedure employed within the DfEE to inform the Secretary of State's decision on reorganisation proposals. At this time, Her Majesty's Inspectors (HMI), the core members of the Office for Standards in Education (OFSTED) who advised ministers on the quality of school provision, would typically visit a school proposed for closure. They would compile a confidential report for the Secretary of State making judgements about the quality of teaching and learning and the effectiveness of management in the school. A decision to approve the closure of a special school in another LEA was challenged in the High Court. The judge ruled that the Secretary of State's decision was against natural justice. The HMI submission included information material to the decision, so it should have been made available to objectors and other stakeholders involved. This ruling set a new precedent, lengthening the HMI reporting process since there was now a requirement for the content to be made public.

The upshot was that officials and local councillors were forced to update their plans, delaying implementation of the second phase for a year and combining it with the third phase. This decision increased the number of schools that officials had to deal with together at the implementation stage. Four applications for GM status were approved but this stage was completed for other schools in all four areas at the beginning of the 1996 autumn term. LEA support for school staff continued into the institutionalisation stage as officials promoted a sustained school improvement effort in each surviving institution.

Outcomes of reorganisation

Both LEA reorganisation initiatives largely achieved their instigators' economic and short-term educational aims – except where inhibited by managerialist central government policies. Most significant were promoting the GM schools system, capping county expenditure, and reducing the central contribution to funding school provision. The target number of surplus places was removed in the borough and in the county (apart from upwards of two hundred in the five new GM schools for which the LEA was no longer responsible). Just how varied the components of the change turned out to be is illustrated by the diversity of proposals and outcomes for individual schools or groups of institutions, each of which had to be managed with account taken of its specific circumstances. Table 4.4 summarises the reorganisation outcomes for all schools in the borough apart from special schools and Roman Catholic schools, which were unaffected. Key outcomes as follows:

- Closures and those mergers where two schools had been combined on a single site had allowed twenty-one sites to be taken out of use and made available for other local authority uses or for sale.
- A diversity of arrangements for merging or changing the character of first, first and middle combined, and middle schools had enabled them to become part of a unified primary-secondary system across the LEA.
- Most primary sector institutions surviving reorganisation were all-through primary schools, so a much lower proportion of younger students now faced two transfers between the ages of 7 and 11.
- All secondary sector schools took students from the age of 11, eliminating all middle to high school transfers at 12 or 13.

An even wider range of merger arrangements was implemented in the county. But fewer arrangements were adopted for changing character, reflecting the fact that there had been only one first-middle-high school system here (Table 4.5). The picture was complicated by arrangements for GM schools. GM high schools changed character to become GM secondary schools, taking in students at the age of 11. Two of the newly established GM primary sector schools changed character after the LEA reorganisation so that the age range for which they catered aligned with that of neighbouring LEA schools. Outcomes largely paralleled those in the borough:

- Closures and mergers where the number of sites was reduced enabled some thirty-one sites to be taken out.
- A unified primary-secondary system was established in the four administrative areas which previously had a first-middle-high school system.
- A higher proportion of primary sector institutions were now all-through primary schools, allowing a single transfer at the age of 11, and as all secondary sector LEA and GM schools took in students at this age, transfer for 12-year-olds had been eliminated.

Table 4.4 Outcomes for schools affected by borough LEA reorganisation proposals

Form of proposal	Type of school(s)	Phase of reorganisation					Total schools
		1	2	3	4	5	
Individual LEA school closed	Infant		1				
	3/4–8 first			1			
	8–12 middle			2	(1c)		
	3/4–12 combined			2			
	3/4–9 first			1	1		
	9–13 middle			2	3	4	
Total number of LEA schools closed		**0**	**1**	**8**	**4(1c)**	**4**	**18**
Merger between two or more LEA schools	Infant + junior →primary (both sites)			2→1			
	3/4–8 f + 8–12 m→3/4–12 f&m (both sites)	2→1a					
		2→1b					
	3/4–8 f + 8–12 m→primary (both sites)		6→3	8→4			
	3/4–9 f + 3/4–9 f→primary (both sites)			2→1			
	3/4–9 f + 9–13 m→primary (one site)					2→1d	
	secondary 9–13 m + 13–18 high →11–18 (both sites)					2→1e	
Total number of LEA schools merged		**4→2**	**6→3**	**12→6**	**0**	**4→2**	**26→13**
Individual LEA school changed character	3/4–8 first→infant	5		8			
	3/4–8 first→primary		1	2			
	8–12 middle→junior	4	1c	7			
	3/4–12 f&m→primary	1	3 (1a)	7(1b)			
	3/4–9 first→infant			1	1		
	3/4–9 first→primary			5	8	11	
	9–13 middle→junior			2	1		
	9–13 middle→primary				2	1	
	12→11–16 secondary			2			
	12→11–18 secondary	2	1	2			
	13→11–18 secondary			1	2	1	
Total number of individual schools Changing character		**12**	**6**	**37**	**14**	**13**	**82**
Total number of schools affected (for the first time)		**16**	**13**	**57**	**18**	**21**	**125**

Key
f = first school, m = middle school, f&m = first and middle combined school
Notes
a A first school and middle school merged in phase 1, changed character to primary in phase 2.
b A first school and middle school merged in phase 1, changed character to primary in phase 3 and the former first school site closed.
c A middle school changed character to junior in phase 2, the school closed in phase 4.
d A first school and middle school merged in phase 5 on the middle school site, the former first school site closed (*case-study schools – Sedge First and Sedge Middle*).
e A split-site high school changed character to secondary in phase 5, the lower school established in a closing middle school site, one of the high school sites closed (*includes case-study schools – Hillside High and Endale Middle*).
A total of 21 school sites closed, leaving 31 fewer schools in the LEA.

The number of LEA primary and secondary sector schools (excluding Roman Catholic schools which were not affected by reorganisation) was reduced from 160 to 129 (1 GM secondary school in the borough LEA area opted out before reorganisation).

Table 4.5 Outcomes for schools affected by county LEA reorganisation proposals

Form of proposal	Type of school(s)	Phase of reorganisation			Total schools
		1 (pilot)	2 +	3	
Individual LEA school closed	3/4–8 first	4		2	
	8–12 middle	1			
Total number of LEA schools closed		**5**	**0**	**2**	**7**
Merger between two or more LEA schools	two primaries→primary (one site)		6→3[a]	2→1	
	two primaries→primary (both sites)		2→1		
	three primaries→primary (one site)		3→1		
	4–8 f + 4–8 f→infant (one site)			2→1	
	4–8 f + 4–8 f→primary (one site)			6→3[b]	
	4–8 f + 4–8 f→primary (both sites)			2→1[c]	
	4–8 f + 8–12 m→primary (one site)			24→12	
	4–8 f + 8–12 m→primary (both sites)	6→3		12→6	
	4–8 f + 4–12 f&m→primary (both sites)			2→1[d]	
	three 4–8 f + 8–12 m→primary (two sites)			4→15	
Total number of LEA schools merged		**6→3**	**11→5**	**54→26**	**71→36**
Individual LEA school changed character	4–8 first→infant	4		28	
	4–8 first→primary	7	2	18	
	8–12 middle→junior	3		25[f]	
	8–12 middle→primary	1		2	
	4–12 f&m→primary	2		25	
	12→11–16 secondary			9	
	12→11–18 secondary	3		9	
Total number of individual schools changing character		**20**	**2**	**116**	**138**
Individual GM school changed character	12–16 GM high→11–16 GM secondary			3	
	12–18 GM high→11–18 GM secondary	1		2	
Total number of GM secondary schools changing character		**1**		**5**	**6**
Individual LEA school became GM	primary→GM primary		3[g]		
	4–8 first→GM 4–8 first			1[h]	
	8–12 middle→GM 8–12 middle			1[i]	
Total number of LEA schools becoming GM			**3**	**2**	**5**
Total number of LEA and GM schools affected		***32***	***16***	***179***	***227***

Key
f = first school, m = middle school, f&m = first and middle combined school

Notes
a (*Includes case-study schools – Lake Primary and Lowrise Primary.*)
b (*Includes case-study schools – Newell First and Moor First, Capston First and Farfield First.*)
c Two first schools merged on one site, with an annex at the other site.
d A first school and a first and middle combined school merged, with an annexe at the former first school site.
e Three first schools and one middle school merged on the middle school site, with an annexe at one former first school site (*case-study schools – Beacon First, Highlane First, St Joan First, Brook Middle.*)
f (*Includes a case-study school – Down Middle.*)

g (*Includes a case-study school – Dale Primary. It had been proposed to merge with Southlip Primary, which therefore remained unchanged.*)
h Subsequently changed character as a GM infant school (*case-study school – Down First*).
i Subsequently changed character as a GM junior school.

A total of 31 school sites closed, leaving 47 fewer LEA schools (including 5 which became GM).
The number of LEA primary and secondary sector schools was reduced from 274 to 227.
(There were 8 GM secondary or high schools in the county LEA area since before reorganisation plus 5 new GM primary sector schools.)

We noted earlier how in both LEAs, but especially in the county, diocesan representatives played a major part in negotiating to realise their sectional interest in protecting the number and distribution of church school places. The partnerships forged between themselves, officials and councillors were reflected in the outcomes for church school provision. In both LEAs reorganisation favoured the economic and religious educational interests of the local CE Diocesan Board of Education. Officials and councillors were able to remove a substantial number of surplus student places, to abolish church first, middle, or first and middle combined schools (Church of England and, in the county, Roman Catholic), to improve the building stock and to reduce the expense of maintaining church schools. Here a confluence was found between the diocesan authority sectional interests and the LEA promotional interest, the compromise reached across both LEAs bringing mutual benefit.

A detailed analysis of the change in surplus church school capacity in the borough (Table 4.6) indicates how five church school closures cut back the number of places, less than two-thirds of which had been filled anyway. But a combination of mergers and changes of status incorporated three institutions (printed in bold type in the table) which had not been church schools. Together they added more than enough church school places to meet existing demand with room for a possible increase in future. The level of diocesan authority was heightened, in that changes of status for the three ex-county schools and one ex-voluntary-controlled school resulted in all Church of England schools in the borough now being voluntary aided, on a par with the Roman Catholic Schools. The LEA contributed to the portion of the building work cost for which the CE Diocesan Board of Education became liable because of the change to voluntary aided status connected with one merger and one change of character. The remaining church schools were larger and so the cost to the LEA of providing each church school place was reduced overall.

The sectional interest in sustaining the provision of church school places was even more prevalent in the county with its higher proportion of church schools. They included Roman Catholic institutions in the first-middle-high school system that changed character in the transition to a primary-secondary system. The CE Diocesan Board of Education concerned with the county LEA's church schools fared well from reorganisation, as the summary of outcomes for Church of England schools there indicates (Table 4.7). Closures and mergers reduced the number of church school places overall, including the capacity that was surplus

Table 4.6 Outcomes of reorganisation for Church of England schools in the borough LEA

Form of change	Phase of reorganisation			Change in capacity and status
	1	2	3	
Closure		VC infant	VC 4–8 first 2 VC 4–12 f&m VA 9–13 middle	– 848 places (510 filled)
Merger and change of status			**4–8 first**+VA 8–12 middle→**VA** primary	+ 180 places
			VC 4–8 first+**8–12 middle**→**VA** primary (capital expenditure)	+ 90 places
Change of character and status	VA 4–12 f&m →primary		VA 4–9 first→ VA infant 2 VA 4–12 f&m→ primary	
			9–13 middle→**VA** junior (capital expenditure)	+ 302 places
Total number of schools affected				**14**

Key
f&m = first and middle combined school

Notes
No church schools were involved in phases 4 and 5.
No Roman Catholic schools were invoved in reorganisation.

Net gain for the Church of England diocese:
• less capacity but fewer surplus student places in VA schools so they were less expensive to maintain
• all church schools VA, so there was greater church authority over their governance
• 3 hitherto 'county' school buildings
• significant LEA capital investment in facilities connected with two reorganised schools
• fewer but larger and higher quality premises (one closed school had a capacity of 89 places, 55 students and over 50% of its accommodation in temporary buildings)
• buildings less expensive to maintain (4 out of 5 schools that closed catered for fewer than 90 students each; the smallest catered for 25 students).

to predicted demand. Since only a single merger and a change of character led to a decline in the level of church authority, the net effect was positive. About half the mergers boosted church authority, as where 'county' (non-church) schools and voluntary controlled schools were combined to form a voluntary controlled institution. A few schools changing character also brought an increase in church authority, one 'county' school becoming voluntary aided. A significant minority of mergers and changes of character created conditions for anticipated expansion, often through investment in new building and refurbishment.

We conclude that both reorganisation initiatives succeeded as a thoroughgoing response to economically driven central government pressure on LEA officials

Table 4.7 Outcomes of reorganisation for Church of England schools in the county LEA

Form of change	Type of school status	Number of schools affected	Change in church linked student places (+/=/−)	Change in church authority (+/=/−)	Building or anticipated expansion (✔)
Closure	VC	6	−	−	
Merger	county+VC→county	2→1	−	−	
	county + VC→VC	6→3	+	+	✔(1)
	county+VC+VC→VC	3→1	−	+	✔
	VC+VC→VC	10→5	= (3), − (2)[a]	=	✔(2)
	VC+VC→VA	2→1[b]	−	+	✔
	VC+VA→VA	4→2	−	+	✔(1)
	VA+VA→VA	2→1	−	=	
	RC+VC+VC+VA→VA	4→1[c]	−	+	
Change of character or status	county→VC	1	=	+	
	county→VA	1	=	+	✔
	VC→VC	23	=	=	✔(8)
	VC→VA	2	=	+	✔
	VA→VA	10[d]	=	=	✔(2)
	VA→VC	1	=	−	
School opted out	VC→GM VC	1[e]	=	=	
Total number of schools affected		**78**			

Notes

a (*Includes case-study schools − Capston First and Farfield First.*) One merger of two VC first schools on one site.

b Two VC first schools merged on a new site with a new building (*case-study schools − Newell First and Moor First*).

c Two VC first schools, one RC first school and one VA middle school merged to form a VA primary school on the middle school site, with the former RC first school site as annexe (*case-study schools − Beacon First, Highlane First, St Joan First, Brook Middle*). Reorganisation of RC schools entailed changes of character within existing sites, so there was no loss or gain of student places except for this merger involving the loss of one RC first school with capacity of 120 places and 66 students.

d (*Includes a case study school − Down Middle.*)

e A VC primary school opted out to avoid proposed merger (*case-study school − Dale Primary, proposed to merge with Southlip Primary which therefore remained a VC primary school*).

Net gain for the Church of England diocese:
- less capacity, but fewer surplus student places in VC and VA schools, so they were less expensive to maintain
- more 'church' schools were VA, so there was greater church authority over their governance
- 5 hitherto 'county' school buildings
- significant LEA capital investment in a minority of schools, including two new premises
- fewer but larger and higher quality premises (one closed school had a capacity of 60 places, 22 students, and 50% of its accommodation in a temporary building)
- buildings were less expensive to maintain (4 out of 6 schools that closed catered for fewer than 90 students).

and councillors to remove surplus capacity. They facilitated the rationalisation of provision and provided opportunities for improving some of the building stock. Contextual parameters for change were set by the accumulation of past and present local and central government policies. The current policy context had become increasingly dominated by the central government attempt to introduce managerialist policies to stay within structural economic limits which expanding public expenditure threatened to overstep. Central government economic considerations were intimately connected with local government educational aims as agency was expressed across all three levels of the education system within these structural limits.

Our summary account of the complexity of these multi-component initiatives as a whole gives little idea of the process of managing such a change. In the next three chapters we examine how agency was expressed within and between system levels at each stage of the change process in turn. We document how change agents attempted to bring off reorganisation, their efforts differentially impacting on users' sectional interests, bringing varied responses.

5 Everything to play for

Managing initiation

The challenge for LEA officials and councillors at the beginning of each initiation stage followed largely from its complexity, generating considerable uncertainty whether it could be successfully completed. Legal parameters for consultation acted as a mandate to officials to ensure that all stakeholders were offered agency to express their views, however divergent, and that their concerns would be taken into account. This stipulation dictated that where any phase of an initiative involved more than a few schools the initiation stage would become *large-scale*. Stakeholders in every school community affected by proposals had to be contacted and their opinion sought. Equally, the scope of the initiatives dictated the range and sequence of *components* that would make up the initiation stage for each phase. Every school to be reorganised would constitute a component throughout the change process. A lock-step series of tasks for managing proposal development, consultation, and approval had to be carried out, to the letter. If central government civil servants were to identify lack of compliance with the rules at LEA level they possessed authority to withhold the decision on proposals.

The *systemic* character of the consultation requirements meant that officials would have to instigate an extensive flow of interaction across system levels to fulfil consultation requirements. They depended on the response of other stakeholders at LEA, school, and central levels over whom they did not have authority, as discussed in Chapter 4. Formative reorganisation proposals would never reach the public domain unless there was sufficient support among councillors and diocesan representatives. Should this hurdle be overcome, proposals had then to be sufficiently acceptable to parents, school staff, governors, and others in each community to dissuade them from seeking to escape through gaining GM status for their school. The downsizing proposals would be bound to make a *differential impact* on other stakeholders according to their incompatible sectional interests and would unquestionably stimulate opposing reactions. We have noted how the likelihood of proposals failing to meet the interest of stakeholders in protecting present provision affecting them made it imperative for LEA officials to seek cultural hegemony through establishing a 'climate for change' so that others perceived reorganisation to be in their interest. Should the proposals survive this second hurdle and reach submission they would be judged by central government ministers with power of decision over their approval. *Contextual dependence* of the initiatives would include their likely interaction with the central government policy to promote the GM sector at LEA expense. The proposal for each school had to take into account its present circumstances, the product of a unique institutional history.

This challenge would be especially demanding during the initiation stage for the first phase of reorganisation. LEA officials were well aware of their legacy of smaller-scale reorganisation failures, the range of stakeholders whose support they must win, and the need to establish a way of operating and safeguards that would win support. This first initiation stage differed from those that followed for later phases because arrangements to protect key stakeholders' interests had to be made then. They could be adjusted subsequently if initiation of the first phase succeeded. Differences in the development of the two initiatives were summarised in Chapter 4. In the borough the initiation stage for the first phase entailed planning for all five phases. In the county the equivalent stage was regarded as a pilot, commitment to initiation stages for phases 2 and 3 coming only after a new local council had been elected.

In this chapter we shall explore how officials endeavoured to persuade other stakeholders to accept components of reorganisation that affected them, and how others reacted. We focus on the management tasks embodied in the initiation stage. The flow of interaction (Figure 3.1) was largely stimulated from central government and LEA levels of the education system. Officials were the main change agents taking forward this stage but it was 'topped and tailed' by central government civil servants and ministers. They stimulated activity at LEA level, liaised to ensure that statutory regulations were followed, and acted as assessors and decision-makers. Stakeholders at school level responded to the push for reorganisation originating at LEA and central levels. Tasks of managing the initiation stage within and between system levels were mostly sequential, in line with statutory requirements for consultation, but the metatask of orchestrating the initiatives was ongoing.

Experience of the reorganisation initiatives at school level varied with the content of proposals for each school and its community. Our school case studies suggested that this diversity had limits and that staff, governors, and parents had to deal with some or all management tasks associated with each stage. We will highlight two mergers to illustrate how the initiatives were managed at school level. The schools represented opposite extremes in terms of size and age range of students but there was overlap between management task areas covered in both. One, in the borough LEA, concerned the expansion of Hillside 13–18 High School to become an 11–18 split-site secondary school by incorporating the site of the closing Endale Middle School (Table 1.3). This merger was complex because of its scale and the possibility of operating on both the existing and a new site. While plenty of staff could share tasks of managing the merger, their work required detailed co-ordination. The other, in the county LEA, concerns a merger between two small rural schools – Capston 4–8 First and Farfield 4–8 First (Table 1.4). Both were voluntary controlled, so reorganisation proposals were the responsibility also of the diocesan authority. Here the scale was smaller but the schools had to be amalgamated on one site and there were few people to share management tasks.

First, we consider the tasks to start the first initiation stage. They included arrangements for protecting the interests of key stakeholders. Officials' priority was to harness the existing network of stakeholders across system levels and expand it to embrace all who must be convinced of the value of reorganisation. Second, we explore the tasks of developing and consulting on formative proposals. Public consultation was difficult for officials to manage where it provided a platform for the airing of conflict between the promotional interest behind reorganisation proposals and the sectional interest of stakeholders concerned with the fate of their school. Here pressure group politics and pursuit of counter-policies came to the fore. Third, we review the tasks of finalising and publishing firm proposals. Fourth, we note how preparations for implementation were made during the initiation stage at both LEA and school levels on the assumption that proposals would be approved. Finally, we turn to the work of central government civil servants who assessed firm proposals and advised the ministers responsible for decision-making.

Our account here and in the next two chapters is organised around a series of matrices summarising the tasks of particular stakeholders involved in managing those components of any stage of reorganisation, or part of it, that affected them. Table 5.1 is the first of these matrices, all of which are structured in a similar way. The first column lists each task area, covering one or more components represented by related tasks. The second column lists the stakeholders who were most centrally involved as change agents in carrying out tasks in this area to bring about some part of the change effort. The third column indicates the extent to which interaction entailed in carrying out each task was systemic. The main direction of the flow of interaction for cross-level tasks is represented by the left-to-right direction of the arrow between two system levels, as in LEA→school. In this example interaction was instigated by change agents based at LEA level who were attempting to impact on the activity of users at school level. (See also the key below this table.) The final column summarises the content of each task within any task area.

Getting started on the first initiation stage

The management tasks to launch the first initiation stage are presented in Table 5.1. The CEOs in both LEAs had realised that surplus student capacity must be reduced for the economic and educational reasons already described. Central government pressure to undertake reorganisation initiatives was expressed in discussions that the senior DfEE civil servant responsible for state school provision held with each CEO. Officials were required to submit statistics to the DfEE annually indicating the extent of surplus capacity. The senior civil servant *prompted* CEOs to consider reorganisation by asking them how the surplus revealed by the statistics could be reduced, a use of authority described by another

Table 5.1 Management tasks to get started on the first initiation stage

Initiation task area	Key change agents	Education system levels involved	Main management tasks
Prompting LEA initiatives	Head of DfEE schools section	Central government→LEA	• Discussing the possibility of an LEA initiative with the CEO in the light of LEA statistics on surplus capacity submitted annually to the DfEE
Orchestrating preliminary planning and consultation	CEO and chair of the education committee	LEA	• Planning in outline the scope, strategy and financial parameters for one or more phases of the reorganisation initiative
		LEA	• Determining the strategy for consultation and liaison
Conducting the preliminary internal consultation	CEO and chair of the education committee	LEA	• Consulting members of the ruling group of councillors in the education committee and other members, including the leader of the council

(Outcomes of preliminary internal consultation: in the borough, commitment to an LEA-wide plan for phases 1–5; in the county, commitment to public consultation on the principle of reorganisation)

Conducting the preliminary public consultation on the principle of reorganisation (county only)	CEO and other senior officials	LEA→school	• Conducting a postal survey, public meetings and focus groups to gather opinions of parents, other community members, school staff and governors
		LEA→school	• Publicising consultation through the local media
		LEA→school	• Collating and publishing results
Conducting the second internal consultation (county only)	CEO and other senior officials	LEA	• Securing the commitment of councillors in the ruling group to the pilot phase 1 of reorganisation

(Outcome of the second internal consultation in the county: commitment to phase 1)

Conducting the preliminary external consultation (borough – phase 1 in detail, 2–5 in outline; county – phase 1)	CEO and other senior officials, civil servants from the DfEE territorial team, district HMI, (minister, borough only)	LEA→school	• Publicising the initiative via local media
		LEA, LEA→school	• Meeting with union and diocesan representatives, chairs of governors and headteachers to discuss strategy and negotiate to protect sectional interests
		LEA→central government	• Liaising with members of the DfEE territorial team and with district HMI about the nature and scope of plans and about statutory procedural requirements
		LEA→central government	• Invited ministerial visit to the LEA (borough only)

Orchestrating the establish-ment of management structures and procedures	CEO and other senior officials	LEA	• Creating reorganisation management structures and procedures
		LEA	• Determining management responsibilities of officials
		LEA	• Allocating specialist tasks to officials with requisite skills and expertise
		LEA, LEA→ school	• Ensuring clear channels of communication including regular meetings with other stakeholders including union and diocesan representatives, chairs of governors and headteachers

Key

Central government→LEA	stakeholders based at central government level instigate interaction with stakeholders based at LEA level
LEA→school	stakeholders based at LEA level instigate interaction with stakeholders based at school level
LEA→central government	stakeholders based at LEA level instigate interaction with stakeholders based at central government level

civil servant as 'a sort of cajoling process . . . softly, softly to begin with, then harder depending on the Authority's [LEA's] response'.

Early on, much interaction was internal to the LEA as each CEO began to broach the issue with senior colleagues and local government politicians responsible for provision of schools: the chair of the education committee and other councillors from the ruling group. Officials' authority to undertake any initiative would be delegated by them. Senior officials were mindful that councillors' support depended on their ability to minimise potential conflict between their promotional interest in reaping economic and educational benefits from reorganisation and their sectional interest in retaining popularity with voters in their ward – which proposals could easily undermine. As one education committee chair put it: 'Politically, there was the fear of alienating elected members [councillors].' A senior colleague confirmed that 'no councillor wanted to close a school in his [*sic*] ward'.

Orchestrating preliminary planning and consultation was the province of the CEO and the chair of the education committee, prime movers of reorganisation. Their preliminary planning focused on the shape an initiative might take: its scope, financial costs and benefits, and management strategy. The imperative to generate a 'climate for change' led to consideration of the stakeholder groups and their representatives who should be consulted at the outset. Early thinking in the borough was to seek commitment of councillors in the ruling group to a first phase of reorganisation. Officials in the county were more circumspect, seeking councillors' commitment only to public consultation on the principle of reverting to a primary-secondary school system. Acceptance of this principle would imply that the extensive reorganisation required to put it into effect must also be accepted.

Both CEOs and chairs of the education committees steered the *preliminary internal consultation*, using their authority to persuade other stakeholders in the

LEAs about merits of an initiative. Word was spread first to those with greatest authority over proposals that might ensue. Informal consultations involved members of the education committee from the ruling group, then colleagues who did not serve on this committee. A councillor in the borough noted: 'It was well sold first to elected members who were shown the advantages.' Winning the leader of the council's support was crucial since this politician could press other members of the ruling group to support or reject an initiative. In choosing an area for the first phase where no closures would be entailed, officials avoided the ward of the leader of the council until phase 2, as closures would be necessary there. By then it was hoped that a culture supportive of reorganisation would have developed. Successful negotiations in the borough resulted in councillors in the ruling group committing themselves to an initiative covering schools in all areas over five annual cycles.

Their counterparts in the county safeguarded the option of turning back should strong resistance be encountered. Their commitment was of a different order: it was to a *preliminary public consultation* exercise on reducing capacity by abolishing the first-middle-high school system existing in all but the southern area. The response reassured councillors that there was moderate public support for reverting to a primary-secondary school system and for reorganisation, despite worries over school closures (Chapter 4). Another round of *internal consultation* led councillors in the ruling group to commit themselves to the pilot first phase in the northern area. They defeated opposition from councillors in the Labour Party in whose wards this area was located. Several councillors also expressed misgivings with a local election due shortly. If the reorganisation policy was unpopular the Conservative Party might lose votes. Others were optimistic, believing that the policy would put 'clear blue water between themselves and their political opponents'. We indicated earlier how at this election the Labour Party gained overall control of the council with support from the Liberal Democrats. It is unclear to what extent reorganisation, as opposed to other national or local issues, was responsible for the swing away from the Conservative Party. But members of the new ruling group did take forward reorganisation by extending it countywide.

Creating conditions for LEA success

Officials' efforts to build a culture of acceptance among stakeholders based at other system levels extended through the *preliminary external consultation* about one or more phases of reorganisation. Press releases were used for dissemination across the network of stakeholders in the LEA. More direct communication was achieved through meetings convened by senior officials with representatives acting as formal intermediaries for stakeholder groups, principally the school staff trade unions. The representatives from these unions shared a sectional interest in protecting their members' jobs, working conditions, and circumstances under which they might accept redeployment or termination of their job. They had considerable authority in respect of their members, being in a position to call for industrial action or to court high-profile media coverage of their case against any threat to members' interests.

The prospect of job losses posed a dilemma for officials. A few school staff would probably leave anyway where they were approaching retirement or the end of a temporary contract of employment. But most had skills suitable for working in those schools whose spare capacity would be filled with students from schools due to close. Officials technically held authority to declare mass redundancies since school staff were LEA employees. But such a strategy would amount to political suicide, as a teacher union representative from the borough confirmed:

> If ever there was something that could have prevented reorganisation going through, it would be the threat of redundancy, which means we would be turning from our support role in easing people through the process to a view of saying, 'There are redundancies threatened at this school, we need to be looking at strike ballots and negotiating strategies around that area.'

Councillors would soon abandon the LEA initiatives if parents in their wards blamed them for causing any disruption to schooling that industrial action might bring about.

We discussed in Chapter 3 how managerialist central government marketisation reforms to promote entrepreneurship entailed devolution of authority over staff appointments from LEA to school level. Since governors (normally with the headteacher) now held authority over appointments, LEA officials did not have authority to guarantee the alternative strategy of redeploying staff to schools where vacancies would arise. Governors and headteachers were unlikely to share the promotional interest of councillors and officials in redeploying staff displaced by reorganisation. Their duty was to seek the best candidate to fill any vacancy in their own school, implying selection from the widest possible field.

Officials used influence and such authority as they did possess to create ameliorative conditions that would safeguard union members' sectional interest. One component of their strategy was to persuade governors and headteachers to compromise over staff redeployment by seeking a voluntary agreement in consultation with union representatives. This approach was designed to shape their professional culture by appealing to their sense of altruism while also encouraging them to reject the more self-interested, entrepreneurial values fostered by central government. Chapter 2 documented how a code of practice was instigated in the county. A similar strategy was adopted in the borough, whose code stated that:

> The responsible body for the management of staff, the governing body or the Authority [LEA], will make every effort to avoid compulsory redundancy, and in avoiding compulsory redundancy will seek, in consultation with the Authority or the governing body respectively and staff representatives, to implement a policy of redeployment.

Each code stipulated that staff vacancies arising from reorganisation should not be used as opportunities for promotion. Staff with no guarantee of future employment alone should be considered for appointments in the first instance. Priority should be given to staff on permanent contracts. The norms encapsulated here would be a source of influence for officials during any implementation stage when staffing decisions would be made. The code had great symbolic significance, interpreted by teacher union representatives as indicating the strength of LEA 'political will' to support their interest and disposing them to accept the reorganisation initiatives. Officials eventually succeeded in persuading governors and headteachers throughout both LEAs to abide by the code.

A second component was to consult councillors in the ruling group over financial parameters for a VPR (voluntary premature retirement) scheme linked with staff redundancies. Once they had agreed to fund the council element of the package, it was discussed with union representatives, ratified by the council, and announced to school staff and governors. The intention was to provide an inducement for older school staff to leave their employment voluntarily. Legal and financial considerations dictated criteria for eligibility: staff had to be aged 50 or over, on a permanent contract, and have at least two years' service in the LEA. Any arrangement had either to avoid the redundancy of a member of staff displaced by reorganisation or reduce the budget deficit where a school was in financial difficulties. Individuals taking VPR would receive a lump sum as part of their pension and a severance payment. Both LEA schemes allowed for pension enhancement. This provision meant that the pension would be increased to the level it would have reached had they stayed in employment and made pension contributions for longer. The borough scheme was the most generous legally possible.

Authority over VPR would enable officials to invite applications from all those eligible for the scheme in closing schools. They sought a confluence of interests between their need to minimise the number of staff whose redeployment they must secure and individuals' personal interest in taking early retirement with a generous pension. One official in the borough dubbed VPR 'the oil in the gearbox' because it would provide an inducement to eligible staff and to school governors. Their sectional interest could be served through the opportunity VPR might offer them to bring in 'new blood', redeploying younger teachers to replace older staff. Equally, they would be empowered to offload an older teacher perceived as marginally competent who could be persuaded to apply for VPR. Another official testified to the potency of VPR as an LEA source of influence: 'VPR is one of the few sources of power left . . . without a scheme we could not, under any circumstances, have done this reorganisation.'

A third component in the county was for officials to use their influence in encouraging governors and headteachers to make new staff appointments on temporary contracts (Chapter 2). The idea was for all appointments to be made on a temporary basis after the point two years before the projected date of reorganisation for schools in the pilot first phase. This arrangement built on practice already emerging in schools with budget constraints following from the central government cap on local taxation (Chapter 4). Temporary contracts offered managerial flexibility. They minimised the number of teachers on permanent contracts displaced by reorganisation.

Other important stakeholder groups were the Church of England diocesan authorities, as illustrated in Chapter 2. They held jurisdiction over all VC and many VA schools. The remaining VA schools were Roman Catholic. We noted in the last chapter how they were incorporated in plans to revert to a primary-secondary school system in the county since there were RC first, middle, and high schools. The reorganisation plan in the borough excluded RC schools since they were already primary or secondary schools with little surplus capacity. Senior clergy and their diocesan representatives responsible for church school provision were consulted while the preliminary internal consultation was under way. Diocesan representatives remained in close contact with senior officials and councillors throughout the initiation stage for all phases. Officials also informed headteachers and chairs of governing bodies of their plans and began a dialogue about how schools might be affected. Reorganisation became a major agenda item at the regular headteachers' meetings and chairs of governors' meetings, which officials facilitated and attended. LEA governors (who were also councillors) relayed information to colleague governors, as did union representatives to their members.

Equally, senior officials fostered a co-operative relationship with central government civil servants and HMI. The Secretary of State's decision on LEA proposals and applications for GM status would rest on their advice. Senior officials held informal discussions with members of the DfEE territorial team and district HMI to inform them and to clarify legal requirements. At the invitation of senior officials in the borough, a minister at the DfEE visited to learn about officials' plans and to see several schools that were likely to be proposed for closure in a later phase. An official indicated how the minister's approach helped generate a culture of acceptance: 'He went down very well . . . he seems to have the common touch with parents and staff, and not many ministers have this.'

Senior officials' other major task area in laying the ground was *orchestrating the establishment of management structures and responsibilities* and ensuring that LEA–school linkages were in place for the extensive dialogue to come. We saw in Chapter 4 how the initiatives constituted an LEA project. Apart from a few new responsibilities allocated for reorganisation, senior officials relied on existing management structures and the distribution of officials' responsibilities and associated expertise in deciding who would contribute to different parts of the process. In the borough a subcommittee of the education committee was set up to deal with reorganisation. In the county a steering group was created, consisting of senior officials and officials responsible for provision in a particular area. Special attention was paid in both LEAs to the structure of regular meetings with different stakeholder groups, so that every stakeholder was given a voice as required by central government regulations. Conversely, senior officials ensured that they could disseminate their vision of reorganisation and detailed information efficiently, monitor evolving concerns of other stakeholders, and respond rapidly to any concerted resistance. Table 5.2 illustrates how the meetings' structure gave representation to the main stakeholder groups.

From preliminary ideas to submitted proposals

Orchestrating initiation continued throughout each initiation stage. Senior officials worked to ensure that communication channels across the network of stakeholders affected by reorganisation were opened up and maintained to give other stakeholders ready access to them. Regular contact was made with civil servants from the DfEE territorial team and district HMI. Meetings with various other stakeholders were complemented by senior officials' efforts to make themselves easily accessible. (Senior officials in the county even publicised their home telephone numbers.) Formal and informal monitoring was ongoing. Activities ranged from checking media output, monitoring how the initiatives were perceived outside the LEA to asking colleague officials how their contribution to reorganisation was progressing. Senior officials remained ever alert, seeking to pre-empt or respond to emerging problems.

Working on proposals required officials to tackle a series of tasks within the LEA and between LEA and school system levels (Table 5.3).

Developing formative proposals was exacting specialist work. Each proposal had demonstrably to meet the aims for reorganisation publicised in both LEAs (Chapter 4). They included reducing capacity by the target amount, reinstating a primary-secondary school system, ensuring that schools were of a viable size, and providing appropriately distributed church school capacity. In drawing up proposals, senior officials drew extensively on colleagues' wide-ranging financial and architectural expertise and the local knowledge of those responsible for schools in each administrative area.

Many contingent factors bearing on options for individual and groups of neighbouring schools might be taken into account. All schools under consideration potentially represented components of reorganisation whose detailed contextual parameters might be unique. Few schools could be considered in isolation from proposals for neighbouring institutions. It was feasible to consider schools individually only where surplus capacity was removed by doing no more than, say, taking out a temporary classroom, so not involving any transfer of students. Factors might include:

- the extent of surplus capacity and the need to retain sufficient empty places to allow parental choice
- the viability of the existing institution, especially where it was small
- the state of repair of school buildings and suitability of older structures for current educational methods
- the predicted demand for school places, complicated in areas where new housing or industrial development were likely
- the predicted redistribution of students from closing schools given the possibility of parental choice, especially in urban districts

Table 5.2 Stakeholder involvement in key regular meetings at LEA level addressing reorganisation

Type of meeting	Purpose connected with the initiation stage of reorganisation	Stakeholder groups or their representatives participating
LEA management team (borough) or steering group (county)	Managing LEA initiatives	Senior officials (and other officials in the county)
Ruling group of councillors	Approving officials' strategy and proposals	Councillors in the ruling group
Education committee of the council (and reorganisation subcommittee in the borough)	Recommending approval of officials' strategy and proposals	Councillors drawn from inside and outside the ruling group, representatives of one or more unions, diocesan representatives
Borough or county council	Approving officials' strategy and proposals	All councillors from inside and outside the ruling group, representatives of one or more unions, diocesan representatives
Unions' co-ordinating committee	Negotiating a shared policy between unions	Representatives of all teacher unions
Unions and LEA joint negotiating committee	Negotiating between officials, councillors, and union representatives acting on behalf of all unions	Representatives of all teacher unions, officials, councillors from the ruling group on the education committee
Officials and diocesan representatives	Negotiating between officials and diocesan representatives acting on behalf of the diocesan board of education	Diocesan representatives, officials
Officials and district HMI	Informing HMI of officials' plans and discussing problems	Officials, district HMI
Headteachers' forums facilitated by officials	Informing headteachers about LEA strategy and proposals, informing officials about headteachers' concerns	Headteachers from one or more types of school and LEA areas, officials
Headteachers' and chairs of governors' forums facilitated by officials	Informing headteachers and chairs of governors about LEA strategy and proposals, informing officials about school level stakeholders' concerns	Headteachers and chairs of governors from one or more types of school and LEA areas, officials

Table 5.3 Management tasks connected with formative proposals

Initiation task area	Key change agents	Education system levels involved	Main management tasks
Orchestrating initiation	CEO and other senior officials,	LEA, LEA→ school	• Maintaining channels of communication
	DfEE civil servants, district HMI	LEA→central government	• Liaising with the DfEE territorial and capital teams and district HMI
		LEA	• Monitoring media output
		LEA, LEA→ school	• Monitoring to sustain an overview of progress
		LEA, LEA→ school	• Coping with emerging problems
Developing formative proposals	Senior officials with specialist expertise	LEA	• Drafting and costing detailed options based on projections of student numbers
		LEA	• Consulting officers and inspectors with responsibility for particular schools
		LEA	• Consulting diocesan representatives on draft proposals
		LEA	• Identifying and evaluating options in drawing up proposals for individual and groups of schools
		LEA	• Consulting councillors from other political parties and MPs with a local constituency
		LEA	• Submitting, with the CEO, formative proposals to councillors from the ruling group serving on the education committee for approval
		LEA	• Writing consultation documents setting out costed options (and, in the borough LEA, preferred options)
Arranging statutory public consultation	Senior officials with specialist expertise	LEA→school	• Setting up public meetings with parents and their communities
		LEA	• Negotiating with councillors about their attendance at public meetings
		LEA→school	• Setting up meetings with staff and governors of schools
		LEA	• Meeting with union and with diocesan representatives
		LEA	• Publicising meetings and circulating consultation documents
		LEA	• Identifying (and, in the county, training) officials who would co-lead meetings
		LEA	• Disseminating information to the local media

Conducting public consultation	Senior officials (and, in the county, officials responsible for particular schools)	LEA→school	• Presenting the LEA case, chairing and taking minutes at meetings
		LEA→school	• Circulating minutes to staff and governors for amendment and incorporating them in the CEO's report with recommendations for firm proposals
		LEA→school	• (In the county arranging a second round of consultation on firm proposals for phases 2 and 3 conducted in writing, and in a few cases, third and fourth rounds)
		LEA	• Recording and analysing written responses
Arranging meetings between central government ministers and other stakeholders	Senior officials, civil servants from the DfEE territorial team, ministers	LEA→central government, school→central government,	• Deputations from stakeholders based at LEA (e.g. diocesan representatives) and school system levels meeting a DfEE minister and civil servants
		central government	• Making a record of meetings

- any impact of reorganising 'feeder' schools catering for younger students on local secondary or high schools
- a transition over two years where first-9–13 middle-high school systems were to be abolished in the borough
- a technical decision with mergers over whether to close the institutions affected and open a new school in the premises of one, or whether to close one or more while categorising the surviving institution as changing character or expanding (in the former case all staff would face the threat of loss of employment, but in the latter case only those in the closing school or schools would do so)
- costs, especially where refurbishment and new building would be involved
- concern whether sufficient church school places would remain to meet demand, and whether the LEA or the diocesan authority would have to borrow capital for building work
- costs that might accrue to the LEA of providing transport where students would have to travel further to school
- any likelihood of councillor or community resistance.

It was vital to negotiate with councillors over draft proposals for their ward before going public. The chair of the borough education committee commented:

> We talked to the members [councillors] individually, ward by ward, about their problems, their individual problems, and then we tried to iron them out. So by the time we got to the public meetings, many of the perceived problems were ironed out.

Phase 2 in the borough entailed closures in the leader of the council's ward. Senior officials were sensitive to the leader's conflict of interests between supporting the initiative as a whole and avoiding loss of votes in the ward by advocating a closure there. They were heavily reliant on the leader's continuing support since their authority was delegated by the borough council. To minimise the risk of losing council backing they offered the leader room to manoeuvre. Their proposal to close a school in the leader's ward contained their preferred option and an alternative. The latter would be more expensive because more building work would be necessary at the school to which students would transfer. The leader favoured the alternative. So it was recast as the preferred option in the public consultation document and eventually implemented. Senior officials had successfully sought a confluence of interests between the leader's concern to retain the support of voters in the ward and their shared strategic concern to promote reorganisation as a whole. The leader subsequently referred to accepting the earliest closure in this ward when persuading other councillors to do likewise.

To illustrate the complexities wrought by the context-dependence of the proposal development task we will dwell on just the first factor in our list. Calculating surplus capacity was far from straightforward. Partially contradictory central government marketisation policies offered different bases for this calculation. Ministers had recently introduced two measures (Table 5.4) relating to school capacity. The first was the 'more open enrolment' (MOE) measure to determine physical capacity. The second was the 'standard number' (SN) providing an annual admissions figure up to which each school could be required to admit students on parental demand (except where VA schools had an arrangement to protect their religious character). The annual statistics on surplus capacity that officials had to submit to the DfEE were based on the MOE measure of physical capacity. Under this measure all unfilled places were technically surplus. There was no direct link between the MOE and SN measures: a school could be full to the MOE capacity figure yet still be required to admit more students because it had a high SN. With LEA agreement governors could even admit students above the SN, as long as the quality of education was not compromised. So officials could not afford to ignore the SN calculation, especially as they would have to consult governors and gain central government approval for any alteration in the SN for schools whose capacity would change.

However, according to the Audit Commission (1996: 12) 'not all unfilled places are surplus, and not all surplus places can be removed'. The borough consultation document stated that:

> Ideally, most local authorities (and central government) would like to see a situation in which all schools would operate, year in year out, at perhaps 90 per cent of capacity, the 10 per cent margin providing the necessary flexibility to cater for educational change and small fluctuations in numbers.

Officials in both LEAs aimed to reduce surplus capacity by an amount that would leave about 13 per cent of unfilled places. But the layout of rooms in any school

Table 5.4 Alternative measures of school capacity

Measure	Origin	Purpose	Basis of calculation (primary sector schools)
More open enrolment	Central government	A measure of physical school capacity	• A DfEE formula allows certain rooms not normally used as teaching bases to be discounted • The floor area of other rooms is measured against a standard of 54 sq m per 30 students • The number of students in the school is subtracted from the MOE capacity figure to produce a statement of surplus places
Standard number	Central government	The minimum threshold for student numbers in the year group where the youngest age group is admitted, so as to maximise scope for parental choice	• The highest of four measures: – the MOE calculation (as above) – the number of students in the school in May 1991 divided by the number of year groups of students in the school – the most recent admission number quoted in a statutory notice which has been approved by central government – the admission number published by the LEA or governors in 1990/1 • The SN is multiplied by the number of year groups in the school to arrive at a capacity figure • The number of students in the school is subtracted from this capacity figure to produce a statement of surplus places
Number of classrooms (county only)	County LEA	A simple and transparent measure of physical school capacity	• Each room designated as a classroom in the school is assumed to have capacity for 30 students • The number of classrooms is multiplied by 30 to give an estimate of school capacity • The number of students in the school is subtracted from this capacity figure to produce a statement of surplus places

and the cost of building new rooms prevented this outcome being sought for every proposal.

In the county senior officials opted for a third, simpler measure of physical capacity, summarised in their consultation document:

> For primary schools, numbers of places . . . are based on the number of rooms in which classes can be formed, not counting specialist and small rooms, and assume maximum class sizes of 30.
>
> For secondary schools, numbers of places are based on an assessment of each school's building stock in relation to the requirements of organising classes for a secondary school curriculum.

Civil servants intimated that the MOE measure must be used for firm proposals submitted to the DfEE and senior officials duly bowed to their authority.

Emergent formative proposals were discussed with representatives of stake-holder groups whose support would ease their passage during the public consultation: from councillors inside and outside the ruling group, through MPs with a constituency in the LEA, to diocesan representatives. Further lobbying, negotiation and compromise occurred at this point. The proposals were written up, finalised, and approved by members of the ruling group on the education committee prior to publication.

Published formative proposals in the two LEAs reflected contrasts in senior officials' consultation strategies. Central government legislation left room for agency at LEA level because a minimum level of consultation was not specified. Formative proposals in the borough related to a secondary or high school and its feeder schools in each pyramid. They contained optional courses of action and concluded with a preferred option and reasons for recommending it. Occasionally two options were given equal weight and public opinion on them was invited. There was to be a single round of public consultation, so it was especially important for senior officials that their documentation would foster a culture of acceptance among stakeholders entitled to consultation. According to one senior official: 'Because we were always producing papers with options in them it did help us to a degree to avoid the criticism, "Oh, you have already decided".'

The approach in the county altered over time. The pilot first phase similarly involved one round of public consultation on groups of feeder primary sector and high schools. Senior officials' preferred option was based on the aim of reverting from a first-8–12 middle-high school system to a primary-secondary system. The alternative of reorganisation without changing the school system was also included for each school. Two rounds of consultation were scheduled for phases 2 and 3. Here most initial formative proposals presented the case simply for the recommended course of action, but feedback was sought on options where proposals were complex. Officials drew up recommendations for revised formative proposals following public consultation, which were discussed in the education committee and reformulated where necessary. This two-part procedure allowed for changes in the light of feedback and for public response on revised formative proposals (illustrated in Chapter 2). Consultation over the latter was conducted in writing except where completely new proposals were put forward. All revised proposals were labelled as being jointly those of the LEA and diocesan authority, each containing one recommendation and its justification for every school in any group affected. In the less settled political context of the county, councillors in the ruling group were keen to consult extensively as a way of strengthening local democracy. The chair of the education committee during consultation for phase 2 and 3 stated:

> If there was one other objective in the process, it was the idea of empowering the community . . . giving them a say in what was to be done . . . If there were sound ideas or issues that emerged, then we were prepared to change and be flexible . . . prepared to change how we implemented things but not changing the fundamental strategy and why we were doing it.

The symbolic importance of public consultation being seen to be genuine was as central to county senior officials and councillors' strategy to empower themselves as in the borough. The extent of the LEA response was publicised in a newsletter for schools. The CEO was quoted as saying: 'One in three of our original proposals have been changed in some way . . . I am sure some people may still say we have not listened – but I can assure you we have.'

Formative proposals affecting Hillside High School

Hillside exemplifies the necessity of considering changes for groups of schools, being a split-site 13–18 high school in an urban area of high surplus capacity. A calculated reduction of 1,650 places was needed across the pyramid of schools including Hillside High (see Figure 1.1) to leave them 90 per cent full. The estimate included an allowance for extra future demand if a housing project proposed for the area were to be approved. Formative proposals were published with recommended options costed according to the number of surplus places removed, annual revenue savings that would be made, the capital borrowing requirement for new building and refurbishment, and the timetable that implementation over two years would entail (see Figure 4.3).

Two sets of proposals affected Hillside High, reflecting different decisions about which schools to link. The first concerned the first and middle schools linked with Hillside to form the primary half of the new school system. Options included closing one or more middle schools. The second contained proposals for Hillside and two other nearby high schools. They would become secondary schools, taking 11–13-year-old students from the middle schools. If Hillside were to expand to absorb the two additional year groups its capacity of 1,350 students would have to be increased to 2,250. Since the present main site was cramped and the cost of extensive building would be prohibitive, it would be cheaper to adapt a middle school site in the pyramid if it should close. The existing subsidiary site of Hillside school was too small for expansion and was separated from the main site by a busy road. Students often had to cross this road unaccompanied.

A summary of options for the primary sector reorganisation and the justification for officials' preference is given in Table 5.5. All options would remove the desired number of surplus places and all would entail some new building. But the first option of closing all middle schools came closest to meeting LEA criteria. The paramount importance attached to the fact that they would also be least costly may be interpreted as an oblique reflection of structural limits imposed by economic conditions. First, a suitable middle school site would become available for expansion of Hillside High to take 11–13-year-old students by forming an 11–14 lower school there. But this arrangement would not alleviate the educational disadvantage of leaving Hillside Secondary as a split-site school. Ironically the middle schools were originally either secondary modern schools or 11–16 secondary schools built slightly more recently at the time of comprehensivisation (see Chapter 1). Science laboratories and other specialist facilities had been removed when adapting them to become 9–13 middle schools

Table 5.5 Summary of formative proposals for primary sector reorganisation in the Hillside pyramid

Options	Points in favour	Points against
Option 1: all middle schools close, all first schools change character to become primary schools	• 1,700 places will be removed if 240 additional places are created through a modest building programme in three of the first schools • First school facilities are more easily adapted than middle school facilities for the primary school age range • One or more middle school sites (including Endale Middle) will become available for the extra secondary school places required • Managing the transition at school level from 3/4–9 to 3/4–11 is easier than from 9–13 to 3/4–11	• None – although some building work will be required, additional accommodation will be needed under all feasible options
Option 2: all first schools close, all middle schools change character to become primary schools	• 1,820 places will be removed if 340 additional places are created through a building programme in two of the middle schools • The cost of maintaining four large schools will be less than seven smaller schools as in Option 1	• Student numbers in two of the new primary schools will far exceed LEA guidelines • Facilities in 9–13 middle schools are not well suited to younger students in the 4–11 age range • No middle school site will become available for the additional secondary school places required • New nursery accommodation (for 3–4-year-olds) will have to be provided at all four schools • Younger students will have to travel further to three of these schools • Managing the transition from 9–13 to 3/4–11 is more difficult than from 3/4–9 to 3/4–11
Option 3: a mixture of first and middle schools close (eleven alternatives were considered)	• Proposals for particular groups of first and middle schools have various advantages including sufficient surplus places removed, minimal building requirements, adaptability of sites, release of middle school sites for the additional secondary school places required	• Proposals for particular groups of schools have various disadvantages including too few surplus places removed, expensive building requirements, unsuitability of sites, increased travelling distance for younger students • Overall, there is a stronger case for closing middle schools than for first schools, except in one area where either Sedge First or Sedge Middle School may equally be closed

Recommendations
- Six of the 3/4–9 first schools change character and expand to become 3/4–11 primary schools
- Either Sedge First School or Sedge Middle School close, and a 4–11 primary school is established in the premises of whichever of the two remains
- The other three middle schools close and the site of either Endale Middle or the second largest middle school becomes secondary school accommodation in accordance with options for the reorganisation of Hillside High School

under the previous reorganisation in this part of the borough. Second, adapting first schools to take 9–11-year-old students from closing middle schools would be cheaper than adapting the latter for the younger primary school students. If former middle school buildings had to cater for the youngest children, cloakroom toilets and washbasins would have had to be replaced with lower units. Specialist areas such as homecraft rooms might have proved too small for conversion into classrooms.

Senior officials, exceptionally, deemed either Sedge First School or Sedge Middle School to be suitable for conversion to a primary school. Sedge Middle was not considered for a lower school site for Hillside because it was further away from the main Hillside site than either Endale Middle or the other middle school contender. So either Sedge Middle or Sedge First would have to close as a contribution to removing surplus capacity in the pyramid. Adapting Sedge First would be straightforward but the buildings were older than at Sedge Middle. Also classrooms were housed on two floors, considered less safe for young children than a single-storey building. As a more recently built former secondary school, Sedge Middle boasted excellent facilities housed on a single level. They included a very large sports hall, representing an irreplaceable LEA investment that councillors in the ruling group were keen to avoid losing, and one that Sedge First could not match. The formative proposals allowed for consultation on either possibility since it was uncertain which way to go.

The other set of proposals covering reorganisation of Hillside and two other high schools is summarised in Table 5.6. Here the concern was to create additional capacity to take 11–13-year-old students. Economic factors were also critical as building work would be inevitable. Options centred on where to build the extra capacity and how best to use middle school sites if they were closed. Ideally no school would end up on a split site because this arrangement embodied educational and moderate economic disadvantages, including:

- co-ordination complexities across sites separated by up to two and a half miles
- timetable constraints
- additional management responsibilities to run the two sites, posing an extra burden on the operating budget
- duplication of specialist facilities

Table 5.6 Summary of formative proposals for three secondary schools including Hillside

Options	Points in favour	Points against
Option 1: build an additional secondary school (three alternatives were considered)	• Most or all additional places required can be provided at the new school, while the other three secondary schools in the central area, including Hillside, can be expanded	• No suitable site is available for a new secondary school of over 1,000 students • A school of 1,000 students established on the site of a closing middle school cannot cater for 16–18-year-old (sixth form) students
Option 2: create two new 11–16 schools and a 16–18 sixth form centre at Hillside (two alternatives were considered)	• Endale Middle and Sedge Middle School sites are suitable for conversion into 11–16 schools • They can be expanded to provide enough places with no new building or only a modest amount at one of the three existing high schools in the central area • The subsidiary site at Hillside High School can be closed	• If Hillside High School becomes a 16–18 sixth form centre, according to central government educational reform legislation it will be removed from LEA control
Option 3: establish an 11–14 lower and 14–18 upper school at Hillside High School, extend two other high schools	• The lower school for Hillside can be accommodated on the site of Endale or Sedge Middle School, so away from the city centre • All 14–18 provision can be accommodated on the main Hillside High School site, enabling the present subsidiary site to be closed • Additional places needed in the other two high schools in the central area can be provided through new building or by converting a closing middle school site	• Hillside Secondary School will still be a split-site school, now with the lower school separated from the upper school by more than 2 miles

Recommendations
• Hillside High School becomes an 11–18 secondary school with the 11–14 lower school on the site of either Endale or Sedge Middle School and the 14–18 upper school on the existing main site
• The Hillside High School subsidiary site closes
• The other two high schools in the central area are expanded to become 11–18 secondary schools

- costs and potential dangers associated with teachers or students travelling between sites
- difficulties with nurturing the identification of students and staff with both lower and upper schools as one organisation.

There was little possibility of building another secondary school. The middle school sites that might be available were too small to house an extension for the specialist facilities needed by sixth form (16–18-year-old) students. Facilities at Hillside High could be upgraded to cater for these students feeding in from 11–16 schools established by adapting two of the middle school sites. But Hillside would then be no longer classed as a school. It would be removed from LEA jurisdiction under central government marketisation reforms in the post-compulsory-education sector – an unwelcome prospect for councillors. The favoured option was a compromise. It incurred the split site but retained LEA control by extending a large middle school site to become the lower school of Hillside. The main Hillside site would gain capacity in becoming the 14–18 upper school, as its 13–14-year-old students would then be educated in the lower school. The present subsidiary site across the busy road could be closed and extra accommodation built at the other high schools so that they could cater for 11–13-year-old students. Capital borrowing of some £2.7 million would be needed to convert the Endale Middle site and expand the main Hillside site.

Governors' written response, also expressed at the public consultation meeting, argued for Hillside High to become a single-site 11–18 school which would move from the present sites to the site of Endale Middle. If the LEA preferred option was to proceed, Endale Middle, being closest to the main site, was the best site for the lower school. This view was reflected in the firm proposal for a split-site school. The present main site for the 14–18 upper school would be retained and Endale Middle would be turned into the 11–14 lower school site. Economics entered here: less new building would be necessary to convert Endale Middle into a lower school site than to build accommodation for the full 11–18 age range.

Formative proposals affecting Capston and Farfield First Schools

These were Victorian church (VC) schools in villages two miles apart in the same parish. The local vicar was a member of the governing body for both schools, proposed for closure under initial formative proposals in the county. They were among several in the locality catering for young children but their estimated capacity of only ninety students each was below half that of the other schools. The central concern was to reduce surplus capacity by closing the smallest institutions since they were disproportionately expensive to run (Table 5.7). The schools were operating well under capacity (fifty-nine students at Capston and fifty-two at Farfield), so were effectively below the minimum financially viable size.

Table 5.7 Summary of formative proposals affecting Capston and Farfield First Schools

Proposals	Points in favour	Points against
Initial proposals: both schools close and students transfer to a nearby infant school and primary school	• 90 surplus student places will be removed in the locality and enough places will remain to meet projected needs • The size of all schools will be within the county LEA's recommended minimum and maximum for primary sector schools • Providing education for the same number of students in fewer schools will make more efficient use of resources as larger institutions are less expensive to run	• Some students will transfer at age 7 from the infant school to a local junior school as well as having to transfer to secondary school at age 11 • Parents in the villages of Capston and Farfield will have a reduced choice of school • Students up to age 7 from Capston and Farfield will have to travel further to school • It may be necessary to change the status of the nearby infant school from a county to a VC school, to replace the loss of VC schools at Capston and Farfield
Revised proposals: the two schools merge to become a new VC primary school on the site of Farfield First School	• 23 surplus places will be removed through closure of the Capston site and transfer of students to the school at Farfield • Establishing a primary school at Farfield will provide both villages with the one 'all-through' primary school • Providing education in one school instead of two will make more efficient use of resources • Students from both villages will have less far to travel to school than under the initial proposal • Students will transfer only at age 11 • The two villages will continue to be served by a VC school	• Additional classrooms will have to be built for the school at Farfield • Existing accommodation will have to be adapted for the full primary age range

Context-dependence was equally significant here. The initial formative proposals would yield the targeted reduction in surplus capacity. But they represented a compromise dominated by the accretion of past changes: the historical legacy of school buildings, church involvement in education, and local demographic trends. They did not match all LEA criteria for reorganisation (especially the aim of avoiding transfer between schools at the age of 7) and would be contentious for stakeholders in the communities concerned because their village school was threatened. Agreement would have to be sought with the diocesan authority about the loss of church school places and whether to replace some by changing the status of the nearby county infant school to which the children from the villages would transfer. The published documents containing proposals for each administrative area also included area-wide costings, rather than being listed school by school. The proposed reduction in surplus capacity was based on the LEA commonsense formula (the third measure of capacity discussed above) and an overall figure covering the north-eastern area was given for annual savings, LEA capital borrowing for county and VC schools, and diocesan authority capital borrowing for VA schools.

The proposal did not find favour with stakeholders in either community. Perceiving that separate attempts to save both schools would be divisive and unlikely to succeed, members of the two communities united to save one school that would serve both villages. Their counter-policy took shape as the vicar, other governors, and senior staff established a pressure group. Members of this self-styled 'action group' conducted a questionnaire survey of parents, whose results informed the alternative proposal they presented to councillors from the education committee. They successfully co-opted that part of the reorganisation policy affecting them. It was accepted that what they put forward met several criteria better than the initial formative proposals, such as students avoiding transfer between schools at the age of 7.

Action group members proposed a VC primary school at Farfield, on a larger site than Capston with more permanent accommodation. Its size would be doubled to give a capacity of 175 students. This counter-proposal expressed values contradictory to the reorganisation policy, in that negligible capacity would be removed and additional capital borrowing would be required to build more classrooms at Farfield. The expansion was actually limited to a capacity of 120 students because officials from the county council planning department and highways department were adamant that the site and access roads could not cope with a larger school and associated extra traffic. Members of the action group realised that their influence was unlikely to hold sway against these officials' authority to recommend councillors to deny the legally required planning permission for an enlarged school. They accepted the limitation imposed, which was reflected in the firm proposal eventually receiving the Secretary of State's approval.

The Public Consultation Process

Senior officials' next task of *arranging statutory public consultation* began when formative proposals were published (Table 5.3). The logistics were problematic because so many public meetings – every one a component of reorganisation that had to be managed – were to be held over the four-to-five-month consultation period. In the borough, three meetings for each school would be arranged for the same day wherever possible. An afternoon meeting for staff was held after students had gone home, then a meeting for governors, culminating in the public evening meeting (which staff and governors could also attend) lasting up to four hours. Well over three hundred consultation meetings were held during the initiation stage of the five phases. A similar number were held in the county, where repeated revision of a minority of the more complex proposals led to one or more further rounds of meetings. Innumerable informal meetings complemented these formal occasions. They involved various officials and other stakeholders, whether in their individual capacity or as representatives of school staff unions, the diocesan authority, or community action groups.

It was a delicate matter to decide which change agents from the LEA should attend the public consultation meetings, and in what capacity. Senior officials were concerned that councillors from the ruling group, on whose behalf the proposals were put forward, might act inadvertently as 'loose cannons' by being drawn into party-political wrangling as they defended reorganisation. The line taken in both LEAs was that ownership of formative proposals lay with officials (and diocesan representatives wherever involved), who put them forward. Whatever proposals emerged from the consultation process would have the status of recommendations to the education committee. Only after adoption there and ratification in the full council would ownership transfer to councillors. After early experience in the borough with councillors fronting meetings, senior officials persuaded them to attend only as observers and representatives of their ward, like any other stakeholder: 'Officers don't mind coping with political questions and taking a certain amount of flak . . . word got around: "Leave it to the officers; they'll cope".' A similar arrangement obtained in the county, where councillors' input was confined to broad policy issues such as overall LEA expenditure on education.

Senior officials at the heart of proposal development led public meetings in the borough, supported by colleagues with specialist expertise, which included calculating capacity and costing building work. Those officers and inspectors also attended who had responsibility for the school that was the subject of any meeting. By contrast, the CEO in the county regarded the experience of sharing leadership of public consultation meetings as a professional development opportunity for officials, particularly in phases 2 and 3. Here the officer with responsibility for schools in the administrative area was required both to lead and to chair meetings, supported by the inspector with pastoral responsibility for these schools. Inspectors were able to help ensure that meetings addressed educational as well as economic benefits to accrue from proposals. As one noted: 'You could increasingly turn the focus of the meeting away from the nuts and bolts of the resource issue and on to quite detailed curriculum issues.'

A consequence of distributing leadership of meetings was to give most officials a new task. In recognition of their learning needs, senior colleagues organised a half-day preparatory training session on the skills of running consultation meetings. Officials with experience of public consultation for phase 1 provided a simulation exercise by acting out a meeting. Additionally, officials were encouraged to attend a public meeting as observers before taking a lead role. The CEO stated: 'I got officers and inspectors trained to be clear, courteous, to listen to what people were saying, to know how to respond but not to be drawn in too deeply, to know how to stick to a prepared script.' The latter consisted of the key messages to get across plus a list of do's and don'ts. It was issued to all officials. A bulletin was produced of the 'twenty most frequently asked questions'.

Once public consultation was under way, officials met frequently to exchange experiences and explore solutions to issues arising from public feedback. These meetings helped to reinforce their professional culture, especially their sense of belonging to a group. One senior inspector recalled: 'We all had to cover each other's backs.'

On the other hand, officers and inspectors responsible for schools in a particular area sometimes disagreed with draft formative proposals. Extensive private dialogue during the development work did not always bring reconciliation. A few officers or inspectors experienced conflicting loyalties where they perceived that senior colleagues were wrong. One official in the borough indicated how the shared norms of officials' professional culture generally ensured that they expressed consistent views in public:

> We have a phrase in this area about singing from the same hymnsheet . . . we all know what we are doing, what we are trying to achieve. It is team-work, you've got to operate efficiently and effectively as a team . . . No one gets a mixed message; that would cause problems with the general public if they were getting mixed messages back.

Senior officials urged their officer and inspector colleagues to adopt the official line but left them to decide whether to express their personal view. Only exceptionally did an official publicly oppose senior colleagues' proposals, suggesting that allegiance to the professional culture normally won out. The county strategy of requiring such officials to lead meetings on proposals they had not formulated could prove even more problematic. Here officials had to 'learn the materials by heart and learn to love and defend them'. They occasionally found themselves advocating a course of action they disagreed with – 'exercising cabinet responsibility for decisions you hadn't taken', as one put it.

Preparation for the consultation exercise extended to press officers in both LEAs briefing local media professionals and keeping them informed through regular press releases and direct contact. They frequently put out 'good news' stories, including those about new building undertaken in an earlier phase. Other senior officials made themselves readily available to respond to journalists' requests. The aim was to ward off negative coverage that might damage the culture of acceptance they sought to inculcate among other stakeholders by convincing media professionals that they were not hiding anything. In the county a journalist would be invited to each public meeting and briefed in advance in the hope that any report would favour the LEA case. However, an issue occasionally arose that suited the journalist's interest but not that of the officials.

The difficulty of *conducting public consultation* meetings varied with the differential impact of proposals on stakeholders connected with particular schools. In many instances stakeholders from all parties perceived that their sectional interests were being served. Here, according to one union representative, the prevailing sentiment was that 'change equals new beginnings'. Proposed closures tended to trigger the greatest confrontation. A senior official who had attended every public meeting in the borough testified to the strong emotions they could arouse:

> One or two meetings became quite heated, with waving of banners and chanting and so on. You've got to enjoy it . . . if you bend under this sort of pressure, it makes it worse. I think you've somehow got to try to get through those sorts of meetings being reasonably cheerful. It's part of the job, isn't it . . . Ribbons and decorations festooned my car at meetings. I'd go outside and I would find they had been putting things on my car, saying 'Save Our School' and so on. No damage was ever done; it was, rather, a good-natured protest.

Officials in the county who led meetings that turned confrontational were generally less positive. One inspector commented that 'being bayed at was very unpleasant'. The two-part consultation exercise entailed further meetings on new proposals arising from public response to initial formative proposals, as noted earlier. They could precipitate even greater conflict. As an official explained:

> The second round became more heated because it was focused on fewer schools and their sense of injustice was heightened by the fact that, whereas in the [first round] everyone was in that boat fighting together . . . in the second round it was very lonely.

Stakeholders from schools serving neighbouring communities had often felt able to combine forces in objecting to initial proposals, knowing that there was to be further consultation. The second round was the last chance to defend individual schools, pressuring stakeholders to fight for their school alone.

A detailed record was made of responses to consultation. Minutes were taken at each consultation meeting in the borough. Staff and governors received the minutes of their meeting and the public meeting for comment and amendment. Written comments were invited and officials wrote a digest of the main points, quantifying them where widespread concerns were expressed. Several petitions were also received. Records of meetings were complemented in the county by records of other forms of response. Members of the project team logged and analysed the key points connected with specific proposals from written responses and telephone calls, tallying them with points raised at public meetings. They responded as necessary, especially if asked for further information. Consultation on phase 2 and 3 produced 8,700 letters or alternative proposals, all of which had to be processed.

Meetings between central government ministers and other stakeholders provided another route for public response to formative proposals. The cross-system-level interaction they entailed kept ministers and civil servants selectively in touch with what was happening at LEA and school levels. On occasion ministers and civil servants would meet a deputation of stakeholders to hear their concerns. Diocesan representatives connected with county proposals brought their case for redistributing church school places in viable-sized primary schools to support their request to borrow capital for building and refurbishment of VA schools. A few groups from school communities were empowered to present their case, typically to avoid closure or merger. Informal lobbying was also reported, where an MP whose constituency covered part of an LEA lobbied a minister on behalf of particular school communities. The CEO in the county accompanied a deputation of councillors from the Conservative Party, by then in opposition, to one such meeting. The councillors attempted to reconcile their conflict of interests between supporting reorganisation as a whole and avoiding local unpopularity. They expressed enthusiasm for the initiative while pleading for the retention of schools in their wards, mostly in the southern area.

LEA containment of pressure group politics

Another formal meeting in the county involved a deputation of stakeholders from a pressure group aiming to save all schools in the southern area which might close. (The same group featured in Chapter 2.) The significance of this pressure group for managing the initiation stage lay in its members' collective and synergistic use of influence and their adherence to norms predisposing them to employ confrontational tactics that others found unjustifiable in opposing officials, councillors from the ruling group, and diocesan representatives.

The deputation exercise was the culmination of intensive pressure group activity during the consultation period for phase 2 and 3. The group originated with three middle-class parents from professional backgrounds whose children attended Dale Primary, proposed for merger with Southlip Primary on the Southlip site (Table 1.4). Three of the four teaching rooms at Dale were temporary classrooms. While it had capacity for 120 students under the common-sense formula, only seventy-eight attended. Southlip was a similar size with even fewer students, but it boasted four permanent classroooms. The three parents had sought room to manoeuvre by forming a pressure group to save Dale Primary (similar to the action group at Capston and Farfield). Group members were addressed at a group meeting by a parent from a neighbouring village school proposed for closure. He had persuaded them that collective action would achieve more than separate factions fighting on behalf of individual schools. Subsequently, he and three originators of the Dale Primary action group formed the nucleus of a pressure group with a wider remit: to save the nine village schools and one secondary school in the southern area whose sites were scheduled to close under initial formative proposals for mergers.

Contextual factors noted in Chapter 4 help explain why an area-wide pressure group formed only in the southern area. Here conditions were ripe for active resistance reaching beyond individual communities:

- It was the one administrative area whose primary-secondary school system had been retained, so downsizing could not be allied with abolishing the first-middle-high school system.

- Surplus capacity was unevenly distributed across a rural district of scattered population, so it was not always obvious which schools to close.
- The district was affluent, the local MP and most councillors with wards in the area were members of the Conservative Party, now (as mentioned above) the main opposition party in the hung council.
- Many parents embraced the spirit of marketisation reforms by travelling to the village school of their choice, making it difficult to predict where demand would rise or fall in future. They were mostly articulate middle-class professionals, many with the expertise, contacts, ability to organise themselves, and motivation to defend the status quo.

Dale Primary was a clear example of the rural 'commuter school' phenomenon. Officials' analysis of the home addresses of students attending Dale Primary indicated that, if it were merged on the Southlip site, a school nearer their home than Dale would be available for about 80 per cent of these children. A quarter came from beyond the county border two miles away. A higher proportion of students attending Southlip came from working-class families in the immediate neighbourhood. The fight to save Dale Primary seemed to be driven, in part, by middle-class parents' wish to avoid their children being educated alongside their working-class peers.

Senior officials were aware that the case for reorganisation was weakest in the southern area. They did judge that population changes had brought a mismatch between capacity and demand for student places in some communities. But phase 3 alone could not meet the higher rate of revenue savings that central government ministers required from 1994 for capital borrowing connected with reorganisation. The insensitivity of this shift of central government policy on capital borrowing towards the LEA reorganisation initiative already under way brought the unintended consequence of forcing senior officials to subsidise phase 3 by including the southern area.

Core members of the pressure group put their professional expertise to use in developing their counter-policy, starting with active resistance. One with public relations experience mounted a sophisticated media campaign. Another with knowledge of operational research management developed a critique of the statistical methods used by officials to arrive at their estimates of surplus capacity in the area and of the results obtained by these methods. Ammunition was provided by the report from the LEA auditors on surplus capacity commissioned prior to the preliminary external consultation on the principle of abolishing the first-middle-high school system through reorganisation, obtained by pressure group members. The auditors' estimate of surplus capacity in the southern area based on standard numbers was lower than the LEA estimate based on the commonsense measure. More ammunition was provided at a public consultation meeting where a senior official claimed that the LEA figures took account of the 'known distribution of population, forecasts of population, parental preference and state of buildings – in other words we do what is known in the trade as a multivariate analysis'. When challenged to demonstrate how this analysis was achieved, the senior official declined. The pressure group statistician calculated surplus capacity across the southern area to be around 10 per cent, half the LEA estimate. He claimed that this modest surplus capacity would soon be filled as the local population was rising.

Senior officials attempted ameliorative action, seeking a confluence of interests by responding positively to pressure group members' request to discuss the evidence behind the LEA analysis. They agreed to work in partnership to produce a more accurate estimate and see if a compromise acceptable to both parties might be reached. Pressure group members agreed to drop their media campaign. But the coalition rapidly broke down because the interests pursued by each party were irreconcilable. According to the pressure group statistician, officials refused access to important statistical information, including the auditors' report. From then on the pressure group strategy was purely conflictual. Its members mounted a sustained campaign against the stakeholders responsible for the proposals, which the latter could only absorb or deflect. The public right to express a dissenting view was enshrined in law, and for the targets of the pressure group to respond in kind would simply court negative media coverage. That would risk undermining such culture of acceptance as was developing.

Pressure group members did their own fact-finding exercise. They published a report, which they also presented to officials. They argued that the LEA statistics were wrong and that small rural schools should receive preferential treatment despite their high running cost. In the report they concluded that sufficient surplus capacity could be taken out by 'removing a total of five temporary classrooms at schools with real surplus places'. They claimed that proposals to close small schools, rather than achieving the same reduction in surplus places by taking out temporary classrooms, were driven by economic considerations to save revenue:

> Taking out surplus places in the school system does save money but this is actually quite small . . . What does however yield proportionately larger savings is if a school can be closed altogether. In this case the 'base allocation' of around £30,000 [annually] per school is saved irrespective of the size of the premises. Logically, it is the smallest schools which can yield the greatest savings.

Their use of influence extended to attending public consultation meetings for schools under threat. On one occasion they put some forty questions to officials, a tactic interpreted by one councillor as 'trying to tie up officers in unreasonable demands for information'. Another tactic was to invite officials and councillors to meet them in the presence of journalists to debate reorganisation. Officials and councillors from the ruling group declined, but the meeting went ahead attended by councillors from the opposition parties.

Senior officials took account of the pressure group along with other feedback in formulating their revised formative proposals. A secondary school and five primary schools down for closure were reprieved, one of the latter now to become the annexe of the other school with which it would merge. An updated LEA estimate of surplus capacity was much closer to the pressure group's figures, down to 13 per cent. After reorganisation, with fewer places removed than under the initial proposals but with the projected rise in the school age population, this surplus would be reduced to 7 per cent. Pressure group members claimed a partial victory. But they perceived officials to have disregarded the heart of their case: proposals for Dale Primary and other schools down for closure remained unchanged.

The revised formative proposals were put forward jointly with the CE and RC diocesan authorities. Pressure group members now targeted them, partly because to sustain an effective campaign 'you have to think of a new theme constantly'. Dale Primary and three other schools still under threat were VC schools, so the CE diocesan authority came under concerted pressure.

Pressure group members continued to attend public consultation meetings where there were new proposals. They gained the support of their local MP, a member of the Conservative Party, who arranged for the meeting with a central government minister mentioned above. A civil servant who was present suggested that they did get their case across, though they ignored the question as to whether schools under threat offered good-quality education. Their final tactic was to exploit the agency they could potentially enjoy under the GM schools policy to persuade governors and parents from these schools to begin the process of applying to the Secretary of State for GM status. In the event Dale Primary was one of three threatened primary schools in the southern area whose GM application went ahead and was approved. The counter-policy of pressure group members who were parents at these schools had proved highly successful. The contradictory GM policy empowered them to reject that part of the LEA reorganisation initiative affecting them.

Norms of behaviour that for core members were justified by their aim lay beyond the bounds of acceptability to many other stakeholders. Their behaviour alienated many headteachers and governors on whose behalf they campaigned. One stakeholder referred to them as 'rent-a-mob'. A councillor hinted at allegiance to the prevalent culture that they had so consistently transgressed, observing that they were 'less than professional in the way they conducted themselves', indulging in 'a lot of misrepresentation'. Their local influence was reduced by their allegiance to a campaign culture that other stakeholders abhorred. Yet their activities were still legitimated by central government consultation requirements entitling them to express their views. Their sectional interest happened to align with the central government GM policy, disposing officials and councillors to take account of their case for fear of stimulating mass attempts to gain GM status. The unequal distribution of authority between the three main system levels meant that managing this part of the change process at LEA level was restricted to containment and amelioration. The confluence of interests between central government and school level stakeholders also disposed ministers to give pressure group members something of what they wanted. The outcome was that five school sites were lost through mergers in the southern area.

Completing the submission process and planning for implementation

Senior officials' efforts to contain the impact of the pressure group on their reorganisation plans illustrate how *orchestrating initiation* had to be continual. Monitoring and liaison activities described earlier were sustained in both LEAs after statutory public consultation was completed. The next sequential component in managing the initiation stage at LEA level was for senior officials with specialist knowledge of the content and costing of proposals to bring firm proposals to the point of submission (Table 5.8).

The scope of proposals for each phase and, in the county, the submission of GM applications led the Secretary of State to 'call in' proposals for all phases and make the final approval decisions. Officials had to demonstrate that they had taken account of the wealth of recorded feedback in *finalising firm proposals*. Any of those affecting church schools were agreed at meetings with diocesan representatives. Officials presented the firm proposals at a sequence of formal committee meetings. Their tasks became more complicated the more proposals were addressed together. The largest tranche was 195 schools connected with phase 2 and 3 in the county presented to the education committee for approval. Diocesan representatives enjoyed an unusual degree of authority as members of this hung council (Chapter 4). They sometimes found themselves with the casting vote on particular proposals when opinion among councillors was evenly divided, whether these proposals concerned church schools or not. A few councillors from the ruling group in both LEAs coped with their conflict of interests over unpopular proposals affecting their ward by using their authority as elected ward representatives to vote against the party line on these proposals. This symbolic gesture was designed to demonstrate to voters in their ward that they supported their case while still backing the council overall. Education committee recommendations were taken forward to a meeting of the full council for ratification. In the county, several recommendations were modified at this meeting prior to the formal decisions being taken on them.

Submitting firm proposals was an exacting endeavour. Senior officials were required to word the statutory notice proposing how each school was to be reorganised in compliance with central government legislation. Objectors could challenge proposals if any loopholes were left. Draft notices were sent to civil servants from the territorial team to ensure that they were acceptable, then a notice was published outside each school and advertisements placed in the local press. Local stakeholders had two months from then to submit objections to the DfEE or the LEA. Submitted documentation was extensive, encompassing:

- a copy of each statutory notice
- a statement of the overall requirement for a reduction in surplus capacity
- a 'statement of case' and maps supporting the firm proposal for each school
- the public consultation documents
- the CEO's report detailing all council-approved proposals, costings, and a breakdown of the views expressed during public consultation

Table 5.8 Management tasks connected with firm proposals and preparing for implementation

Initiation task area	Key change agents	Education system levels involved	Main management tasks
Orchestrating initiation		(Ongoing activity, see Table 5.3)	
Finalising firm proposals	Senior officials with specialist expertise	LEA	• Taking account of feedback in drafting firm proposals • Presenting firm proposals for formal LEA and council decisions
Submitting firm proposals	Senior officials with specialist expertise	LEA LEA→central government LEA LEA→central government school→LEA→ central government	• Drafting statutory notices for each school affected • Checking with the DfEE territorial team that statutory requirements for notices would be met • Displaying statutory notices in local newspapers and at the schools concerned • Submitting a copy of statutory notices, CEO's report • Forwarding written objections to the Secretary of State
Capital borrowing	Senior officials with specialist expertise	LEA LEA→central government LEA→central government	• Developing detailed capital expenditure plans connected with firm proposals • Liaising with the DfEE capital team about parameters for the scheme • Submitting a bid for each phase
Planning implementation for all schools affected	Senior officials with specialist expertise	LEA LEA→school LEA→school	• Planning implementation tasks including building work, procedures for setting up temporary governing bodies, phasing of bids for capital borrowing, finalising allocation of transitional funding for schools affected by proposals • Setting up temporary governing bodies for merged schools (county) • Liaising with headteachers and governors
Planning implementation for individual schools affected	Senior staff and governors	School School	• Planning implementation tasks depending on the content of formative and firm proposals for the school • Appointing the headteacher-designate for merged schools (county)

- a list of all 'statutory objections' to firm proposals (written statements signed by at least ten voters among local residents) and objections from individuals, with a summary of their content and the LEA response
- petitions (which counted as a form of statutory objection).

Two months later they forwarded any written objections received during the period allowed after submission, together with the LEA response. Conversely, territorial team civil servants sought the LEA response on any objections they had received directly.

Officials with responsibility for finance and building work began separate negotiations with the DfEE capital team over *capital borrowing* requirements connected with proposals, as did diocesan representatives over building work for VA schools. Since they effectively sought permission to borrow money, the detailed basis of their estimates went largely unquestioned. Approval for capital borrowing tended to come some time after the decision on reorganisation proposals was announced, forcing officials in the borough to arrange with councillors temporarily to borrow this money from local authority reserves until the central government money came through.

The final initiation stage task falling to senior officials and their colleagues, senior staff in schools, and governors alike was to start *planning implementation* on the assumption that proposals would be approved. Planning dovetailed the concern of officials over the differential impact of proposals for schools across the phase of reorganisation with the concern of school staff and governors over implications of the proposal for their school. It led to intensive communication across the network of these stakeholders based at LEA and school levels. Activity for this part of the initiation stage for later phases built on lessons officials had learned in an earlier phase. We will discuss preparatory efforts in the next chapter since they were taken into the implementation stage wherever proposals were approved. However, it is worth noting how extensive the preparatory planning was at Hillside High School in the borough because of its projected expansion as a split-site school. Preliminary activities included:

- holding a weekend conference for members of the senior management team (SMT) and the chair of governors to plan how to consult other stakeholders, to articulate guiding principles (e.g. that the school would have a 'secondary school ethos'), and to consider what consultation and planning must cover (e.g. the curriculum and the structure of the school day)
- undertaking a questionnaire survey of staff at Hillside and the four feeder middle schools to determine their view of what the school ethos should be
- arranging a half day in-service training session for Hillside staff to consider curriculum and pastoral care issues
- fact-finding, where the headteacher and other senior staff visited several split-site schools in other LEAs and secondary schools in the borough which had already been reorganised
- holding a meeting between SMT members, the chair of governors, and LEA officials to discuss logistics, the budget, and staffing.

Similarly, preparation at Capston and Farfield in the county was far advanced long before their merger was confirmed. Not anticipating the long delay over the decisions for proposals for schools in phase 2 and 3, officials set up a temporary governing body. It contained representatives from the existing governing body of each school contributing to a merger. Officials advised members of the temporary governing body on advertising and appointing a headteacher. The headteacher at Farfield retired shortly before the firm proposals were submitted to the Secretary of State. Subsequently the acting headteacher at Capston (appointed on a temporary contract) was asked by the governors at Farfield and officials to become acting headteacher of both schools until reorganisation. She agreed, and later applied for the permanent headship of what was proposed to become Bigtree Primary School on the Farfield site. She was appointed as headteacher-designate four months before the central government decision was announced.

Reaching the big decisions

The initiation stage was out of officials' hands once firm proposals had been submitted. Central government civil servants were the key change agents, assessing proposals and advising ministers responsible for decision-making (Table 5.9). *Assessing applications for GM status* from schools in the county was carried out simultaneously. But decisions on approving GM status had to be taken first because a positive decision on GM status precluded whatever was proposed for their reorganisation. The use of a mandate as the policy instrument for the consultation process and the inducement of capital borrowing to encourage LEA initiatives meant that LEA compliance had to be checked. It was also important to avoid jeopardising the quality of educational provision. Accordingly, civil servants employed criteria for *assessing submitted proposals* of three kinds:

- *legal* – that requirements for public consultation were met, objections were taken into account, and statutory notices were correct
- *economic* – calculating that a sufficient proportion of surplus student places would be removed, capital borrowing requests were justified, schools would be financially viable, and the proposals offered value for money
- *educational* – judging the quality of provision in existing institutions and the likely quality in those scheduled to survive reorganisation, and checking the feasibility of complex transition arrangements including those at Hillside High School where reorganisation would take place over two years (Chapter 4).

Territorial team members checked the legal and economic acceptability of proposals through the documentation submitted, liaising with colleagues from the capital team over calculations for borrowing. A copy of the documentation was sent to the district HMI who reported on educational quality.

The professional approach adopted by LEA officials contributed to their empowerment in relation to central government. Their efforts to liaise with civil servants had symbolic value in demonstrating willingness to comply with legal

Table 5.9 Management tasks entailed in making decisions on submitted proposals

Initiation task area	Key change agents	Education system levels involved	Main management tasks
Assessing applications for GM status (county only)	Members of the DfEE territorial team, district inspectors (HMI)	Central government→ school	• District HMI visiting schools where an application had been submitted and writing a report on its educational quality and viability for the DfEE territorial team, recommending whether the application should be approved
		Central government	• Compiling documentation for the Secretary of State with recommendations on whether the application should be approved
Assessing submitted proposals	Members of DfEE territorial team, district inspectors (HMI)	Central government→ school	• District-based HMI visiting schools affected by LEA firm proposals and writing a report on their educational quality for the territorial team, recommending whether individual proposals should be approved
		Central government→ school	• A senior member of the territorial team visiting communities in the LEA to gain a detailed understanding of local situations (county only, phases 2 and 3)
		Central government	• A meeting between the members of the territorial team and district HMI to agree on their advice to the Secretary of State
		Central government	• Compiling documentation for the Secretary of State with recommendations on whether individual proposals should be approved
Capital borrowing	Members of the DfEE capital team	Central government Central government	• Checking that LEA bids meet financial requirements • Liaising with members of the DfEE territorial team
Decision making on GM applications (county only)	Minister, senior member of the DfEE territorial team	Central government	• A meeting between the schools minister and a senior member of territorial team where the minister makes formal decisions on behalf of the Secretary of State
Decision making on LEA firm proposals	Minister, members of the DfEE territorial team	Central government Central government	• Submitting documentation including recommendations to the schools minister • A meeting between the schools minister and territorial team where the minister makes the formal decision on behalf of the Secretary of State
Announcing decisions	Members of the DfEE territorial team	Central government→ LEA	• Writing to the CEO and diocesan representatives

and economic requirements and their capacity to manage the initiation process. Civil servants became favourably disposed towards officials because of a shared belief in their competence, the accumulation of positive experience from one or more earlier phases, and awareness of the confluence of LEA and central government interests in making reorganisation initiatives succeed. A civil servant said of borough officials: 'They seemed to have it all under control and they were quite happy to keep us informed as to where they were at in terms of consultation.' Another commented of county officials: 'We don't have to keep throwing proposals back at them . . . they provide good, well worked through capital bids and they make good, sensible judgements. They're well in touch with their schools.' Consequently civil servants supported LEA officials wherever they could. Referring to the borough, a civil servant observed: 'Our questions helped them to a certain extent in expressing the proposals in a way which would help them to win acceptance.'

The central part played by district HMI reflected their role across the network of stakeholders based at the three levels of the education system. They acted for the national inspectorate in advising central government ministers but also had regional responsibility. Their location enabled them to develop an ongoing relationship with LEA officials and knowledge of the schools in their district as a foundation for judging educational quality. Table 5.10 summarises the district HMI's contribution in assessing proposals for the pyramid of schools which included Hillside High, giving some idea of the amount of work that complex proposals could entail.

Part of the material to be assessed was a statutory objection received since submission. It came from governors and parents at Sedge First School, proposed to merge with Sedge Middle by closing both schools and opening a new one on the Sedge Middle site. They argued that Sedge First should merely change character so that the staff would not have to apply for jobs in the new institution. The LEA response was to justify the closure on grounds of fairness to staff from both schools, as had been done previously with similar mergers. There were also several letters expressing concern about the proposed transition year arrangements for 12–13-year-old students, due to transfer to Endale Middle from the other three middle schools for this school's final year before it became the lower school site of Hillside Secondary School. Governors and headteachers feared that parents with younger children at those three middle schools would try to place them at Endale so that they would not have to transfer the following year. Staff at Endale would already have to cope with extensive building work on the site and the influx of 12–13-year-old students. Their preferred alternative was for 12–13-year-old students to remain in their middle school for the transition year. The rationale was to avoid overcrowding at Endale and haemorrhaging of students from the other middle schools in their final year of existence. The LEA response agreed by members of the education committee was to accede, proposing a 'minor amendment' to that effect should the proposals be approved (see Figure 4.3). The district HMI included the statutory objection and representations in the assessment, recommending approval of all LEA proposals.

Table 5.10 Tasks of district HMI to assess proposals for the Hillside pyramid in the borough

Task	Contribution to assessment of proposals
Analysing proposals and objections	• Examining details of specific proposals • Checking facts about accommodation, calculations of surplus capacity and the amount of capital borrowing required • Assessing the financial viability of reorganised schools • Evaluating objections and officials' response
First meeting with senior LEA officials	• Gathering information about the context of proposals • Setting up a programme of visits to schools
Visiting all schools affected by proposals	• Assessing the quality of provision, including accommodation, capacity and staffing levels • Assessing the standards of education achieved, taking account of past HMI inspection reports • Checking the feasibility of what was proposed
Second meeting with senior LEA officials	• Checking whether sufficient surplus places would be removed • Asking how higher standards would be achieved in the lower years of secondary schools than were currently achieved in the upper years of middle schools • Raising issues about individual proposals • Feeding back views expressed by school staff about LEA management of reorganisation
Compiling a report for the DfEE territorial team	• Drafting the report and updating it in the light of investigation • Judging the quality of present and proposed provision and present and predicted educational standards • Recommending whether proposals should be supported

Shortly before submission of proposals for phases 2 and 3 in the county, civil servants from the territorial team had identified twelve schools where there might be difficulties, whether because proposals were complex, transport to school might prove problematic, or GM applications were involved. The team leader had been prompted to visit the locality by the pressure group activity discussed above and the exceptional number of statutory objections and applications for GM status in the southern area. The team leader admitted: 'We were a bit nervous at this point.' The initiative would collapse if more than a few schools were allowed to escape by achieving GM status. An unusual step had therefore been taken to check out on the ground details such as distances between schools and the condition of school buildings to complement school visits made by the district HMI.

Members of the capital team received separate applications for *capital borrowing* from officials and diocesan representatives. In contrast with the detailed scrutiny of proposals by their counterparts in the territorial team, the brief of this team was mainly to check that the bids met financial requirements. The mandatory minimum rate of LEA revenue savings had to be achieved by removing surplus capacity as a condition of releasing the capital for building and refurbishment. Their feedback was taken into account in the advice put forward to ministers. Territorial team members and district HMI met to review all recommendations and formulate their joint advice.

Nine applications for GM status were associated with county phase 2 and 3 proposals, causing much of the delay that resulted in the timetable for implementing phase 2 being postponed for a year (Chapter 4). The schools minister responsible on behalf of the Secretary of State for *decision-making on GM applications* and LEA and diocesan authority reorganisation proposals had given civil servants 'a very useful steer', advising them to offer a judgement on each GM application and reorganisation proposal on its own merits. The overtly political 'trade-off' between the GM and reorganisation policies was thus retained as a matter for politicians alone. Civil servants' advice was to reject the bulk of GM applications because the LEA case for closing or merging them was judged on legal, economic, and educational criteria to be almost uniformly strong. But for the schools minister, additional political criteria were paramount: boosting the GM policy versus supporting the reorganisation policy. The minister made each GM application decision or a provisional decision that the Secretary of State was 'minded' to make at a meeting with the senior civil servant from the territorial team. The joint advice from members of the territorial team and HMI on this application and the associated LEA reorganisation proposal were taken into account. The eventual outcome was a balance struck between the two contradictory policies. Restricting the number of schools approved to gain GM status to five was calculated to ensure that the revenue savings for the rest of phase 2 and 3 remained above the minimum threshold for the necessary capital borrowing to be allowed. Here, inconsistency inside the state channelled the agency of central government policymakers towards seeking a compromise that would minimise one policy undermining the other.

Provisional or firm *decisions on LEA firm proposals were made* at the same meeting. Further fact-finding and analysis followed where there had been provisional decisions, leading to a final decision. Decisions on proposals for the less contentious phases in this LEA and the borough were reportedly made without a face-to-face meeting. Civil servants from the territorial team dealing with the later phases of reorganisation in the borough sent a file with their recommendations and the other documentation to the schools minister with an invitation to discuss them, which the minister deemed unnecessary. Once decisions were made, their *announcement* fell to civil servants, who formally notified the CEO and diocesan representatives. They in turn informed governors and headteachers directly. The decisions were publicised through the local media and, in the county for phases 2 and 3, the reorganisation newsletter. From then on central government was no longer involved with the reorganisation initiatives, apart from ongoing links between officials and members of the capital team over the release of capital to pay for building and refurbishment.

Implications of complexity for managing initiation

The expression of characteristics of LEA reorganisation initiatives as a complex educational change during the first and subsequent initiation stages shaped the approaches to their management that brought them to a successful conclusion. Senior officials, acutely aware of the *large scale* of their project, prioritised facilitating formal and informal communication with the thousands of people whose voice was heard during internal and external consultation. For support as change agents, they relied heavily on their different individual specialist knowledge required to formulate and consult on proposals. They also sought expert feedback and advice from civil servants. They instigated partnerships with other local stakeholder groups and attempted, within limits, to accommodate divergent sectional interests.

Senior officials had to plan for all *components*, whether the sequential management tasks to set up the first phase, the range encompassed by the proposal for each school targeted, or the long series of management tasks for each phase dictated by legal parameters governing consultation. Each component had to be planned incrementally with an eye to what had to be done beforehand, what would also be happening elsewhere at the same time, and what was to follow. These components embodied a flow of interaction through the network of stakeholders based at all three *system* levels. Much was mediated, most strikingly perhaps where central government ministers were informed at third hand about concerns at school level through civil servants' advice based on LEA summaries of issues raised at public consultation meetings. Managing initiation across system levels necessitated linkage roles, such as the district HMI and officials responsible for groups of schools, and tasks promoting cross-level communication, most notably the diversity of consultation meetings. Senior officials largely succeeded in nurturing a culture of acceptance among stakeholders inside the LEA and at school level despite the unequal distribution of power between system levels reflected in their lack of authority to make the decision to implement proposals. They also succeeded early on in demonstrating to central government civil servants their commitment to reorganisation and competence to manage the LEA initiatives, enabling both stakeholder groups to work together synergistically.

Senior officials made some allowances for the *differential impact* of their strategies for managing the initiation stage and the content of proposals made on the various stakeholders at LEA and school level. An attempt was made in the county to prepare officials for the exceptional tasks of leading public consultation meetings. In both LEAs the partnerships with other stakeholder groups were designed to protect their sectional interests where possible. But certain conflicting interests turned out to be irreconcilable, and here a strategy of containment was employed. Senior officials and their colleagues had to make the running for the initiation stage yet few could dedicate themselves to the reorganisation project. Most experienced significant intensification of their work during the public consultation period. The degree to which different stakeholders either understood or cared about the totality of the proposals for each phase varied enormously, reflecting the contrast between officials' promotional interest and the diverse sectional interests of other groups. In their interactions with other stakeholders officials had to allow for this difference, explaining how particular proposals fitted into the targets and financial parameters for the initiatives as a whole. *Contextual dependence* impinged on all activity to manage the initiation stage, from the encounter with the GM policy to the import of historical factors affecting individual schools.

The complexity of the change required a sophisticated approach to the management of initiation, and that is what the main change agents proved capable of achieving through their agency, despite the difficulties of coping with complexity. But success in getting proposals approved was merely the start. Implementation was a very different business, as we shall see in the next chapter.

6 Working to a deadline
Managing implementation

Stakeholders had been concerned throughout the initiation stage for each phase whether LEA proposals should or would get as far as implementation. From the beginning of this next stage the concern of change agents responsible for putting approved proposals into effect was much narrower: to complete preparations before the immutable deadline of the stipulated reorganisation date. Once central government ministers' decisions were announced they were universally accepted as authoritative. The widely shared assumption about the naturalness and legitimacy of the present order of authority delimited the agency of those whose sectional interests would not be served by these decisions. Far from challenging ministers' entitlement to decide the fate of individual schools, they very largely acquiesced. The structural limit imposed by this assumption bounded their choice of alternative courses of action. Further resistance was rare. Ministers were thus empowered to respond to the underlying economic conditions delimiting their own and other stakeholders' agency by making decisions that would contribute to curbing public expenditure. They could rely on the compliance or support of most stakeholders based at other levels on whom they depended to implement these decisions.

The single-school-level example of a counter-policy continuing during implementation was where a number of diehards at Moor First School found room to manoeuvre to reject the reorganisation policy by exercising their legal right to set up a school outside the state education system (Chapter 2). Universal belief in the finality of central government decisions on applications for GM status and LEA proposals also served to channel the agency of stakeholders managing implementation, encouraging them to work hard to meet the reorganisation deadline. The potential alternatives of postponing or abandoning parts of the initiatives affecting particular schools were never entertained, even where the timescale proved uncomfortably tight or unpredictable problems caused delays.

The clarity of what had to be done to prepare schools for reorganisation belied the complexity of the management tasks involved. Under the legislative framework implementation was down to change agents at LEA and school levels (Figure 3.1), subject only to continuing liaison with the DfEE capital team over the annual release of funds for new building and refurbishment. The challenge of acting as change agents passed largely to headteachers, their senior colleagues, and chairs of their governing bodies. While LEA officials continued to drive the initiatives forward, they depended on co-operation from those with management responsibility at school level because it was there that changes in personnel, premises, and practice were to take place.

Expression of the characteristics of complexity was to shift during the implementation stage as the management tasks and people responsible for them shifted. The scope of these *large-scale* initiatives would be greatest during implementation. Preparation would affect most parents whose children attended schools undergoing reorganisation, all teachers and support staff whose jobs would cease or alter, their union representatives, governors, diocesan representatives, councillors, and LEA officials with diverse specialist responsibilities. A priority for change agents would be to ensure adequate communication across this network, to co-ordinate the contributions of the many specialists, and to juggle with competing priorities.

The *componential* nature of implementation would also differ from the previous stage. Where proposals had implied the possibility of alternative fates for particular schools, they were now certainties. Each school represented a change component with specific implementation requirements. Outright closure, merger, expansion, or a change in character would entail a specific sequence of management tasks, most with implications for tasks in nearby schools, implying a complex logistical exercise where multiple tasks had to be carried out together and in order. Building work had to be completed before furniture could be moved in. But furniture could be identified from stock in closing schools or ordered in advance so that the removal or delivery could be timed accordingly. The 'critical path' of management tasks across each phase and within each school was likely to tax change agents' finite resources of time and energy. Emerging problems might have knock-on consequences for later tasks but the deadline date would impose tightening limits on flexibility as it drew closer. At school level a range of sub-innovations such as curriculum developments would have to be initiated during the implementation stage of reorganisation in preparing for its institutionalisation, comprising additional components to be managed.

The *systemic* character of the implementation stage had to centre on the intensive two-way flow of interaction between LEA and school levels required for senior officials to orchestrate and for officials to support preparation in all reorganising schools and for headteachers, their senior colleagues, and chairs of governors to orchestrate the detailed preparation for those components affecting their institution. Power was distributed variably between change agents at the two system levels for different components but they were still mutually dependent. LEA officials' approach would have to take into account the divergence between the LEA promotional interest in phase-wide implementation and local community stakeholders' interest in protecting themselves and their school, combined with the lack of LEA authority over staffing. They had to continue to seek a confluence between LEA and school-level interests wherever possible in order to guarantee acceptance and to nurture endorsement. Officials stood to be empowered wherever the school-level interest coincided with an area of LEA authority, as with requests for VPR packages and new building and refurbishment. The implementation stage was to be marked by an iterative process of negotiation and compromise among officials and school-level change agents as they sought to realise their respective interests with and through each other.

The *differential impact* on stakeholders during implementation would reflect the evolution from proposals to permanent change on the ground. All would face some form of learning experience. But it would vary according to the part they were to play as change agents, users, or both (Table 3.3). Whereas officials could draw on their specialist expertise and engage mainly with a single task area, headteachers and governors in schools scheduled for radical change had more to learn as generalists dealing with a wider range of tasks affecting their institution. The reality of the change would produce winners and losers. Most stakeholders at school level shifted their attention to realising as much of their individual or group interests as they could once the possibility of protecting the status quo appeared to have gone. The negative emotive force of reorganisation was likely to remain high for them until they were sure of their own, their colleagues', or their children's future, perhaps lasting into the institutionalisation stage. Those in expanding schools would probably continue to perceive implementation as a welcome opportunity and so be disposed to give it their full endorsement and energy. All officials, staff, and governors would experience further intensification of their work, implementation having to be dovetailed with their other tasks. Few enjoyed any remission from these duties. Some were to find themselves with several jobs, as where the headteacher at Sedge First School was appointed as headteacher-designate of what was to become Headland Primary School. He was responsible for running the first school, preparing to close it and transfer furniture and equipment to the middle school site, while also preparing for Headland's opening. Managing implementation was to be affected by frequent disjunction between stakeholders' perceptions in such varied circumstances. All had to base their understanding of what was happening on a more or less limited knowledge base.

Context-dependence would continue to feature strongly, interaction with the evolving profile of other policies altering as their salience for this stage increased or fell away. The central government policy of promoting the GM sector was to fade into the background. But for schools affected, the insensitivity of the external inspection policy would loom large where staff had to cope with a full inspection alongside preparation for reorganisation. In the borough three middle schools, including Endale and Sedge Middle, would be subjected to a full inspection in the last six months of their existence even as staff prepared for closure. The headteacher at Endale Middle stated afterwards:

> Apparently we do have to do an action plan. I know what my action plan is. It has got to be to maintain the quality of education for the children; it has got to be organising resources coming in and out; it has got to be to retain as much sanity as we can while the building works are in progress; and it's to close the school. With one term to go, what else can I do?

Implementation would also build directly on the extremely recent history of the preceding initiation stage, such as the final form taken by particular proposals or diocesan authority involvement with church schools. The outcomes of senior officials' negotiations with central government civil servants, headteachers, and chairs of governors over capital borrowing and transition funding resulted in the generally tight resource parameters discussed in Chapter 4.

This chapter, like the last, is organised around matrices describing the management tasks linked with these characteristics of complexity entailed in completing the implementation stage. We first examine LEA officials' endeavours to bring about implementation for schools across a particular phase of reorganisation. They were concerned with circumstances in each school and with the interrelationship between them all. Second, we consider the management tasks for stakeholders at school level. These tasks were in part a reflection of the administrative emphasis of LEA tasks but they also embraced the content and quality of educational provision in each school. We will illustrate such tasks by exploring implementation at Hillside High and Endale Middle in the borough and Capston First and Farfield First in the county. Senior staff and governors there laboured right up to the day of reorganisation, frequently contending with difficulties beyond anyone's control.

LEA management of implementation

Officials were widely empowered to wield influence where they did not possess authority over headteachers and governors because of the success of their earlier endeavours to nurture a culture of acceptance among stakeholders at school level. So well established was the climate for change, especially for later phases, that a majority of other stakeholders perceived officials to have their interests at heart. The more powerful among them with much to gain – especially headteachers and governors in expanding schools – readily worked with officials. Even those who were relatively powerless and with much to lose – such as displaced staff from closing schools – frequently reported how hard officials had worked to support them at a difficult time. Uncertainty over their future brought by the initiation stage had already lowered their morale. The certainty that their present job would soon terminate depressed them further until they became equally certain what their situation would be after reorganisation. According to one teacher at the closing Endale Middle School:

> It is a very traumatic process altogether; you can't plan your future, that's the trouble! You can't plan very far ahead at all because you don't know where you will be, what you will be doing or what the circumstances will be.

The management structures and procedures created during the first initiation stage served officials well in promoting the communication between LEA and school levels that was vital for the necessary co-ordinated yet flexible action and response. A huge amount of information had to flow through the network of stakeholders who were centrally involved in managing implementation, and beyond them to all the individuals affected whose practice must change in some way. Face-to-face interaction continued to be supplemented with indirect forms of communication, including the dissemination of copious LEA guidance documents. Intermediaries in a position to represent the concerns of other individuals and groups played a key role in giving them a proxy voice in these intermediaries' face-to-face negotiations with officials. Most forms of regular meeting at LEA level featuring in the initiation stage continued throughout implementation so as to ensure that all major groups were represented and kept informed of progress and problems arising (Table 6.1).

Senior officials in the county feared an upsurge of resistance from teaching staff immediately after the central government decisions on phase 2 and 3 proposals were announced. Seeking to pre-empt such a response, senior officials held frequent meetings with teacher and headteacher union representatives. They worked proactively to reinforce the culture of acceptance by demonstrating that they were listening to union concerns, addressing them where possible, and keeping representatives informed. They also lobbied groups of headteachers, mainly from the secondary sector, to head off a possible second wave of GM applications. Senior officials sought their views, ready to respond by putting the case for staying with the LEA. A new forum was created in the guise of area network groups where teachers and headteachers from all schools in the same administrative area could engage in dialogue with officials.

The range of management tasks was similar for officials in both LEAs (Table 6.2). Senior officials dealt with *orchestrating implementation* through their management or team or reorganisation steering group. They also met regularly with colleagues who held specialist responsibility for a group of schools, exchanging information so as to sustain an overview of phase-wide progress and planning how to solve problems such as delays connected with building work. They endeavoured to ensure that their combined efforts were consistent and mutually reinforcing. Their press officers continued to monitor the mass media and put out 'good news' stories about aspects of implementation. The culture of acceptance among governors, school staff, and parents could easily be undermined by negative publicity.

Orchestration was complemented by the equally important task of *administering finance* connected with reorganisation. Economic factors discussed earlier precluded officials allowing financial commitments to go over budget, whether they related to capital borrowing for building work, formula-based transition funding drawn from the LEA coffers, staff appointments to reorganised schools financed by their LMS budget, or the number and generosity of VPR packages. Administration for each area of finance was accompanied by continual monitoring of overall expenditure. The central government requirement that the size of a school's LMS budget must rest very largely on a combination of student numbers and floor areas amounted to policy insensitivity. Regulations did not allow for the unusual temporary circumstances of reorganisation, exacerbated by the policy of promoting parental choice. The precise number of students could

Table 6.1 Stakeholder involvement in key regular meetings at LEA level addressing implementation

Type of meeting	Purpose connected with the implementation stage	Stakeholder groups or their representatives participating
LEA management team (borough) or steering group (county)	Planning, monitoring progress and expenditure, problem-solving	Senior officials
Officials with schools responsibility	Exchanging information on progress, planning solutions to problems arising	Senior officials and officials responsible for particular schools
Education committee of the local council	Monitoring progress, approving capital and transitional funding expenditure, approving officials' request for short-term borrowing from council reserves (borough)	Councillors drawn from inside and outside the ruling group, representatives of one or more unions, diocesan representatives
Unions' co-ordinating committee	Exchanging information on progress and staffing issues arising, negotiating joint policy	Representatives of all teacher unions
Unions and LEA joint negotiating committee	Informing union representatives of progress and staffing issues arising, informing officials of union concerns	Representatives of all teacher unions, senior officials, councillors from the ruling group on the education committee
Senior officials and diocesan representatives	Making transfer arrangements where schools were to change status (from or to VA, VC, or county schools)	Senior officials, diocesan representatives
Headteachers' forums facilitated by officials	Informing headteachers about implementation tasks and progress, informing officials about headteachers' concerns	Headteachers from one or more types of school and LEA areas, officials
Headteachers' and chairs of governors' forums facilitated by officials	Informing headteachers and chairs of governors about implementation tasks and progress, informing officials about school level stakeholders' concerns	Headteachers and chairs of governors from one or more types of school and LEA areas, officials
Area network groups (county)	Informing school staff about implementation tasks and progress, exchanging experiences, informing officials about school level stakeholders' concerns	Teaching staff from all school sectors in an administrative area, officials

not be known until the reorganisation date itself since parents could express a preference as long as schools had places available. Where extensive building work was involved, the exact floor area would not be known until plans were finalised. The indicative budget had to be calculated and staff appointments made long before the reorganisation date, encouraging headteachers and governors to leave some staff appointments to the last moment. An unintended consequence was inadvertently to prolong the uncertainty of displaced staff over their future. Officials had to revise and adjust the budget after reorganisation.

Governors of schools undergoing radical changes faced an unprecedented set of one-off management tasks, especially those individuals appointed to the temporary governing bodies to prepare the way for new schools being created through closure and merger. Temporary governors would remain in office until the first term after reorganisation when the permanent governing body was established. Officials endeavoured to set up temporary governing bodies as early as possible. Members of these bodies were responsible for a sequence of management tasks that could not begin until the temporary governing body had been inaugurated and had established subcommittees, most significantly for staffing and finance. Lack of familiarity with tasks to implement reorganisation in schools gave rise to an urgent need for *training and support for governors*. Membership of temporary governing bodies was drawn from governors in the schools involved in each merger. Governors had often responded to LEA proposals at the initiation stage by attempting to save their own school at the expense of the other school or schools with which it was merging. Now, as members of temporary governing bodies preparing the way for opening merged schools, many had to learn to work with governors of other schools in their merger whom they had formerly opposed. At the same, as governors of their present pre-merger institution they continued to work with some colleagues who remained unreconciled to the merger decision.

Their most pressing tasks were to prepare a budget and staffing structure for the new school and to appoint all the staff. But they also had to establish official school aims, oversee the construction of a school development plan and consider policies in key areas such as the curriculum and student behaviour. There were governor training sessions and regular update meetings in both LEAs. Support was wide-ranging, from officials in the borough acting as clerk to the governing body and so providing a direct link between officials and governors, to officials in the county writing and disseminating guidance documents on such management tasks as creating a staffing structure or closing a school.

Equally urgent was *training and supporting school staff*, reflecting the differential impact of reorganisation on individuals and groups and the learning that their new circumstances might dictate. An extensive programme of short training courses was provided in both LEAs. Target groups included:

- specialist teachers from middle schools taking on responsibility for a class in a primary school
- class teachers taking older or younger students than they had in the past

Table 6.2 LEA officials' tasks to manage the implementation stage of reorganisation

Implementation task area	Education system levels involved	Main management tasks
Orchestrating implementation	LEA LEA LEA LEA LEA LEA→school LEA→school LEA→central government	• Continuing to plan implementation tasks • Monitoring media output, informing local media professionals • Advising the education committee • Liaising with diocesan representatives over church schools • Liaising with school staff union representatives • Monitoring to sustain an overview of progress • Coping with emerging problems • Keeping the DfEE territorial team informed
Administering finance	LEA LEA LEA→school LEA→school LEA→school LEA→school	• Monitoring overall expenditure related to reorganisation • Administering approved capital expenditure • Arranging transition funding for schools • Monitoring LMS budget expenditure in closing schools • Calculating the indicative LMS budget for reorganised schools and advising headteachers • Administering approved VPR packages
Training and supporting governors	LEA→school LEA→school LEA→school LEA→school	• Setting up and servicing temporary governing bodies • Arranging training, especially in relation to staffing • Providing guidance on reorganisation-related tasks • Keeping governors informed
Training and supporting school staff	LEA→school LEA→school LEA→school LEA→school LEA→school LEA→school	• Offering targeted preparatory training programmes • Facilitating exchange of information between staff from different schools • Facilitating visits to other schools • Disseminating lessons from earlier implementation experiences • Counselling individuals about their career, attempting to boost their morale and acknowledging their efforts • Keeping headteachers informed
Facilitating the redeployment or VPR of displaced staff	LEA→school LEA→school LEA→school LEA→school LEA→school LEA→school	• Advising headteachers and governors about staffing structures • Monitoring the evolving profile of displaced staff and redeployment opportunities • Consulting displaced staff about their redeployment or VPR preferences • Informing headteachers about redeployment preferences • Negotiating VPR offers • Assembling and circulating vacancy lists

	LEA→school	• Attending appointment interviews in an advisory capacity
	LEA→school	• Arranging temporary employment for unallocated staff
Capital borrowing	LEA→central government	• Liaising with the DfEE capital team over bids and release of capital
	LEA	• Easing cash flow by seeking approval to borrow from council reserves (borough)
Organising new building and refurbishment	LEA	• Obtaining planning permission
	LEA→school	• Drawing up and costing building plans
	LEA	• Consulting governors and senior school staff
	LEA	• Arranging tendering and negotiating building contracts
	LEA→school	• Instructing builders about safety for staff and students
	LEA→school	• Monitoring progress and liaising with school staff over their detailed requirements and safety issues
	LEA→school	• Liaising with builders
	LEA→school	• Authorising the handover to schools
Arranging the redistribution of furniture and equipment	LEA→school	• Conducting an audit in closing schools
	LEA→school	• Identifying material surpluses and related needs in different schools
	LEA→school	• Arranging removal, storage, transfer and disposal
Arranging closure of sites	LEA→school	• Providing guidance, including winding up accounts, archiving records, shutting down premises
	LEA→school	• Organising security and maintenance of closed premises
Arranging school transport	LEA	• Calculating costs for LEA-funded transport
	LEA	• Negotiating with bus and coach operators to alter services
	LEA→school	• Determining individual students' eligibility for free transport
Informing parents	LEA→school	• Providing information about reorganisation dates and arrangements, revised school catchment areas and the proposed destination for each student, revised transport arrangements

- class teachers or semi-specialist teachers from middle schools who were transferring to secondary schools where they would become specialists
- subject co-ordinators from first or middle schools transferring to primary schools where they would have to advise on their specialism across the full primary school age range
- senior staff in high schools due to receive 11-year-old students for the first time.

Officials' support activities were similarly differentiated. They included facilitating visits of displaced middle school staff to primary or secondary schools to help them decide in which kind of school they wished to seek redeployment; disseminating lessons learned from an earlier phase of reorganisation; career counselling; helping staff to prepare a job application and to perform well at interview; holding regular update meetings for headteachers; and visiting staff who were highly stressed by reorganisation to help them think through problems and to boost their morale. Training and support of governors and staff enabled the officials involved to monitor progress and problems arising, reporting this information back to the group responsible for orchestrating implementation.

Dealing in staff futures

Facilitating the redeployment or VPR of displaced staff was perhaps the most complex task area for officials to manage. As discussed in earlier chapters, central government system-changing policies had devolved officials' authority over appointments to governors while pressuring them to downsize provision on a scale that would require a reduction in staffing. Officials were, however, sometimes supported indirectly by councillor-nominated 'LEA governors' who formed a minority on each governing body. These governors had authority to contribute to appointment decisions and to advocate that the governing body should act on officials' advice. However this source of power was limited in respect of any governing body, as governors representing other stakeholders far outnumbered the LEA nominees.

Officials' influence derived partly from their negotiating skills and partly from their working relationship with governors and headteachers long preceding central government intervention to reduce their authority. The contextual dependence of the LEA initiatives featured a cultural legacy disposing most governors and headteachers to invite officials' opinion or respond positively to their requests, even when asked to follow the voluntary code of practice in appointing displaced staff – against their legitimate sectional interest in securing the 'best person for the job'. Many continued subscribing to a subliminal and outmoded belief in LEA authority over staffing despite being aware that it had passed into their hands (a 'historical lag' in Hargreaves's terms that enhanced officials' agency – see Chapter 3). Habitual deference to the LEA lay behind governors' readiness to use their authority and headteachers' willingness to wield influence with governors to compromise their sectional interest. The headteacher at Hillside High School reiterated his assumption that '[the CEO] is my boss'. He was willing to accede to officials' requests to take staff from middle schools in the pyramid. Yet he was equally clear that he and governors were now their own bosses:

> No local authority can make us do what we don't want to do. We have generally accepted the principle, because [the borough] is a good authority, that we will accommodate as far as possible the staff in closing middle schools.

With the proviso that if they can't do the job we want, or if we feel that they can't do the job we want, then we are not forced to appoint.

The formal shift in the locus of authority over staff appointments had failed so far to bring about a parallel cultural shift, especially in the borough. Most headteachers and governors apparently held two contradictory beliefs, perceiving that they were in charge of staffing while regarding officials' staffing opinions or requests almost as instructions. At a conscious level, such stakeholders in both LEAs generally respected officials, appreciating their detailed knowledge of schools and staff enabling them to match any views they expressed on staffing with school level priorities. As the headteacher at Endale Middle School commented: 'You know that there is always somebody at the end of the phone at [the borough office] who will help you out.' Officials were aware of this perception, one stating: 'We have between us a lot of detailed experience about handling staff change and redeployment . . . and credibility because we have been around a long time and we are well known.'

To achieve the necessary staffing reduction by the reorganisation date officials had to identify, consult, and try to meet the needs of a continually evolving profile of displaced staff on permanent contracts from any schools within the phase of reorganisation concerned. Officials attempted to secure their redeployment or, where eligible, VPR. Every member of staff in most schools due to close outright or to merge through closure of the merging institutions and the establishment of a new school (as at Capston and Farfield) would technically lose their present job. Only where there was a change of employer in the transition to or from VA status (as at Newell and Moor in Chapter 2) were governors legally obliged to give displaced staff first refusal.

Once temporary governing bodies had been established for the new schools being created, officials were in a position to advise their members and the headteachers and governors of expanding schools about the structure of staff posts and the number of staff they could afford to employ according to their indicative operating budget. Officials in the borough also attended appointment interviews, where they were entitled to offer advice but governors were equally entitled to ignore it.

Appointments had to be made in sequence, starting with headteachers, progressing to deputy headteachers, class teachers and support staff on permanent contracts, and then finally to staff on temporary contracts who did not enjoy the same employment protection. Central government legislation required all vacancies for headteachers and deputy headteachers to be advertised nationally. This was another instance of policy insensitivity where the exceptional circumstances of reorganisation did not appear to have been taken into account. The top priority had to be securing appointments for displaced headteachers and deputy headteachers in the LEA, except where a VPR offer could be arranged. Otherwise there would be redundancies, and union industrial action and parental backlash against officials and councillors would surely follow. The legal framework was designed to avoid nepotism and promote equal opportunities. But how governors should shortlist or interview applicants was not specified, leaving room for an informal LEA counter-policy. Staff selection was conducted according to a belief in following the letter, but not necessarily the spirit, of the law. Often a verbal agreement would be reached first between borough officials and governors over which displaced headteacher or deputy headteacher should be appointed. Job advertisements were then constructed to signal to outsiders that the priority was to reallocate displaced staff. One for a deputy headteacher post in the borough declared that the school would change character, and that:

> a number of local schools will close. In this situation the Authority must look to protect the interests of all employees under threat of redundancy. The governors see the deputy head vacancy as an opportunity to assist the LEA in this task.

Typically there were no applicants other than the individual identified for the job under the informal agreement, a testimony to officials' success in co-opting the central government policy of national advertising for such posts. In the county, officials and governors generally agreed tacitly that selection would be made from a shortlist of displaced headteachers and deputy headteachers, but that governors were not precluded from selecting someone else if they wished.

Different phasing of the two LEA reorganisation initiatives affected officials' room to manoeuvre between phases. Borough officials were able to arrange temporary employment in schools as an interim measure for any phase except the fifth and final one. They persuaded headteachers and governors to take on staff for a year who were on permanent contracts, were not eligible for VPR, and had not been placed in a new permanent post by the reorganisation date for the phase in question. These posts were LEA-funded for a year at a time, allowing officials to carry forward unplaced staff in the hope that they would find permanent redeployment by the end of the next phase. It was most difficult to persuade headteachers and governors to accept staff whose reputation locally was of marginal competence. In the county there were fewer phases, and central government delay over the decisions on phase 2 proposals meant that the relatively small pilot first phase was two years ahead of the combined phase 2 and 3 where the bulk of staffing changes occurred. It was a major logistical exercise for officials to arrange for all appointments and VPR offers involved in phases 2 and 3. They were empowered by wide adherence among governing bodies to the voluntary code of practice. Staff in all reorganising schools were invited to apply for VPR, but relatively few offers were actually made because most of the necessary downsizing was achieved through the policy of making the most recent appointments on a temporary basis.

Table 6.3 illustrates how the componential character of implementation required officials in the county to co-ordinate the planning of linked management tasks. Provision of training and support for managing implementation and of information about indicative LMS budgets had to be timed so that they were available before the relevant place in the sequence of staff appointments was

Table 6.3 Timetable of training support and staff appointments for phases 2 and 3 in the county

Time	Governor and school staff training and support	Staff appointments and VPR offers
Au 94	• Temporary governing bodies set up • Briefings for displaced headteachers on headship appointment procedures • Staff informed about the availability of individual counselling support • Retraining for displaced teachers	• The first invitation to eligible staff in reorganising schools to apply for VPR
Sp 95	• Briefings for displaced deputy headteachers on deputy headship appointment procedures • Briefings for teachers and for support staff on applying for posts • Training for governors on selection of headteachers and deputy headteachers, establishing a new school, creating a staffing structure and budgeting • Indicative budgets for 1996/7 issued to governors and headteachers • Retraining for displaced teachers	• Headteacher appointment interviews and VPR offers
Su 95	• Training for governors on policy development in new schools • Retraining for displaced teachers	• Deputy headteacher appointment interviews and VPR offers
Au 95	• Repeat of training for governors previously offered (see above) • Training for governors, headteachers and deputy headteachers on closing and merging schools, managing a change in character or expansion • Retraining for displaced teachers	• The second invitation to eligible staff in reorganising schools to apply for VPR • Applications for the first ring of appointments to posts in new schools (available to staff on permanent contracts in merging schools due to be replaced by the corresponding new schools)
Sp 96	• Retraining for displaced teachers • Revised indicative and actual budgets issued to headteachers and governors	• First ring appointments and VPR offers • Applications for the second ring of appointments to posts in new schools unfilled through the first ring (available to all displaced staff on permanent contracts in schools in the same administrative area) • Applications for the third ring of appointments to posts in all reorganising schools including those unfilled through the second ring (available to all staff on permanent contracts)

Table 6.3 (Continued)

Time	Governor and school staff training and support	Staff appointments and VPR offers
Su 96	• Retraining for displaced teachers	• Second ring appointments and VPR offers • Applications for the fourth ring of appointments in all reorganising schools unfilled in the third ring (available to staff on permanent and temporary contracts) • Third ring appointments and VPR offers • Fourth ring appointments and VPR offers

reached. Consequently, most of this training and support was offered during the last part of the initiation stage after proposals had been submitted for central government approval. It was supplemented by training available throughout the implementation stage focusing on the curriculum and on learning and teaching.

Staff appointments other than those for headships and deputy headships were made during the implementation stage in the second year once these decisions were known. The 'ring fence' arrangement allowed for a sequence of 'rings', giving a hierarchy of priorities favouring displaced staff on permanent contracts. VPR offers were made at the end of each ring of appointments to eligible staff who had responded to officials' invitations to apply and who had not found redeployment in that ring, or whose retirement could be linked with avoiding the compulsory redundancy of someone else on a permanent contract. Officials consulted staff about their preferences, informed headteachers and governors, consulted them about vacancies in their schools, and circulated lists of vacancies to schools across the county.

VPR was used more extensively in the borough where a greater reduction of staff on permanent contracts was needed. Authority over VPR enabled officials to invite applications from all those eligible for the scheme, the parameters of which had been agreed during the first initiation stage. The VPR rules allowed officials to employ negotiating tactics reflecting a confluence between LEA and school interests of which governors would otherwise not have been aware. Officials frequently suggested that a VPR arrangement in one school could be linked with avoiding redundancy in another. One particularly complicated negotiation concerned a deputy headteacher who applied for VPR and was eligible on grounds of age, but not on grounds of avoiding a compulsory redundancy. This person worked in an expanding first school, so no staff would be displaced there. Officials brokered an informal agreement with the governors and headteacher that they would promote another teacher in this school to the deputy headteacher's post falling vacant if the existing incumbent's VPR application was approved. They had also to agree to fill the promoted teacher's place by appointing a second teacher from a closing school elsewhere in the borough who was under threat of redundancy. The agreement was not binding but it effectively delimited governors' agency. If they had failed to abide by the agreement, say, by appointing a replacement deputy headteacher from outside the LEA, they would have become liable for financing enhancement of the pension of the person taking VPR out of their school's LMS budget – which was too small to bear such a commitment.

Confluence of interests extended to individual staff seeking VPR. Freedom in the borough from the central government cap on local taxation which affected the county meant that sufficient finance was available here for the VPR package to be based on the maximum legally permitted financial investment. This inducement was enhanced by the fact that it was a time-limited offer. In the words of one official: 'The scheme may be revised following reorganisation; it will certainly be managed very differently and therefore it may be almost their [staff's] last opportunity to be released with very generous benefits, and it's to their advantage to take it.'

One unforeseeable central government-induced problem emerged in late 1996 during the implementation of phase 5 in the borough. Officials had made commitments to a series of VPR offers that would be taken up the day before the reorganisation date of 1 September 1997. The Secretary of State unexpectedly announced a forthcoming change in policy from April 1997 to increase the proportion of pension enhancement payments that must be underwritten from individual LEA funds rather than being paid centrally. This contradictory central government policy shift threatened to undermine the LEA VPR policy. On it depended the success of the LEA reorganisation initiative that had been demanded by central government ministers. Yet through various policies for curbing LEA expenditure, ministers had ensured that the borough council did not possess the capital to foot such a bill. Senior officials had to make time to respond through intensive lobbying. They eventually persuaded ministers to defer the date when the policy change would come into force until September 1997 – after reorganisation.

Reorganising material provision across the LEA

Since improvement of school buildings and facilities was universally valued in school communities, officials were empowered to carry out the sequence of tasks involved with little risk of resistance at school level. However, the context-dependency of their work featured interaction with a mixture of facilitating and inhibiting central government policies which affected the scope and pace of this aspect of implementation. Congruence between the central government policies of reducing surplus capacity and the concern of councillors, diocesan representatives, and officials alike to improve the building stock for which they were responsible led to demonstrably better provision in those schools due to benefit. The significance of the opportunity for *capital borrowing* was underlined in the county. The contradictory central government capping policy meant that there was no source of LEA finance to do more than the minimum required for implementation of reorganisation proposals. A guidance document for school staff and governors carried the warning:

> The building projects are to provide new accommodation or adapt existing accommodation for alternative uses. Unfortunately we simply haven't the resources to provide your school with a complete facelift. You could well be left with a situation where the new paintwork or carpet dramatically finishes half way down a corridor.

Securing DfEE capital was not without problems. The central government policy governing its release was insensitive to the length of time that major building projects took. LEA dependence on central government narrowly delimited officials' room to manoeuvre. Capital was not released until the beginning of the financial year (in April) when building was to be completed (by September). Most building work could begin only a few months before schools were to be reorganised because builders would have to be paid by regular instalments. Little allowance could be made for possible slippage in the building schedule.

A temporary shortfall of capital resulted in the borough just when finance was most needed. It was caused by a combination of three factors: the extent of new building in phases 4 and 5; reorganisation with associated building work over two years for schools reverting from the first-9–13 middle-high school system to a primary-secondary system (Figure 4.2); and a restriction on capital borrowing arising since outline LEA proposals were costed when getting started on the first initiation stage. The recent central government policy shift to raise the rate of revenue savings that had to be achieved by removing surplus places (Chapter 4) entailed a new formula. It allowed less capital borrowing for the LEA proposals than the earlier formula on which officials' calculations had been based. Consequently, allowable capital borrowing for the first year of implementing phase 5 was insufficient to complete the building work scheduled. The upshot was more work for officials, persuading councillors in the education committee to authorise borrowing of the shortfall from council reserves so that planned building work would not be delayed. The money would be paid back when the DfEE allocation for the next financial year was received.

Organising new building and refurbishment was more straightforward for officials because they had sufficient authority to wield a high degree of control within the limits imposed by the short timescale for construction. A similar sequence of tasks had to be carried out for most building projects. The complexity of this task area lay in the sheer number and size of simultaneous projects scheduled for completion by the reorganisation date – in the county there were over fifty projects for phases 2 and 3. Borough architects and consultant architects employed by the local council in the county worked closely with officials who held specialist responsibility. Together they secured planning permission where necessary, brought plans forward, consulted staff and governors, completed the tendering process, and saw the building work through to the point of handover to school governors and staff. The invariably tight timetable left little room for unforeseeable contingencies such as bad weather. Storms quite frequently caused late completion – more a school problem than an LEA problem.

Similarly, *arranging the redistribution of furniture and equipment* was rendered complex because the number of schools involved meant that officials must undertake considerable school liaison work just to identify and match up surpluses with needs, followed by the logistical headache of arranging for their movement. Officials requested headteachers in closing schools to provide them with a full inventory. Details were then circulated to headteachers from schools due to survive. These headteachers indicated what they wanted and officials negotiated who was to receive what. Pressure on officials peaked as the reorganisation date approached. Many items could be transferred only at the end of the term preceding reorganisation as they were in use until then. A large amount of old furniture and equipment was not wanted, but could not easily be destroyed despite LEA authority to do so. One borough official referred to belief in the importance of 'making sure that you are not criticised by other schools, the public or anyone else if you are disposing of what they sometimes see as valuable property'. A large amount of furniture and equipment in closing borough schools was consequently taken to an LEA warehouse to be stored. Contingency plans for temporary storage had to be made incrementally in the county as it became increasingly apparent that some building projects would not be completed on time.

Many detailed tasks were entailed in *arranging for closure of sites* in addition to clearing them of furniture and equipment. Headteachers and governors were offered detailed guidance. In the county it extended to provision of a comprehensive checklist. A variety of LEA responsibilities related to closing down school premises depending on their site-specific circumstances. Most could be implemented only at the end of the summer term before reorganisation. They included:

- taking possession of school documents such as the logbook and passing them to the LEA record office for archiving
- identifying and cancelling contracts such as photocopier leases
- ensuring that mail was redirected
- arranging for premises insurance to be adjusted where buildings would no longer be occupied
- arranging for keys to be handed over and a new keyholder designated
- making security arrangements such as boarding up windows
- isolating gas, electricity and other services and collecting relevant information, such as on the running of school boilers.

Finally, two task areas directly affected students and parents. *Arranging school transport* had to be undertaken wherever reorganisation would change the pattern of student attendance. Students living at least three miles (and those under 8 years living at least two miles) from the school proposed for them were entitled to free transport to and from school. This factor was costed into LEA proposals during the initiation stage. Officials had to negotiate with bus and coach operators where it would be necessary to realign services to match anticipated demand and work out which students would be eligible for free transport. It was also essential to *inform parents* through letters and occasional meetings about all reorganisation arrangements that would affect their children, including changes in transport arrangements.

The frenetic pace that officials had to maintain throughout this stage reflected the central government policy vacuum over allowing for all the extra work it embodied. One informant claimed to have worked up to a hundred hours per week. Most had to achieve their specialist tasks for all schools in the same phase of reorganisation and support their colleagues on top of their ongoing duties. The latter often included managing different stages for other phases of reorganisation. Economic strictures precluded any expansion of LEA staffing so, in the words of an official in the county: 'You just did whatever was required.' Multi-tasking, monitoring the evolving profile of their tasks for different schools and frequent troubleshooting were the order of the day.

Implementation in schools: closure and expansion at Hillside

The pace for senior staff and governors was similarly frenetic in schools facing extensive changes. Here though the pace tended to increase steadily from the point when the Secretary of State's decision was announced, reaching a climax at the end of the summer term preceding the reorganisation date on 1 September. We saw earlier how complex the LEA formative proposals were for the Hillside pyramid, comprising Hillside High and its feeder first and middle schools. The LEA-preferred option 1 had prevailed for the middle schools (Table 5.5) and option 3 for Hillside High (Table 5.6). This institution would become an 11–18 split-site secondary school, its lower school site catering for 11–14-year-old students to be created on the closing Endale Middle School site. The present main site would cater for the 14–18 upper school age range and its nearby subsidiary site would close. Extra accommodation and specialist facilities would be provided through an extensive building programme on both sites throughout the year and a half leading up to reorganisation. All students transferring from closing middle schools to the secondary school would do so at the beginning of term following the reorganisation date. So three year groups – some nine hundred students aged 11 to 14 from four middle schools including Endale Middle – would transfer together to the secondary school (the alternative arrangement for reorganising the first-9–13 middle-high school system depicted in Figure 4.2).

Since implementation was systemic across LEA and school levels, the range of implementation task areas falling to senior staff and governors reflected in part officials' task areas for all schools in any phase of reorganisation. But change agents at school level were more narrowly focused on the implications of proposals for their institution and any neighbouring schools whose reorganisation arrangements impinged on their own. Their tasks extended beyond those of officials because they were directly responsible for educational provision in the school. They were charged with making all administrative arrangements for the reorganised institution to function as effectively as possible from day one. As mentioned in Chapter 5, planning for implementation had begun long before the firm proposal was approved. The mix of management tasks comprising the components affecting Hillside is summarised in Table 6.4.

The headteacher and chair of governors were the key change agents with responsibility for *orchestrating implementation*. The large size of the school meant that they were empowered to share this burden by delegating many management tasks to senior staff, especially the two deputy headteachers. It even proved possible to advertise throughout the borough for two new senior posts – head of lower school and head of upper school – which staff at Hillside were successful in securing almost a year before the reorganisation date. The designated head of lower school immediately took on detailed preparations for the move to the lower school site even though he did not officially take up post until the move was over. The headteacher acknowledged that 'without good people to delegate to I would have sunk without trace'. Middle managers with curriculum or pastoral responsibility were change agents for their domain. Heads of science and technology departments were especially heavily involved because of the necessity of replacing and updating specialist facilities in the lower school. Those had been removed or downgraded a decade and a half earlier when Endale Middle had been created from an 11–16 secondary school (Chapter 5).

The co-ordinated approach to bringing about implementation was very much a team affair. It was underpinned by a cohesive managerial subculture among senior staff and middle managers featuring shared commitment to completing implementation tasks in building towards the institutionalisation of an expanded split-site school serving the full secondary age range. Much planning for strategic decisions was undertaken during dedicated meetings, especially the annual SMT weekend conference, attended also by the chair of governors. It was in this forum that consideration was given to matters such as the staffing structure, how far to restrict movement of staff between the two sites during the school day, the structure of the curriculum and pastoral system, and how to consult other staff at Hillside High and the middle schools in the pyramid. Planning was equally incremental, dealing with the multitude of task areas which must be progressed simultaneously, in frequent dialogue with officials over particular issues and in the light of ongoing internal monitoring.

Several core beliefs gave direction to this concerted effort. First, there was a shared belief in the need to extend the 'secondary school ethos' in the present institution throughout the lower school. Taking in 11–13-year-old students for the first time would empower staff to induct them from the beginning of key stage 3 into a 'secondary school' way of working. In the words of the headteacher:

Table 6.4 Managing implementation of the LEA proposal for Hillside High School in the borough

Implementation task area	Key change agents	Education system levels involved	Main management tasks
Orchestrating implementation	Headteacher, chair of governors, other senior staff	School School School LEA→school LEA→school school school School	• Planning and delegating • Allocating transition funding • Monitoring to sustain an overview of progress • Receiving information from officials • Negotiating with senior officials • Promoting a secondary school ethos • Making a good start after reorganisation • Creating the sense of a unified school
Liaising with headteachers in the pyramid	Headteacher, deputy head-teacher (pastoral)	School School	• Meeting headteachers of middle schools • Meeting headteachers of first schools
Administering finance	Office manager	School School	• Administering expenditure of transition funding • Administering the budget related to ordering furniture and equipment and appointing staff
Staffing the reorganised school	Headteacher, governors, deputy head (curriculum)	School School School School→LEA School School School, LEA→school	• Planning the staffing structure, taking account of the indicative LMS budget and the two sites • Consulting heads of department about staffing needs • Consulting eligible staff about taking VPR • Negotiating with officials over VPR for staff • Consulting staff from closing middle schools seeking redeployment at Hillside Secondary • Negotiating with staff at Hillside High to base themselves at the lower school site • Appointing staff to new posts based at the upper school site and almost all posts based at the lower school site
Training and supporting staff	Deputy headteacher (pastoral), heads of department, senior teacher (systems)	School School School	• Inducting new staff into departments • Organising a training day for preparing Hillside staff and introducing any new staff • Organising training days for moving furniture and equipment and setting up teaching rooms

		School	• Planning training days for staff to consider short and longer-term developments
		School	• Arranging for staff training to use new administrative software
Contributing to new building and refurbishment	Headteacher, chair of governors, heads of department	School→LEA	• Negotiating with officials about the extent and timing of building work
		School→LEA	• Monitoring health and safety issues and liaising with officials
		School	• Consulting staff about requirements for new and refurbished areas
		LEA→school	• Liaising with officials over provision of fixed furniture and equipment
		School	• Ordering new furniture and equipment
Developing systems for split-site administration	Senior teacher (systems), office manager	School	• Planning split-site administration arrangements
		School	• Extending the computer network
		School	• Transferring data
		School	• Setting up the lower school office
		School	• Planning telephone and computer links within and between the two sites
Redistributing furniture and equipment	Heads of department, designated head of lower school	School	• Negotiating with first and middle school staff over furniture and equipment from closing middle schools
		School, LEA→school	• Arranging for removal of furniture and equipment from the main site and the closing middle schools to the lower school site
		School	• Ordering new furniture and equipment
Arranging closure of the subsidiary site	Heads of department	School	• Arranging for removal of furniture and equipment from the Hillside High School subsidiary site
		LEA→school	• Liaising with officials to shut down the site
Informing parents and their children	Headteacher, deputy headteacher (pastoral)	School	• Visiting middle schools to meet students
		School	• Publishing and distributing newsletters and letters for present and prospective parents
		School	• Updating the school prospectus
		School	• Holding evening meetings for prospective parents and students to meet staff
Arranging school transport	Headteacher	School	• Negotiating with the local bus company chief executive to increase services to the rear of the lower school site

Table 6.4 (Continued)

Implementation task area	Key change agents	Education system levels involved	Main management tasks
Planning and resourcing the curriculum	Deputy headteacher (curriculum), heads of department	School	• Designing the lower school curriculum in consultation with departmental colleagues
		School	• Planning the integration of students from middle schools with different curriculum experiences
		School	• Ordering resources for the lower school and refurbished specialist rooms in the upper school
Planning and resourcing pastoral care	Deputy headteacher (pastoral), heads of year	School	• Planning transfer arrangements for three year groups from closing middle schools to the lower school site in September 1997
		School	• Liaising with first school headteachers about future transfer arrangements
		School	• Designing a new students' uniform and arranging for local shops to supply it
		School	• Convening a staff working party to draw up a students' code of conduct and reward system
Timetabling	Deputy headteacher (curriculum)	School	• Establishing principles, such as minimising staff and student movement between sites
		School	• Consulting senior staff about the structure of the school day and time for each subject
		School	• Consulting staff
		School	• Planning and publishing the detailed timetable

We are hoping that if we can instil a secondary atmosphere and attitude to work – the whole range of things that you think of as the ethos of the school – it may mitigate some of the problems that we find when we get some of them at 13 when they're already turned off . . . we would like to get some really good study skills established in year 7 [encompassing 11–12-year-old students] so that they will know how to study.

Specialists would teach students for each curriculum subject; students would experience specialist facilities of secondary-school quality; they would be expected to follow a full timetable; and they would be supported through a separate pastoral care system. Second, a top priority was to 'make a good start' after reorganisation, especially in the lower school, by completing all preparations so that staff and facilities were ready for the influx of new students. Third, both senior staff and middle managers with cross-school responsibility were equally concerned to develop a sense among staff and students of belonging to the one institution, rather than to either the lower or the upper school. They worked to compensate as far as possible for the location of most staff and all students on one or other site for almost the whole time.

The network of stakeholders impinging on each other at school level as implementation progressed was to include staff across the Hillside pyramid. It was essential for senior staff at Hillside High to *liaise with other headteachers in the pyramid*, key intermediaries through whom arrangements affecting their staff could be made. The deputy headteacher responsible for pastoral support at Hillside High prepared for institutionalisation by meeting with the headteachers of the first schools (due to become primary schools) to arrange for transfer of students in future years.

The considerable extra work of *administering finance* devolved to the school and related to reorganisation could be delegated to the office manager and her support staff colleagues. They dealt with expenditure of the allocated transition funding, claims on the operating budget made by the exceptional purchasing of furniture and equipment for the lower school site, and the projected salary burden of new appointments.

Staffing and staff support

One very time-consuming task area that the headteacher could not delegate was *staffing the reorganised school*. Work had begun during the initiation stage on planning a new staffing structure. It was a potentially hazardous undertaking because the staff salary bill was by far the largest element of the school's LMS budget, and running up a deficit through overstaffing was inadmissible. Yet not all parameters could be known until after reorganisation, when student numbers – on which the budget rested – were definite. The headteacher commented:

> My baseline as a head has always been never to have to go into a staffroom and say, 'Sorry, we got the figures wrong. We want three or four of you to put your hands up to be redundant.' . . . That's my nightmare . . . so I have got to err on the side of caution.

The indicative budget received a year before reorganisation suggested that there would be an increase of £0.5 million, but economic factors affecting LEA resource parameters meant that this figure could not be guaranteed:

> This, of course, does not allow for any further budget cuts either nationally or locally. With a [central government] election approaching, it is difficult to decide whether tax cuts, combined with strict public spending limits, will be seen as more politically attractive than improvements in the financing of public services such as . . . education.

Staffing needs in each department had to be established in order to teach the curriculum. The number of existing staff who might wish to apply for VPR had also to be ascertained. Nine staff who were eligible on grounds of age indicated such a wish, most being attracted by the generosity of the package that staff in the middle schools had received. The headteacher was keen for their VPR applications to be approved because the possibilities for redesigning the staffing structure would be broadened. There was a confluence of interests inside the school, but the headteacher did not possess authority over the necessary decision. The nine applications for VPR engendered protracted negotiations with officials because their promotional interest in facilitating reorganisation was not well served in this instance. The sticking point was that the rule for enhancement of pensions did not apply (see Chapter 5). Hillside High was expanding and, if these staff were to retire, over thirty vacant posts would then be available while no more than twenty displaced middle school staff with appropriate expertise had expressed a wish to be redeployed to the school. There could be no link with avoiding a redundancy and the existing budget was healthy. Officials were under no obligation to make a VPR offer with or without any enhancement. A resolution finally came just six months before the reorganisation date when an LEA offer was accepted which entailed modest pension enhancement.

There was a strong element of incremental sequencing among components of the staffing task area. Few staff appointments could be made until the VPR issue was resolved. It was uncertain till then how many posts and what range of expertise would be required. The situation was exacerbated because of an internal conflict of interests that was equally intractable, contingent on the unusual context presented by the split-site character of the expanded school. The decision to minimise staff movement between lower and upper school sites meant that most staff based in the lower school would not be able to teach older students. A substantial minority of existing staff at Hillside High would have to go to the lower school. But the prevailing staff culture accorded high prestige and valued career prospects to teaching examination classes – which would happen only on the upper school site after reorganisation. Heads of department supported the headteacher in delicate negotiations with departmental colleagues to persuade enough of them to opt for the lower school, at least for the next three years. Younger staff with career aspirations feared that their eligibility for future promotion would be compromised if they did not take examination classes. These negotiations also had largely to be resolved prior to appointing staff from the closing middle schools or elsewhere.

The upshot was to prolong uncertainty over the future of most of these middle school staff. They were not offered a post until the summer term immediately before reorganisation, after having anticipated that appointments would be made up to a year earlier. The delay over appointments contributed very significantly to the build-up of reorganisation activity as the reorganisation deadline approached. The headteacher was acutely aware how interviewing for some thirty-five appointments in the six months before reorganisation had led to him being 'less accessible to staff than I hope I normally am and like to be'.

Extensive delegation had proved vital in empowering him to concentrate on this task area.

Training and supporting staff was a related task area which also came to the fore as reorganisation approached. We referred earlier to the way officials provided preparatory training and other forms of support to governors and staff across the LEA, and facilitated meetings between headteachers in the pyramid. Displaced staff from middle schools had benefited from LEA provision. Once the future of those wishing to be redeployed to Hillside was assured, they were supported by Hillside staff who facilitated their induction into their departments and helped them prepare for their new teaching and pastoral responsibilities. In-house support for existing Hillside staff focused on giving them opportunities to work with the new staff, arranging for the latter to visit their new department and organising a training day (when the school would be closed to students) in the summer term preceding reorganisation when present and new staff could meet. A second, shorter-term priority was to support the move to the lower school site. Two training days were set aside at the end of that term for packing and moving. Further training days at the beginning of the term after reorganisation were planned for unpacking and getting rooms ready for students.

Reorganising material provision for two sites

All the task areas connected with material provision featured a sequence of components, dictating a lock-step approach to implementation. Delay in completing an early component could lead to slippage. The closer to the deadline delay occurred, the more it militated against meeting the deadline and so being ready to open the school to students on time. *Contributing to new building and refurbishment* was particularly difficult to control at school level, partly because of the systemic nature of this task area where school staff and governors were dependent on officials and architects to manage the work. But they in turn were dependent on central government ministers and civil servants for the loan of capital, and on officials from the council planning department, builders, their suppliers – even the weather. Most of the extensive building and refurbishment work necessary to accommodate the planned expansion and lower school site would have to be carried out while the schools were in operation. Staff and students would therefore be occupying the existing accommodation. A complex sequence of building and refurbishment was designed to enable staff and students at Endale Middle and Hillside High to move to newly completed accommo- dation, so freeing up more elsewhere for further work throughout the year and a half leading up to reorganisation. Table 6.5 summarises the planned sequence and what actually happened.

Officials' intention was to create more teaching space by the beginning of the 1996/7 academic year (Reorganisation Part 1) by building on the main site and the future lower school site. Staff and students from Hillside High and Endale Middle could move into the new accommodation on their site, freeing up existing rooms where refurbishment was required so that this work could be

Table 6.5 New building and refurbishment for the split-site Hillside Secondary School

Time	Main site	Subsidiary site	Endale Middle (lower school) site
Sp–Su 96	• Building of a 17-room teaching block • Refurbishment of science laboratories, a drama studio and business studies rooms	• Move to the main site at the end of the summer term (except chemistry, examinations, physical education, some sixth form teaching)	• Building of a 17-room teaching block
		Reorganisation (part 1)	
Au 96	• Move into the 17-room teaching block and refurbished rooms at the beginning of term • Refurbishment of the careers building		• Move into the 17-room teaching block at half term
Sp–Su 97	• Building of the assembly hall and sixth form block delayed because of DFEE constraints on capital borrowing • Refurbishment and expansion of the office block delayed because a listed building, planning permission to add a second storey refused • Move the school office into the careers building • Refurbishment of the office block	• Move to the main school site at the end of the summer term • Closure of the site	• Building of a sports hall, art, music and drama block • Move out of rooms to be refurbished and into rooms vacated because no intake of 9–10-year-old students • Refurbishment of science laboratories and technology rooms, library and office block • Storm damage to building and refurbishment work during the summer holidays
		Reorganisation (part 2)	
Au 97	• Move into the office block • Move into rooms vacated because intake of 13–14-year-old students accommodated in the lower school • Building of an assembly hall and sixth form block		• Completion of building and refurbishment work delayed, move in after half term
Sp 98	• Move into the assembly hall and sixth form block		

completed by the deadline a year later (Reorganisation Part 2). The drop in the number of students at Endale Middle for its final year of existence because there was no intake from first schools of 9–10-year-old students also helped to ensure that sufficient accommodation was available. The extra space at Hillside High enabled a partial move to be made from the closing subsidiary site nearby at the same time, completed the following year. At this point accommodation at the main site, needed until then for 13–14-year-old students, became free because they were now housed at the new lower school site. More new building was originally scheduled for the main and lower school sites throughout 1996/7. The order of this sequence did not alter but slippage did delay completion on both sites until well into the institutionalisation stage. Major factors beyond school level control causing the slippage were:

- constraints on capital borrowing (noted earlier) that held back planned building work on the main site for 1996/7 until the following year
- borough council planners' refusal to give planning permission for a second storey to be built on to the main site office block because it was a 'listed building'. Special legal protection was in force to preserve the external appearance of the existing single-storey building (an instance of policy insensitivity where the integrity of the original building was preserved for aesthetic and historical reasons at the expense of its expansion to meet a changing school-level need)
- ingress of water during a severe storm three weeks before reorganisation which damaged rooms at Endale Middle where re-roofing had been under way.

The contribution of staff and governors at Hillside High to this work entailed negotiating with officials early on. They were pursuing the school-level interest in securing maximum enhancement of accommodation and facilities, and a sequencing of tasks that would minimise disruption for students and staff before reorganisation. Here and at Endale Middle, senior staff were equally concerned with ensuring safety for students and staff whose normal activity had to continue while both schools were also building sites. They spent much time monitoring the builders' and their suppliers' access arrangements and provision of fencing to keep students away from building work. Their negotiations with builders had to take place by liaising with officials as intermediaries since the builders were under contract to the LEA. Internal consultation at Hillside High established the detailed requirements of heads of department and the office manager for building and refurbishment connected with their management responsibilities. Architects also consulted them over provision of fixed furniture and equipment.

Contrasting assumptions of architects and school staff, coming from rather different 'lifeworlds', sometimes caused unanticipated communication difficulties. The head of science at Hillside High requested lab benches with storage cupboards beneath for the refurbished lower school laboratories. He made a point of showing the LEA architect this arrangement in his laboratory on the main site. Subsequently the official responsible for building work removed the cupboards from the plans. The head of science had first been shown a plan where the cupboards had been marked with dotted lines, then later a plan where the dotted lines had been removed. But since he was not an expert on architectural plans, he did not realise the significance of this alteration. He returned from his summer holiday immediately before reorganisation to find that benches without cupboards had been installed. 'Nobody told me that they [the cupboards] had been removed. So I've got all this equipment in the lower school and suddenly not the amount of storage space that I thought I should have had.' He then faced a longer-term problem at the beginning of the institutionalisation stage over how to create additional space for storing this equipment.

The task area of *developing systems for split-site administration* indicated how significant the LEA and school-specific contexts could be for managing implementation. An ostensibly unrelated LEA policy to install a new computerised administrative system in schools throughout the borough impacted on the planning of information systems for the new split-site arrangement and the associated refurbishment of the two offices it required. As the office manager noted: 'It's not really about reorganisation, it is a reorganisation of the computer system which seems to have just fallen at the same time as our reorganisation.' The system entailed new hardware and software, and staff training was to be provided by LEA officials. A senior teacher was allocated the responsibility of managing information systems. She worked closely with the office manager to work out support staffing and equipment requirements for each site and provision of adequate communication links between the sites. Planning issues included administering the annual round of public examinations, to be confined largely to the upper school site; invoicing, where the office manager consulted officials who advised her that they should be dealt with at one point (the upper school site); and twice-daily student registration, to be carried out separately on each site as few students would move between sites. The senior teacher took responsibility for extending the school's computer network, negotiating with telephone contractors to see if a single computer and telephone network could be created between the sites. The cost of laying cable for the two and a half miles between sites proved prohibitive, so the decision was made to opt for separate systems even though the running costs would be higher.

Implementation was delayed until after the reorganisation date for unpreventable reasons beyond the bounds of staff agency. The lower school site was most affected. First, additional wiring would have to be installed at Endale Middle for the internal computer and telephone links. Officials offered the work to the electrical contractors already working on that site. They declined, however, because they were too busy. But they refused to allow electricians from another company on to the site. So the work could not be done and the newly purchased computers could not be connected. Second, electrical wiring had to be replaced after the storm during the summer holiday period. Only when this was complete could a telephone engineer start to connect telephones and computer terminals. Third, the sole official in the LEA who could install the new administration software was much in demand at other schools, and so was not readily available. Fourth, staff training was held up because consultants from the software company had failed to complete the training of officials who, in turn, were supposed to train school staff.

Delay was less tolerable for most other task areas. The designated head of lower school and heads of department were responsible for *arranging the redistribution of furniture and equipment*. Items at Endale Middle designed for younger students (aged 9–11) and the entire stock at the three middle schools in the pyramid due to close outright were to be redistributed among the seven first schools and Hillside. The designated head of lower school led the necessary liaison with first and middle school staff and with the official responsible for removals and storage. There was a confluence of interests between first school staff and high school heads of department, enabling the latter to be generous in giving first school staff first refusal. Since the first schools possessed little specialist equipment, their staff were keen to improve the stock. High school heads of department were equally keen that young students in feeder schools should have the opportunity to experience using such equipment. The secondary school would then benefit from the higher standard of learning they were likely to achieve at primary school. The more generous funding level of the secondary school sector meant that heads of department could better afford to purchase new equipment than their first school counterparts. Consequently the negotiations were generally harmonious.

Work on the move itself built up rapidly towards the reorganisation date. All furniture and equipment was packed and its destination labelled. Removals took place at the end of term. A major component of *arranging closure of the subsidiary site* was to clear the building at the same time. But much of the furniture and equipment destined for the lower school site could not be taken to where it would be needed because of the delay in completing the building and refurbishment at Endale Middle School. Consequently, the school hall had to be used as a temporary home. The designated head of lower school testified to the sheer volume that would then have to be moved again: 'You can't describe it but I have seen it. It is a big hall and it was floor to ceiling; the whole place was just full of furniture.'

Officials had responded positively to middle school headteachers' request to close three days early so that students would no longer need furniture and equipment. Staff could then complete the packing. In law, schools were required to open to students for 190 days and staff had to attend for training purposes on another five days per year. The training days allocation had already been used in the middle schools. This is another instance of policy insensitivity, illustrating the contextual dependence of reorganisation as it affected these schools. Central government legislation did not allow for the exceptional circumstances of this change. Officials decided to authorise the early closures, however, because it was simply not feasible to complete the removal work otherwise. Legislation equally protected school staff against being required to work during their holiday period. In adopting this one-off, short-term counter-policy, officials used their agency to counter the letter – but not the spirit – of national reform legislation. The law was unlikely to be enforced. Ministers' attention could have been drawn to the transgression had parents complained, but few parents would be aware of the number of days the middle schools had been open that year.

Preparing to operate as a secondary school

Great effort went into *informing parents and their children* about how the impending changes would affect them, focusing on the students currently in the three year groups in the four middle schools. Most would enter the lower school at Hillside Secondary on reorganisation. This effort also built up incrementally towards the deadline as information on progress became available and the time came for final arrangements to be made. Senior staff visited each middle school to talk to the students there, and information was disseminated through newsletters and circular letters to parents. The new school prospectus was written and a series of evening meetings convened by the deputy headteacher with pastoral responsibility. There she and senior colleagues met with parents and their children from different age groups. The headteacher put considerable time into *arranging school transport*, negotiating for the local bus company to adjust its services to meet the increased demand represented by the larger number of students converging on the lower school site. He also sought re-routeing to create a bus stop at the rear of this site away from the residential area at the front through which students would otherwise have had to walk.

The three remaining task areas were those most directly connected with the core educational purpose of the school and included the initiation of various sub-innovations to be implemented after reorganisation. *Planning and resourcing the curriculum* were largely the province of heads of department, frequently in collaboration with a senior colleague who would be co-ordinating work in the lower school. They designed the curriculum for the early years of key stage 3 and ordered associated resources in consultation with other members of the department. A short-term issue was how to integrate students from different middle schools whose key stage 3 curriculum experience had been rather different until now. Heads of department decided that the first term after reorganisation would focus on compensating for any gaps in coverage becoming evident among particular students.

Planning and resourcing pastoral care concerned heads of year, especially those appointed to work in the lower school. The deputy headteacher responsible for pastoral care assisted them with planning the transfer and record-keeping arrangements for the once-only simultaneous intake of three year groups. She also convened meetings with the feeder first school headteachers to discuss primary–secondary school transfer arrangements for the following year and beyond. A new students' uniform intended to help reinforce the sense of identification with the school as a whole was designed by staff and approved by governors. Arrangements were then made for the uniform to be available for purchase through local shops. A staff working party was convened to draw up a code of conduct and rewards system for students to foster behaviour in younger students appropriate to the aspiration of creating a secondary school ethos throughout the institution.

Finally, *timetabling* was a particularly intractable management task area that fell to the deputy headteacher with curriculum responsibility. Much of his time was taken up with incremental design work, once principles that set parameters for the timetable were established early in the implementation stage. This timetable would be of unprecedented complexity to accommodate the decision to minimise movement of staff and students between sites. Frequent consultation with other staff over their needs for time and specialist facilities on the two sites continued until a few weeks before reorganisation when the finished timetable could be published and disseminated.

The multiplicity and sequencing of these management tasks at Hillside dictated that the headteacher and his senior colleagues had to focus on several components simultaneously while also planning for the next components, and always with an eye to the logistics of what must be completed by the deadline date. The headteacher likened the task area of appointing staff alone to a 'very big jigsaw puzzle'. As at LEA level, the metatask of orchestrating implementation in schools implied ensuring that all components were completed in the required sequence by the deadline. We discussed earlier research in Chapter 3, suggesting that key change agents in schools are faced with a similar metatask in coping with multiple innovations (Wallace 1991b). The present research indicates that, when an innovation is complex enough, juggling with the profile can include multiple components *within* the one innovation.

Yet this was only part of the workload for the headteacher and his senior colleagues. Orchestrating reorganisation was just one element of the wider metatask of orchestrating all the work of staff across the school. Coping with the first full external inspection of Hillside High School under the regime of the new central government agency, OFSTED, in the autumn of 1996 represented another innovation that had to be implemented alongside reorganisation. By the beginning of that autumn preparing for the inspection had to take precedence over preparing for reorganisation, already less than a year away. Thanks in part to the thorough preparation, it turned out that the school received a favourable inspection report. An unintended consequence of the inspection was to delay the appointing of staff, contributing to the anxiety for those in closing middle schools hoping to secure a future at Hillside Secondary School. Alongside all this work, the wider metatask of orchestration included ensuring the smooth continuation of the normal round of teaching, examinations, and publication of examination scores in national league tables of results. Despite their efforts, senior staff could not prevent several implementation task areas for reorganisation remaining unfinished by the beginning of the autumn term 1997. Making a good start on the institutionalisation stage was not going to be straightforward.

Implementation in schools: merger at Capston and Farfield

At the other end of the scale of institutional size and complexity, the metatask of orchestrating implementation of the merger between two small village schools in the context of ongoing work was highly complicated for the headteacher-designate. She found herself taking the lead not only with school staff but also with governors on the temporary governing body set up to oversee implementation. She had recourse only to influence if they were slow in fulfilling their responsibilities. She had no authority in her position as headteacher-designate because she was not yet in post.

Already the headteacher of Capston First and the acting headteacher of Farfield First, she had successfully applied for the headship of what was to be called Bigtree Primary School. Establishment of the temporary governing body and her appointment were completed during the initiation stage prior to the announcement that the proposed merger was to go ahead (Table 6.3). As headteacher-designate of Bigtree, she had less than a year and a half to ensure that preparations were completed by the reorganisation date. The many components of this work had to be fitted in alongside class teaching for part of each week, running both the pre-merger schools, and preparing formally to close them. Table 6.6 summarises the main implementation task areas. The chair of temporary governors contributed as a change agent in so far as the temporary governing body was responsible for oversight of preparations and staff appointments. Otherwise the headteacher was on her own. The merger of two VC schools into one meant that a third of the temporary governing body was made up of 'foundation governors' nominated by the diocesan authority: one person from each pre-merger school governing body and the vicar, whose parish encompassed both communities.

Orchestrating implementation reflected the extent of work required to set up a new school in the expanded premises of one of the merging institutions. A long-term concern was to develop the capacity for educational provision as a 4–11 primary school. Bigtree was to cater for students aged 4–9 in its first year (1996/7) by retaining the oldest students from the first schools, 4–10 in its second year, and the full 4–11 range in its third year. The short-term priority was to develop provision for 8–9-year-old students from the point of reorganisation. Members of the temporary governing body were responsible for ensuring that the full set of formal policies required for the new school were written (including those covering the curriculum, and student behaviour and discipline), together with a school development plan. Accordingly, the headteacher made a start on several policies. She also worked on securing an increase in the LEA transition funding for the reorganisation year. Further tranches would be available in the coming years while Bigtree was still a 'growing school', expanding to cater for older students. She also prioritised fostering the identification of staff, governors, and parents with the new growing institution. One means of doing so was to consult parents from both communities about a new school name.

Table 6.6 Managing implementation of the LEA proposal to merge Capston and Farfield in the county

Implementation task area	Key change agents	Education system levels involved	Main management tasks
Orchestrating implementation	Headteacher-designate, chair of temporary governors	School	• Planning for the school to serve the full primary age range
		School	• Monitoring to sustain an overview of progress
		LEA→school school	• Receiving information from officials • Starting on development of written policies that the new school would be required to possess
		School→LEA	• Negotiating with officials to increase the level of transition funding and deciding its allocation
		School	• Fostering identification with the 'growing school'
Administering finance	Headteacher-designate, chair of temporary governors	School	• Setting the first budget for the new school
		School	• Administering expenditure of transition funding
Staffing the reorganised school	Headteacher-designate, chair of temporary governors	School	• Advising staff about redeployment and VPR
		School	• Planning the staffing and class structure, included mixed-age classes, taking account of the indicative LMS budget
		School	• Negotiating for the headteacher not to have full responsibility for a class for two terms
		School→LEA	• Consulting officials about employment legislation and seeking information on applicants for posts
		School, LEA→school	• Appointing staff to all posts, beginning with the headteacher, in compliance with the LEA ring fencing arrangement
Training and supporting staff and governors	Headteacher-designate	School	• Advising support staff who were not offered posts in the new school
		School	• Arranging regular meetings and training days for staff from the merging schools to plan together
		School→LEA	• Encouraging members of the temporary governing body to attend LEA training sessions
		School→LEA	• Participating in a 'self-help' group of staff from local schools

Table 6.6 (Continued)

Implementation task area	Key change agents	Education system levels involved	Main management tasks
Contributing to new building and refurbishment	Headteacher-designate	School→LEA	• Negotiating with officials about the programme of building work
		School→LEA	• Monitoring progress and health and safety, and liaising with officials and consultant architects
		School	• Consulting staff about new and refurbished classrooms and play areas
Arranging the redistribution of furniture and equipment	Headteacher-designate	School	• Consulting staff about furniture and equipment
		School, School→LEA	• Negotiating with governors for the schools to close a day early to give staff time for packing
Arranging formal closure of both the merging first schools	Headteacher/ acting Headteacher and chair of governors	School	• Winding up the finances of both schools
		School→LEA	• Negotiating for the Capston premises to be vacated and made secure
		School	• Organising ceremonies to mark the passing of both schools and the retirement of several staff
		School	• Liaising with the parent-teacher associations of both first schools and arranging for the transfer of funds to the new school
		School	• Clearing the Capston site
Informing parents	Headteacher-designate	School	• Meeting with prospective parents from both village communities
Planning the curriculum	Headteacher-designate	School	• Designing the curriculum and detailed schemes of work in consultation with other staff, including a focus on key stage 2 for 8–9-year-old students
Planning routine organisation	Headteacher-designate	School	• Determining the length of the school day and procedures for morning and lunchtime breaks
		School	• Allocating classrooms to age groups and staff

Administering finance linked with reorganisation included firming up the indicative LMS budget for the initial months of the new school's operation (September 1996 to March 1997). This budget, coupled with the amount of transition funding, set parameters for the staff complement. *Staffing the reorganised school* was a particularly difficult task in a small, class-teacher-based institution because the salary cost of each teacher represented a large proportion of the annual budget. The maximum number of full-time class teachers who could be afforded for the first year without risking over-expenditure was four, but the students likely to attend would span the age range 4–9, a total of five year groups. The decision was made to divide the students into four classes, three containing students of mixed age from two year groups. The headteacher persuaded governors to agree that she should not take full responsibility for a fifth class because there would be so much managerial work to be done after reorganisation. Her regular teaching commitment would still be three days per week, where she would take colleague's classes to empower them to undertake their management tasks during the school day.

The headteacher-designate's time was equally taken up with *training and supporting staff.* She looked after her own learning priority by visiting other merging schools in the locality to gather information. She also took advantage of her unusual situation as headteacher of one merging school and acting headteacher of the other by arranging regular joint staff meetings to discuss plans for Bigtree. She accompanied governors to LEA training sessions where they were briefed on their duties in an effort to impress on them the extent of their responsibilities for preparatory tasks. The headteacher-designate was also instrumental in promoting a 'self-help' group for local schools, mainly attended by headteachers, to which officials were also invited. It was instigated as a means of exchanging experiences and solving each other's implementation problems.

Expansion of the Farfield premises to accommodate the influx of students from Capston embroiled the headteacher-designate in *contributing to new building and refurbishment.* Two new classrooms were to be added. Her work included iterative consultations with officials and architects, ensuring the safety of students and staff while building was in progress, and consulting staff about their needs. Poor weather brought delays. Whilst classroom spaces were completed just before the reorganisation date, installation of fitted furniture such as shelving was not. Most of the existing stock of furniture, equipment, and teaching resources in the pre-merger schools was to be re-used. *Arranging the redistribution of furniture and equipment* necessitated identifying everything on the Capston site that was required and arranging for it to be moved to Farfield as soon as space was available there. The headteacher-designate pressed temporary governors to support closing both schools early in order to give staff some time for packing and removals. While this measure could not possibly compensate for the extra work these tasks required, she perceived that it would have symbolic value as a token of support. The outcome was that the schools closed to students one day before the end of the summer term preceding reorganisation.

The related task area of *arranging formal closure of both the merging first schools* built up towards the end of term. In her unusual position of responsibility for both merging schools the headteacher-designate 'had double doses of everything'. All finances, including money raised by the parent–teacher association of each school, had to be accounted for. The first school LMS budgets were terminated, a small surplus being carried forward to the initial budget for the new school, together with transition funding and the total of both parent–teacher association funds. The headteacher-designate believed that the merger and staff retirements should be marked ceremonially. Her arrangements included a farewell service in each village church, especially poignant at Capston where there would no longer be a school in the community; open afternoons and a picnic to which past members of each school were invited; educational trips out of school; and a commemorative bookmark for each student. These celebrations signified the end of the old order, paving the way for promoting identification with the new school. The Capston premises were to be cleared, ready for the site to be made secure and the windows of the school boarded up. The single-day closure proved very inadequate, as had been expected. Staff spent the first two weeks of their summer holiday filling a large container that the headteacher-designate persuaded officials to have delivered so that material could be stored in it over the summer. Little space was available at Farfield while building work was still going on there.

The headteacher-designate perceived that some parents, especially from the middle-class community in Capston, might choose to send their children to another school rather than to Bigtree. A quite widely held view among these parents was that the quality of educational provision was lower at Farfield. The headteacher followed her interest in attracting them to the new school by making time to *meet with individual parents* to discuss their concerns over reorganisation, to reassure them that the new school meant a new start, and to update them on progress. The quality of provision itself was equally a priority. She was acutely aware of the 'very different ethos' in the two schools, staff at Capston being 'lively, bubbling, enthusiastic' whereas staff at Farfield were 'very loyal, very committed, but there is not a lively, bubbly atmosphere in the classroom'. She attempted to foster a unified culture among staff coming together at Bigtree, pairing a teacher from each of the existing schools with contrasting approaches to learning and teaching as the 'key stage 1 team', and engaging them all in *planning the curriculum* and *planning routine organisation*. But incompatibilities between the two staff professional cultures did surface over such curriculum issues as the reading scheme. After extensive consultation the headteacher-designate used her authority to decree that the Capston scheme should be employed, securing agreement from the teacher at Farfield to do so. Organisational issues over which the headteacher-designate had to negotiate included different preferences over procedures for morning and lunchtime breaks. Just as at Hillside High in the borough, implementation tasks dependent on the building work could not be completed by the reorganisation date. Institutionalisation was not going to be straightforward here either. In both post-reorganisation institutions, careful preparations had been made to foster unified practices. Yet cultural transition had scarcely begun.

Implications of complexity for managing implementation

This was the stage where it was imperative for LEA officials to bring about irreversible change in schools by the set date for each phase of reorganisation. The complexity of implementation was reflected in the management strategies adopted by the key change agents at LEA and school levels to make the multiplicity of approved proposals a reality. The *large scale* of the operation to bring schools to the point of reorganisation in time dictated the co-ordinated activity between officials, well versed in their specialist responsibility for some or all schools affected, and headteachers and their senior colleagues (except in the smallest institutions) supported by their governors. Officials' continuing strategy of communication, negotiation, and compromise to find a confluence of interests across LEA and school levels was paralleled now by headteachers' and governors' efforts to protect their sectional interests. They 'managed officials' on the one hand and negotiated with school staff colleagues on the other. They drew on their expert knowledge of their institutional context and accepted responsibility for all the changes affecting their school, looking to officials for assistance.

The implementation stage proved even more intricately *componential* than the initiation stage, with much greater implications for school-level change agents' management strategies. The logistical complexity was exacerbated where delays were caused by uncertainty which inhibited action, or by other factors outside change agents' control. Ongoing incremental planning at LEA and school levels for the critical path of components to be completed by the deadline had to assimilate slippage and its knock-on consequences for other components and the sequencing of activity. Some components such as building work could generally be worked around. Others had to be completed on time, such as appointing enough staff to teach all the students. Since implementation was *systemic*, the key to co-ordinating this incremental planning process across LEA and school levels was the metatask of orchestration at both levels. It entailed ongoing monitoring, feedback between change agents based at each level, and their mutual adjustment. Tables 6.2, 6.4, and 6.6 demonstrate just how much cross-level interaction was required to achieve all implementation task areas, except those connected with educational provision which were an internal school level concern. Officials' dependence on change agents at school level for implementation made it imperative to maximise their capacity to deal with the unprecedented bundle of management task areas that implementation demanded. Officials gave high priority to providing them with sufficient and practical preparatory training and ongoing support, aware that they in turn depended on officials' expertise and authority over task areas such as building work.

The *differential impact* of implementing reorganisation on stakeholders in schools necessitated the differentiated approach to officials' support they received. Provision of information, preparatory training, and proactive and reactive support was carefully targeted according to needs identified through ongoing monitoring. Headteachers of institutions undergoing radical changes were undoubtedly the school-level stakeholders who experienced the steepest learning curve as change agents. Those experiencing the steepest learning curve as teachers were displaced staff whose redeployment entailed moving to a different school sector, specialising in a different curriculum area, or working with an unfamiliar age range of students. Officials' provision for such people was complemented by school-based provision and self-help activities which officials were ready to facilitate.

No significant resistance surfaced among staff or parents whose sectional interests were transgressed by the implementation of reorganisation affecting their school. Officials' earlier success in nurturing a culture of acceptance was reinforced by the dominant assumption of both groups that implementation was an inevitability. The legislative framework left members of both groups with comparatively little room to manoeuvre as individuals. Senior officials' early agreement with staff union representatives on means of protecting their members (Chapter 5) helped to channel the agency of displaced staff towards meeting their top-priority individual interest in securing their own future, rather than call for collective action. Implementation had greatest negative emotive force for these people, who had least power to protect themselves. They were heavily dependent on others to decide a 'least worst' fate for them. Management strategies were designed to help them as individuals with seeking redeployment or VPR. Parents were most concerned with their own children's well-being. School staff worked hard to enable them to realise this interest by making the reorganisation as smooth as possible for them, keeping them informed, and consulting them on matters directly affecting their children. Otherwise, parents were bystanders as the technical business of putting proposals into practice progressed.

The intensification of work experienced by officials continued throughout the implementation stage. But the added pressure was unprecedented for school-level change agents coping with major changes alongside their routine activities. Managing the extra work meant putting in extra time. Central government financial strictures precluded the provision of sufficient transition funding to employ enough additional staff to compensate for the added burden. Moreover, school-level stakeholders were largely concerned with their immediate circumstances. Officials continued to acknowledge the contrast in breadth of perspective between themselves and those in schools, frequently highlighting how these stakeholders' situation and officials' provision for it fitted into the context of reorganisation as a whole.

The *contextual dependence* of the implementation stage remained very significant. A range of other policies continued to interact, and bad weather made a strong impact. Outcomes of the initiation stage had shaped the resource parameters for building or transition funding that change agents at LEA and school levels alike had very largely to accept. Room to manoeuvre to improve resource parameters was marginal, exemplified by officials' informal counter-policy to create extra time for packing and unpacking through sanctioning additional training days.

The approach of senior officials and their colleagues to managing implementation was as sophisticated as that for the initiation stage. The approach of school level change agents varied more, depending on their sectional interests, their competence in fulfilling reorganisation tasks, and their ability to juggle with this exceptional priority on top of their other work. Compensatory action where necessary enabled this stage to be largely completed on time, whether offered by officials, by headteachers pressing dilatory governors, or by school staff working voluntarily through their holiday. But successful reorganisation in terms of the physical rearrangement of school sectors, buildings, staffing, resources, and student intakes did not automatically mean success in terms of the quality and coherence of educational provision in reorganised schools. Much remained to be done in reorganised schools where change had been radical, as we discuss in the next chapter.

7 Establishing the new order

Managing institutionalisation

When the reorganisation date arrived for schools in a particular phase of the LEA initiatives most stakeholders at the school system level were preoccupied with short-term priorities: making a start in reorganised schools, and dealing with the legacy of any unfinished implementation tasks. But there were fewer of these stakeholders, as displaced staff who had taken VPR or who were on a temporary contract had gone. Reorganisation had changed their professional lives and they no longer had a stake in its success or failure.

The flow of interaction at the outset of the institutionalisation stage centred on face-to-face encounters at school level, LEA officials with specialist responsibility offering back-up support (Figure 3.1). While the LEA initiatives for any phase technically ended on the reorganisation date, adapting to the new situation in schools had a long way to go. In legal terms the downsized and reconfigured primary-secondary school system had been established through an overnight event. Students and the bulk of staff were redistributed to a smaller number of schools, some featuring new buildings and facilities. Establishing the new order of educational provision in these reorganised schools was a gradual process with a clear beginning but no obvious end, as it came to be perceived as normal practice. Longer-term institutionalisation tasks would eventually become aspects of ongoing work constituting the context for future changes. Staff in schools where a major change had brought together people from different types of institution experienced considerable cultural fragmentation. The transition to a new staff professional culture and shared identification with their reorganised school could prove quite rapid and harmonious. But it might also be very slow and conflictual if staff attempted to perpetuate incompatible practices or to introduce new ways of doing things that ran counter to colleagues' longstanding professional beliefs and values.

The emphasis of LEA support and of practice in schools eased away from reorganisation and towards addressing new demands for change as institu-tionalisation of the final phase of reorganisation in both LEAs proceeded and the wider policy context continued to evolve. We stated in Chapter 1 how our fieldwork timetable enabled us to follow institutionalisation of the final phase of reorganisation in the borough for just one term. In the county, the equivalent phase happened a year earlier so we were able to track LEA and school institutionalisation activity there for over a year. Consequently our account is based mainly on experience in the county.

Managing the institutionalisation stage would be less complex overall than the initiation and implementation stages had been. Yet it could still be complicated enough while implementation tasks remained undone or where conflict ensued among school staff or between them and governors. Though diminished, the LEA initiatives' aftermath would still be significantly *large-scale* as the focus of activity shifted firmly into the surviving schools. A new start must be made in every reorganised institution. Many parents would have to get used to different teachers, a different building, or a different type of school for their children. LEA officials' workload remained quite substantial, whether in finishing off implementation tasks, in supporting staff and governors in the reorganised schools where problems arose, or in assisting them with implementing new LEA and central government initiatives. The first months of the institutionalisation stage were likely to be as hectic as the final months of the implementation stage had been for headteachers in merging or expanding schools. An enduring priority for headteachers was to channel their staff colleagues' agency by promoting their own beliefs and values as educators, attempting to build a cohesive professional culture among staff that would accord with their existing view of good practice.

This stage would also be *componential*. Officials continued to monitor every reorganised school and to provide support where needed. Various management tasks at school level begun during implementation were still to be completed, whether the short-term residue of delayed building work or the longer-term development of educational provision through curriculum policies. In many instances staff had instigated specific sub-innovations during the implementation stage of reorganisation, now to be implemented as part of the institutionalisation stage of this complex change. Most staff coming together in merged or expanded schools had not been able hitherto to work collectively on what they would do in the post-reorganisation school. But far less lock-step sequencing of components would be required than featured throughout the initiation and implementation stages, apart from the early short-term concentration on making a good start. How far activities were still linked to reorganisation would become increasingly uncertain as it receded into the past as just one aspect of the context affecting further changes.

The process of moving on in schools would still be *systemic*, though the network of stakeholders implicated in reorganisation-linked management tasks would progressively shrink as the flow of interaction centred more exclusively on the school level. While headteachers and chairs of governors were the key change agents driving the normalisation of practice in their schools, they would remain dependent on LEA officials while there was any building work to finish. Headteachers remained generally ready to turn to officials for support, particularly in primary sector schools. Complementary LEA initiatives to promote improvement in the quality of educational provision in newly reorganised schools were launched by officials, embracing the new agenda of the incoming New Labour central government in the summer of 1997 when our fieldwork ended.

The lasting *differential impact* of reorganisation was to be a strong feature of institutionalisation. Staff coming together as a result of merger or expansion were likely to face a steep learning curve, particularly where individuals were teaching a different age group of students or an unfamiliar curriculum subject. So much of their post-reorganisation experience was unfamiliar and it would take time to develop new working practices and staff relationships. Officials would have to support school staff in novel situations of uncertainty and possibly of conflict. Some in expanding secondary schools had realised their sectional interest in extending their authority over younger students. A few had even gained promotion to posts created to manage the expansion. Yet many staff from primary sector or middle schools had already endured years of insecurity over their job before being forced to accept redeployment in another school. A significant minority were to face some disjunction between their habitual practices reflecting their professional culture and what would be deemed acceptable in the new regime. For most staff the tasks of contributing to educational provision did not so much occur in the context of other work as constitute the central focus of normal work. A minority of headteachers and other staff who were directly affected by incomplete building and refurbishment work would have to cope with the institutionalisation tasks imposed by the delay alongside their work as educators. Links across the network of stakeholders would become looser as those at school level reverted to their normal concern with what was happening in their own school and their community.

The cumulative impact of earlier stages contributed to the *contextual dependence* of institutionalisation. Interaction would continue with other policies, whether the OFSTED inspection regime or the forthcoming New Labour educational reforms. Resource parameters similarly had been largely established before reorganisation. However, adjustment of each school's LMS budget was scheduled wherever a significant discrepancy was found between the estimated number of students and those actually attending after reorganisation.

We conclude the reorganisation story by considering the management tasks to deal with its aftermath as they were affected by these characteristics of complexity. The same approach as in the last two chapters is employed here, the account being organised around matrices describing these tasks to carry out the institutionalisation stage. First, we summarise officials' support activity and its shift of focus towards new initiatives to promote school improvement in the context of new central government policies. Second, we portray the main management tasks at school level to create a new normality of practice in the expanded Hillside Secondary School in the borough and the newly established Bigtree Primary School in the county. Senior staff in both these institutions drew quite extensively on officials' support.

LEA management of institutionalisation

Central government managerialist policies curbing the impact of LEA officials on 'self-managing' schools had left them with very limited authority over institutionalisation, with the exception of building work and transition funding. But most school staff and governors remained favourably disposed towards them. Officials continued to be empowered by the 'historical lag' represented by the subliminal belief that they retained the extent of authority that obtained prior to central government reforms, by widespread approval of their actions in accord with their professional culture, and by the success of their efforts to build a culture of acceptance of reorganisation. There was greater cross-level dependence on LEA support and provision of services such as training programmes in primary sector schools than in the generally much larger secondary schools. The size of the in-service training budget in the latter institutions gave senior staff and governors greater power to choose where to purchase this service. Also, officials had targeted primary and middle schools for most of the more radical changes and no secondary sector school staff had been faced with merger or closure. Most work on developing educational provision and positive staff relationships was required in reorganised primary sector schools where problems were also most likely to arise. Officials were empowered to wield considerable influence, whether reactively by giving advice on request or more proactively by offering training and taking new initiatives. One such in the county was a scheme of classroom observation conducted jointly by headteachers and inspectors. This scheme was a subsequent innovation that partially overlapped with reorganisation, being implemented during the institutionalisation stage of phase 2 and 3 of the LEA reorganisation initiative.

Supporting institutionalisation in schools was a metatask falling primarily to the senior official responsible for the LEA teams of inspectors (Table 7.1). As the chief inspector in the county noted: 'We've tried to focus very tightly on where the turmoil of reorganisation has left schools fragile in terms of curriculum or management, or whatever, and what we can do in support.' One important management task was to offer advice to headteachers who had moved to a different school or who were new to headship. The focus for primary school headteachers at newly established schools included their responsibilities for school-wide development, especially writing, resourcing, and implementing new curriculum policies and schemes of work. For secondary school headteachers it included coping with the exceptional intake of two (and exceptionally at Hillside Secondary School in the borough, three) year groups of students from middle schools. Inspectors' efforts were supplemented by those of officials with pastoral responsibility for particular schools who liaised with specialist media relations officials to generate material for 'good news' stories. They included the ceremonial opening of new or substantially refurbished schools, disseminated to local media professionals. Officials' intention was to communicate to parents and others in school communities throughout the LEA that reorganisation had brought tangible benefits. In the county this image-management exercise was designed to compensate for the frequently negative media coverage during the initiation stage for phases 2 and 3 when the parents' pressure group in the southern area had been most active (Chapter 5).

Table 7.1 LEA officials' tasks to manage the institutionalisation stage of reorganisation

Institutionalisation task area	Education system levels involved	Main management tasks
Supporting institutionalisation in schools	LEA→school LEA	• Advising headteachers on working strategically • Monitoring media output, informing local media professionals, providing 'good news' stories
	LEA→school	• Monitoring to sustain an overview of progress in schools and intervening to solve problems
	LEA→central government	• Keeping the DfEE territorial team informed
Supporting school administration of finance	LEA→school	• Advising headteachers on their school financial problems arising from reorganisation (county)
Concluding VPR and redundancy of displaced staff (borough, phase 5 only)	LEA→school	• Honouring VPR offers made to staff who would become eligible in the year after reorganisation
	LEA→school	• Making temporary LEA funded appointments in schools
	LEA	• Initiating compulsory redundancy proceedings for two displaced teachers ineligible for VPR who had failed to gain redeployment
Supporting governors	LEA→school	• Advising on the winding up of temporary governing bodies and the establishment of new permanent governing bodies
	LEA→school	• Intervening to improve relationships where tensions emerged among governors and between governors and headteachers
Training and supporting school staff	LEA→school LEA→school	• Providing guidance to under-performing teachers • Counselling individuals, attempting to boost their morale
	LEA→school	• Advising headteachers and teachers with additional age groups of students on curriculum development (county)
	LEA→school	• Intervening where tensions emerged between school staff to improve relationships and to promote a shared culture
	LEA→school	• Identifying development needs of school staff and designing a training programme to meet them (county)
	LEA→school	• Fostering the leadership development of headteachers and facilitating headteacher meetings to reduce isolation (county)
Capital borrowing (borough phase 5 only)	LEA→central government	• Liaising with the DfEE capital team over a bid and release of capital for new building during the year after reorganisation
Organising new building and refurbishment	LEA→school LEA→school	• Chasing progress with unfinished building work • Supporting headteachers over 'snagging', ensuring that contractors rectified faults in completed building work

	LEA→school	• Organising new building to be completed a year after reorganisation (borough)
	LEA→school	• Negotiating with headteachers over requests for supplementary building and refurbishment (county)
Arranging the redistribution of furniture and equipment	LEA→school	• Arranging transfer between schools and from storage
	LEA→school	• Negotiating with headteachers and governors in newly built voluntary aided schools to provide grants for them to purchase new furniture (county)
Arranging the disposal of Accommodation and closed sites	LEA→school	• Setting up new uses for redundant buildings (borough)
	LEA→school	• Arranging for demolition of buildings and the sale of redundant sites
	LEA→school	• Organising the removal of temporary classrooms (county)
School transport	LEA, LEA→school	• Monitoring the altered transport arrangements and negotiating adjustments where necessary

Inspectors with pastoral responsibility for a group of schools monitored them unusually closely immediately after reorganisation, reporting any problems to senior officials and taking ameliorative action. As the chief inspector in the county had predicted: 'Lots of the things that I'm picking up are personnel-type issues which are emerging, as I imagined they might do now, once people were exposed because they've changed their workplace.' The inspectors visited reorganised schools early in the first term to monitor short-term progress. A more long-term reason was to foster a staff professional culture where their future efforts to influence practice would continue to be accepted. Their visits symbolised the importance they attached to each school. They also acknowledged staff efforts to open schools on time. The sole contact with DfEE civil servants in the territorial teams, who had been so central to the initiation stage in both LEAs, was to provide them with feedback at their occasional meetings with senior officials.

We discussed in Chapter 6 how ambiguities over the first LMS budget for reorganised schools affected planning in schools. *Supporting school administration of finance* became necessary for those headteachers finding it difficult to stay within budget. Inhibitory economic factors in the county included the high running costs of retaining an annexe some distance from the main school site. This solution to mergers of two or more village schools offered officials a means of minimising travelling distances for young students and avoiding some building work on the main site that would otherwise be required, as at Ridge Primary School in the eastern area. The costs of maintaining separate buildings and travelling between them came on top of the already high running costs they incurred as small primary schools. Another financial problem arose where 8–12 middle or 4–12 first and middle schools had changed character to become junior or primary schools. Their new budget no longer included a tranche for the

11–12-year-old students, calculated at the advantageous rate to which secondary-school-age students were entitled. Existing budgetary commitments, especially to the present number of teachers, could become unsustainable where this more generous allocation was lost. The financial viability of the smallest primary schools came once again under threat where the predicted minimum number of ninety students failed to materialise. In such cases, officials put considerable effort into helping headteachers to reach a financially workable solution.

Officials in the borough, where the required reduction in staff was achieved through the VPR scheme, *concluded VPR and redundancy of displaced staff*. They honoured offers that had been accepted prior to the change in the central government rules governing VPR, together with any for staff on permanent contracts who would reach the minimum age of 50 during the first year after the final phase of reorganisation. Three teachers who could not be placed by the reorganisation date were given LEA-funded temporary appointments while efforts continued for two more terms to redeploy them. One secured a job, but redundancy proceedings were undertaken with the other two. They were too young to be eligible for VPR. The teachers concerned exercised their right of appeal to a subcommittee of the borough education committee with their union representative in attendance. According to an official, the teachers claimed to have been given 'a cast iron guarantee that no one would be redundant as a result of reorganisation. And we had to say then, while some very strong commitments were made, it could never actually be cast iron'. Officials had been careful in framing the code of practice during the first initiation stage (Chapter 5) to prevent themselves being held responsible for more than they had authority feasibly to deliver. They perceived that they had indeed made 'every effort to avoid compulsory redundancy' according to the code. This strategy paid off in empowering them to realise their interest in the single instance where, as a last resort, they made staff with permanent contracts redundant.

In both LEAs *supporting governors* continued for the first few months following reorganisation. The authority of the temporary governing body for mergers entailing formal closure of the amalgamating schools ceased on reorganisation. The permanent governing body for the new institution had to be elected. Its members' post-reorganisation duties included writing a raft of policies and overseeing the production of a school development plan and administration of the operating budget. Officials also intervened where monitoring indicated that headteachers and governors or the governors themselves were failing to develop constructive working relationships.

Provision of *training and support for school staff* was the responsibility of the team of LEA inspectors. Their work similarly included reactive intervention in the light of monitoring by colleague inspectors carrying out their pastoral responsibility, as where former middle school teachers in the county had been redeployed to teach as specialists in a secondary school and were struggling to teach older students. An inspector identified the problem during a monitoring visit and offered these teachers individual guidance. Inspectors offered counselling support to many headteachers and other staff who were either overwhelmed by the volume of work as they endeavoured to establish practice in newly created schools or were otherwise unhappy with their situation. They also advised staff from former first schools which were 'growing' incrementally by retaining the oldest students over the next three years to become 4–11 primary schools. The focus in the first year was on the curriculum for 8–9-year-old students.

Occasionally, inspectors were made aware of cultural conflicts arising between staff where individuals who might otherwise not have chosen to work together had found themselves in the same school. Inspectors' interventions where there was cultural conflict included advising headteachers to avoid introducing further innovations until they had worked for longer on developing positive staff relationships. They also talked through the conflictual issue with each party and raised the awareness of all protagonists as intermediaries, relaying each other's feelings and views. Support even extended to professional development activities. In one case a teambuilding workshop was offered in a school where the head-teacher was perceived by other staff to operate too autocratically.

A longer-term proactive strategy complemented troubleshooting in the county. Professional development needs of school staff were identified to inform the focus of the LEA training programme. One route was for the inspector responsible to survey the profile of staff in reorganised schools to identify possible areas of weakness in, say, curriculum expertise. Another was for the inspector to convene a steering group of twelve headteachers from schools across the county to advise on priorities for development. Information from these sources was collated and training courses designed accordingly. One was targeted on secondary school teachers catering for 11–12-year-old students for the first time.

The chief inspector was responsible for developing a new LEA curriculum policy that would frame inspectors' training and support activity through and beyond institutionalisation of reorganisation. Headteachers were viewed as the key to improving curriculum quality and educational standards, so several activities were designed to promote their development as leaders of the improvement process. It was arranged for new headteachers to engage with an inspector in a 'guided conversation through aspects of school improvement chosen by the headteacher . . . a challenging dialogue about mutual responsibilities'. Needs identification exercises established that 70 per cent of headteachers had served in this capacity for eight or more years. They were offered a course entitled 'keeping the vision' which, as the chief inspector explained, was about 'how you retain that leadership and visionary quality and regenerate it, perhaps in a new context'.

Headteachers were informed about collecting evidence of students' learning as a basis for management decisions and encouraged to monitor teaching and learning more closely. One activity was for a headteacher and inspector jointly to observe teachers at work using the national published OFSTED inspection criteria as a basis. Another was for inspectors to carry out a 'work trawl' of a sample of students' written work and to judge its quality and quantity. The chief inspector's intention was for inspectors to model the systematic approach they wished headteachers to undertake for themselves in future. Inspectors introduced systematic assessment of the performance of headteachers, secondary school heads of department, and school staffs as a whole. This monitoring activity was designed to inform inspectors' response, especially where any underperformance was identified. Their response might entail allocating additional time to work with the headteacher in such schools, drawing up an action plan, and monitoring its implementation.

A further thrust was to provide support to mitigate the professional isolation often experienced by headteachers of rural primary schools. Officials organised regular area-based meetings for them and facilitated contact with comparable schools whose staff were facing similar challenges.

Completing the reorganisation of accommodation and facilities

Most building work was finished before or soon after the reorganisation date. However, restrictions on *capital borrowing* affecting the borough forced officials to hold back the building of the new assembly hall and sixth form block at Hillside Secondary School until the 1997/8 financial year (Chapter 6). Negotiating the bid with civil servants from the DfEE capital team occurred prior to reorganisation but liaison continued over the release of capital. This and other building work in both LEAs occupied officials with specialist responsibility for *organising new building and refurbishment* for several months. They were mostly concerned with finishing overdue building work scheduled for completion by the end of the implementation stage. The final component of each building and refurbishment programme was 'snagging', a time-consuming process where officials supported headteachers in checking for faults in contractors' work that they were obliged to rectify before they received their last payment. A few headteachers in the county began pressing officials to fund additional building work where experience in the reorganised schools indicated that further improvement of facilities was desirable.

Officials also continued *arranging the redistribution of furniture and equipment* for schools where slippage over building work had left rooms unusable until the beginning of the first term or beyond. Several headteachers in the county sought extra funds to purchase new furniture for their new or refurbished buildings. They did not wish to have to make do with what had been transferred from closing schools. The severity of the central government capping of county expenditure militated against major investment, even after the cap was finally lifted in 1997. Eventually senior officials authorised the purchase of new furniture for new classrooms. Responsibility for provision of furniture and equipment in newly created VA schools (as at Newell) lay with the LEA, so officials were involved in negotiating grants for this purpose.

A substantial number of school buildings had been taken out of use. Officials *arranged the disposal of accommodation and closed sites*. During the initiation stage in the borough councillors and officials had frequently promised that new community uses would be found for redundant buildings, rather than the sites being sold for housing or commercial development to recoup as much money as possible. They had compromised their promotional interest in maximising savings by selling sites as part of reorganisation to help generate a culture of acceptance among parents and other members of school communities. The aim was to meet their sectional interest in enhancing community facilities. Where sites were sold, officials had to avoid flooding the local property market so that a reasonable price could be obtained. In the county, a substantial number of temporary classrooms were removed from schools that were staying open.

A final task area for officials concerned *school transport* arrangements for conveying students to and from school. Occasionally it was necessary to negotiate with bus and taxi companies on behalf of headteachers and governors. Officials were responsible for making sure that the LEA obligation was fulfilled to fund transport for students now living some distance from their nearest school.

Early institutionalisation at Hillside Secondary School

All preparations that staff could control had been completed by the summer holiday period before the reorganisation date. The building contractors were scheduled to hand over the lower school site at the end of August 1997 after completing all building work except the new sports hall. The headteacher and governors had secured officials' permission in such exceptional circumstances for the lower site to remain closed for the first four days of the autumn term. This decision reflected the informal LEA counter-policy prompted by the insensitivity of the central government policy requiring that schools be open for 190 days each year (Chapter 6). Staff and removal contractors needed the additional time to move furniture, equipment, and other material resources out of the lower school hall into teaching rooms and to get them ready for teaching. As the headteacher at Hillside reflected, just two weeks before the handover a severe storm had put paid to the reorganisation timetable:

> It caused a great deal of damage because the roofs which were not completed allowed enormous amounts of water to go through, particularly in the admin block in the lower school. It did damage to the phones, the computers, the flooring, and virtually had to be started again . . . We lost another four days because of health and safety – there was just no way that 900 kids could have come in.

While the upper school site opened normally, the lower school site stayed closed for eight days until building work was completed and the site declared safe. However, the further delay did align with the staff interest in having sufficient time to prepare for opening. Short-term priorities dominated institutionalisation activity at the lower school site for the first two months. Changes at the upper school site were relatively minor, bringing the luxury of extra space and refurbished facilities that had been finished on time. But both sites constituted the reorganised school, and *orchestrating institutionalisation* was a metatask for senior staff, with support from governors, embracing both sites and the relationship between them (Table 7.2).

Table 7.2 Managing institutionalisation of reorganisation at Hillside Secondary School in the borough

Institutionalisation task area	Key change agents	Education system levels involved	Main management tasks
Orchestrating institutionalisation	Headteacher, chair of governors, other senior staff	School	• Making a good start after reorganisation
		School	• Monitoring progress with institutionalisation
		School	• Operating the split-site management structure
		School	• Coping with problems, including unfinished building and mislaid furniture and equipment
		School	• Promoting a secondary school ethos for the lower school
		School	• Promoting a shared staff culture and identification with the split-site school
Training and supporting school staff	Deputy head (pastoral), other senior staff	School	• Arranging training days for staff
		School	• Rescheduling staff training in the use of new administrative software
		School	• Monitoring how new staff were settling in
		School	• Inducting and counselling new staff
		School	• Acknowledging efforts to make a good start
Contributing to new building and refurbishment	Headteacher, both deputy heads	LEA→school	• Liaising with officials over 'snagging' connected with completed building work
		LEA→school	• Liaising with officials over building work to be undertaken on the upper school site
Redistributing furniture and equipment in the lower school	Head of lower school, heads of department, other teachers	School	• Moving furniture and equipment in the lower school and getting rooms ready for students
		School→LEA	• Retrieving mislaid furniture and equipment from LEA storage
		School	• Receiving deliveries of new furniture and equipment, unpacking and installing it
Developing systems for split-site administration	Senior teacher (systems), office manager	School	• Coping with delayed installation of the computer network and telephone links
		School	• Liaising with installation engineers
Arranging school transport	Headteacher	School	• Negotiating with a bus company to change its bus route past the lower school site

Informing parents	Senior staff	School	• Disseminating letters to parents and responding to enquiries
		School	• Holding a lower school open evening for parents and students
Managing the curriculum in the lower school	Heads of department, lower school co-ordinators	School	• Teaching the curriculum for the first two years of key stage 3
		School	• Unpacking equipment and ordering to plug gaps in what was received
		School	• Setting up specialist and storage facilities
		School	• Coping with problems
		School	• Promoting communication between lower and upper school within each department
Adjusting the timetable	Deputy head (curriculum)	School	• Making minor adjustments to the new timetable in the light of problems emerging
Establishing routine organisation in the lower school	Senior staff based in the lower school	School	• Establishing rules for student behaviour
		School	• Implementing the students' reward system
		School	• Implementing procedures for break and lunchtime supervision
Establishing pastoral care in the lower school	Deputy head (pastoral), heads of year	School	• Implementing procedures for pastoral care
		School	• Using the student exclusion procedure to control students' disruptive behaviour

It proved difficult to make a good start. The headteacher reflected:

> The biggest problem was the sheer logistics. The actual logistical exercise that the head of lower school oversaw was quite enormous. And it really took us almost till the end of September to find the last television and the last box.

More resources kept arriving from the LEA furniture store as those already stacked in the hall were being shifted, along with new items ordered. The head of first-year students observed: 'The delivery lorries were coming, it was like a famine relief expedition. There were convoys . . . they literally just disgorged their contents into every possible storage area of the building.' All items from middle schools and the upper school site had been labelled but staff soon discovered that many had failed to arrive, including drawers and their contents for the science storage units that had been delivered safely. The lack of laboratory storage space resulting from the installation of benches without cupboards (Chapter 6) meant that many material resources could not be put away. The lower school science co-ordinator voiced frustration over being blocked from setting up the laboratories properly: 'Rather than coming and seeing a brand new lab, tidy and businesslike, it wasn't. There were boxes everywhere. Although they weren't a safety problem, it just didn't look a good start.'

The deputy headteacher based at the lower school site noted how exceptional it was for staff to begin a term knowing neither their colleagues nor the students: 'Most of the staff in the lower school are new to the school and are struggling even to remember everybody's name.' The head of lower school, whose entire professional career had been at Hillside High, described his first encounter with younger students as a 'culture shock', recalling how on the first day the lower school opened to students: 'There must have been twenty [11-year-old students] who asked if I would fasten their tie. And in all the eighteen years' of teaching I have never, ever, been asked to fasten someone's tie.'

The staff response was to collaborate in the face of their common adversity, empowering senior staff to orchestrate as good a start as possible in these circumstances. The headteacher used the metaphor of the 'Dunkirk spirit' to acknowledge how 'people were really mucking in and pulling together and not putting problems our way'. This synergistic deployment of authority and influence to achieve a shared short-term goal helped to shift the initial cultural fragmentation experienced by staff towards transition to a lower school site subculture.

Senior staff based at this site monitored progress and reported back to the SMT, which now included the head of lower school and the head of upper school. Plans were made in this forum to deal with problems identified. A short-term concern was locating mislaid resources. Many turned out to have been taken in error to the LEA furniture store. A longer-term issue was the lack of indoor areas in the lower school where students could be supervised during wet morning and lunchtime breaks. An ongoing priority was to establish a secondary school ethos, impressing staff expectations of behaviour on the students. The youngest had found it difficult to follow their timetable. The deputy headteacher based at the lower school site declared: 'I felt like a policeman on point-duty. I used to go out there [into corridors] every single change of lesson to make sure they knew where they were going.' Senior staff had told middle school staff seeking a post at Hillside that they would be expected to operate as wholly specialist secondary school teachers. After two months the head of first-year students, a former Endale Middle School teacher, confirmed that:

> I cannot say that there is a great deal of a legacy [of the middle school ethos].
> I think that the fact that all the middle schools were amalgamating to become this school, there was a fair amount of burning of boats. Once you know you've got a new system you work for the new system . . . I think it's counterproductive to always be harking back to, 'It wasn't like that in the old days' . . . It is a new entity.

Cultural transition among staff based in the lower school was rapid, partly because few staff faced a major challenge to their existing beliefs and values. A small majority were former staff from middle schools in the pyramid who had worked as semi-specialists, teaching a few subjects only. A significant minority were taking up their first post after initial training and had yet to firm up their professional beliefs and values. Examination classes did not dominate teaching in the lower school and most staff had experience of teaching at least two out of the three year groups for which the lower school catered.

The deputy headteacher based at the lower school site acknowledged that senior former high school staff were partially dependent on former middle school staff who 'can teach us a lot – they've been used to key stage 3 and younger children'. The deputy headteacher and the head of lower school had 'tried very hard on the pastoral side to always ask staff what they think, to ask for suggestions'. Former middle school staff were favourably disposed towards the secondary school ethos. All depended on senior high school staff for their redeployment. Many had worked in such schools before their middle school post and readily re-identified themselves with a secondary school professional culture. Soon staff across the lower school site had been through the experience of pulling together to make a good start. One former Endale middle school teacher indicated how her professional values were changing: 'There was more regulation in the middle school than there is in the secondary school. As long as I deliver the course it is up to me the best way I would like to do it, which I like.'

There was even evidence of balkanisation between departments that is common in secondary schools, despite senior staff efforts to encourage colleagues to mix through such means as the twice-weekly staff briefings. Refurbishment of the lower school staffroom was incomplete at the beginning of term and staff had developed the habit of taking breaks in their departmental offices. The head of lower school commented ruefully: 'One colleague described it [the staffroom] as like the ballroom on the Titanic: beautiful but no one goes in it.'

The longer-term attempt to forge a unified professional culture across the two sites where staff would identify with the whole school had progressed slowly. The increased number of teaching staff (totalling 137) inhibited culture building efforts. There was limited feasibility for colleagues based at different sites to mix. A former middle school teacher admitted that at the occasional school–wide staff meetings 'you tend to stick with the people you know'. Heads of department were based at the upper school site and generally spent only a minority of their time in the lower school. Even those who did identify strongly with the notion of the expanded school found it difficult to stay in close touch with colleagues based at the lower school site. The head of science noted how he and the head of lower school science were 'drifting apart'. Teachers working in the upper school tended to value their examination classes more than teaching younger students. Senior staff organised occasions to bring staff together across the sites, such as a whole-school training day and a staff Christmas dinner at the end of term. But the deputy headteacher based at the lower school site indicated how the upper school professional culture could not be directly manipulated, observing: 'You try all the normal things really and you can only offer these, can't you? You can't make people take these things up. There are still some people in the upper school who have never been down here.' Senior staff authority and influence had proved inadequate so far to head off some balkanisation of lower and upper school staff subcultures in this unusual context marked by a split-site reorganised school and the examination-oriented subculture of many upper school teachers.

Arranging training days was one of several ways of facilitating *training and supporting school staff*. A day had been allocated about six weeks into the first term to enable staff to meet in their departmental teams to discuss curriculum issues. Training targeted on specified needs was planned, including provision to use the belatedly installed administrative software. The deputy headteacher based at the lower school and the head of lower school monitored how colleagues from middle schools and newly qualified staff were settling in, ready to provide counselling support. Senior staff also spent time continuing to *contribute to new building and refurbishment*. They scrutinised contractors' work on the lower school site, reported 'snags' to officials, and liaised over plans for constructing the assembly hall and sixth form block on the upper school site. Early on, the head of lower school and heads of department were much occupied with *redistributing furniture and equipment in the lower school*, which extended to locating the items that had gone missing. A head of department discovered most of them in the LEA furniture store three weeks after the start of term, returning with the headteacher to check everything there that belonged to Hillside. Staff from other schools had already taken several items including a television set, which had to be retrieved. Another short-term task area was completing the *development of systems for split-site administration*. The senior teacher responsible worked with the office manager to get hardware and wiring into place, software installed, data entered, and the office staff inducted into running the systems.

Arranging school transport was a problematic task area that staff did not have authority to resolve. The headteacher continued negotiations with the chief executive of the local bus company to alter the route serving the lower school site. The bus stop nearest to the school was on a main road across from a residential area to the front of the school. Students had to walk through this area, and several residents soon complained about the behaviour of a small minority. The headteacher perceived that the bus route should be modified and the bus stop sited on a quiet road behind the school, but the decision was out of his hands.

Several task areas were devoted to establishing normal educational provision in the lower school. In most instances changes had been initiated during the implementation stage of reorganisation and were now to be implemented as part of its institutionalisation. High priority was given to *informing parents* about routine organisation and progress with reorganisation. Prospective parents had not been able to view the lower school site before reorganisation. It had then still been operating as Endale Middle School, and building and refurbishment was ongoing. An initial open evening was therefore organised where present and prospective parents could see their children at work using the new facilities.

Managing the curriculum was the central concern of heads of department and their lower school co-ordinators. They had designed the curriculum for the younger students and now relied on the expertise of former middle school staff to implement it. Short-term priorities to create sound conditions for teaching included ordering material resources. During the implementation stage first refusal had been given to feeder first school staff for material resources from closing middle schools (Chapter 6). This strategy had knock-on consequences for resourcing the curriculum after reorganisation. The material resources actually redistributed to the lower school excluded many required items which had then to be ordered. Longer-term problems had to be addressed once the specialist facilities were in operation. Sufficient storage had to be created in the science laboratories and the electrical installation had to be completed in the technology rooms. For several weeks, staff teaching technology had to adjust the order in which they taught the course to avoid activities dependent on the availability of a power supply. As we have seen, the split-site character of the school made it imperative to develop ways for staff to communicate effectively across each department, whether face-to-face or by telephone and e-mail.

The deputy headteacher based at the upper school site faced the short-term task of *adjusting the timetable* to resolve unforeseen difficulties as work began on the longer-term task of thinking through improvements for the following year. *Establishing routine organisation in the lower school* was top priority for senior staff during the first weeks of term. The student code of conduct and reward system developed by the working party at Hillside High during the implementation stage (Chapter 6) were sub-innovations that could now be implemented. *Establishing pastoral care in the lower school* was equally important at the outset of institutionalisation. Exclusion of students from school was an existing procedure that senior staff employed more extensively than they had anticipated. The deputy headteacher based at the lower school site noted how 'we have had to really try and press down on anti-social behaviour' in enforcing staff expectations of students as they sought to establish their desired secondary school ethos.

Great progress was made during the first term with achieving the short-term priorities. Staff were beginning to focus on longer-term issues but recognised that there was some way to go. The head of science considered that the tasks of establishing educational provision (and implicitly, therefore, the institutionalisation stage) would take at least three years, by which time the first intake of 11–12-year-old students would have experienced the whole of key stage 3 and transferred to the upper school.

Institutionalisation at Bigtree Primary School

The headteacher was bestowed with full authority for Bigtree Primary School when she formally took up post from the point of reorganisation. She continued to be the sole change agent pushing ahead with most reorganisation-linked tasks at the onset of the institutionalisation stage (Table 7.3). As at Hillside Secondary, institutionalisation in this growing school would also take at least three years. By then the oldest students would have been through the whole of key stage 2 and transferred to secondary school. Catering effectively for older students was a

Table 7.3 Managing institutionalisation of reorganisation at Bigtree Primary School in the county

Institutionalisation task area	Key change agents	Education system levels involved	Main management tasks
Orchestrating institutionalisation	Headteacher	School	• Monitoring progress with institutionalisation
		School, school→LEA	• Encouraging members of the new governing body to fulfil their responsibilities
		School	• Allocating teachers' curriculum responsibilities
		School, school→LEA	• Consulting staff and an official and drafting the school development plan
		LEA→school, school	• Deciding transition funding expenditure for the 'growing school'
		LEA→school	• Introducing a system of classroom observation
		School	• Sustaining staff morale
		School	• Promoting a shared staff culture, consistent practice and identification with the school
Staffing the reorganised school	Headteacher, chair of governors	School	• Appointing staff to replace teachers who took VPR and to create a fifth class
		School	• Negotiating for the headteacher's continued exemption from class responsibility
Training and supporting school staff	Headteacher	School	• Counselling individual staff
		School	• Organising training days and staff visits to other schools
		School	• Participating in a self-help group of 'growing schools'
		School, school→LEA	• Encouraging staff to attend LEA training courses
Contributing to new building and refurbishment	Headteacher	LEA→school	• Liaising with officials over 'snagging' connected with completed work
Redistributing furniture and equipment	Headteacher	School	• Setting up rooms ready for students
		School	• Ordering furniture for the fifth class
Liaising with parents	Headteacher	School	• Meeting with parents to hear their concerns
		School	• Drafting a new school prospectus

| Managing the curriculum | Headteacher, School teachers | School | • Ordering resources, especially for older students
• Drafting curriculum policies and developing unified practice |
| Establishing routine organisation | Headteacher | School | • Implementing agreed procedures |

prominent example of a sub-innovation imposed by the approved LEA merger proposal, initiated during the implementation stage of reorganisation and implemented during its institutionalisation stage. Staff had spent some of their summer holiday in school, getting classrooms ready as far as possible while builders worked around them. During the first days of term fixed shelving was still being put up in classrooms. Staff had to spend the next few weekends unpacking boxes from the Capston site and moving furniture into their classrooms.

The metatask of *orchestrating institutionalisation* was the province solely of the headteacher. Her ability to monitor progress and respond accordingly was greatly facilitated by her exemption from any responsibility for a class for two terms. Most members of the temporary governing body were duly elected to the new permanent governing body for the school. She used influence to persuade them to be more proactive, stating that they would be 'questioned and monitored about what's going on in school when we have our OFSTED inspection'. That it was not due for almost two years indicates how much impact the managerialist thrust to increase such accountability measures was making on practice in schools. At the inaugural governing body meeting the headteacher attempted to 'open their eyes to quite an extent' by referring to the requirements imposed on governors by central government legislation, including the establishment of subcommittees. She also arranged for an official from the LEA governor training unit to visit, who informed governors about their responsibilities. Her use of influence here resulted in governors accepting that they must take initiatives rather than rely on direction from the headteacher.

She distributed school-wide responsibility for advising on different curriculum subjects among her teacher colleagues. Responsibility for each subject included writing curriculum policies, furthering her longer-term interest in achieving high-quality educational provision. The newly appointed teacher, for instance, was made responsible for advising on physical education and information technology. The headteacher also led the production of a school development plan. She consulted staff during a training day at the start of the second term and discussed priorities with the LEA inspector who had pastoral responsibility for the school, then presented the plan to governors for ratification. As a growing school Bigtree was allocated a tranche of LEA transition funding for each of the first three years after reorganisation. The headteacher decided that priority for expenditure should be given to material resources for the older students for whom the school now catered.

She capitalised on the LEA classroom observation initiative by contacting her inspector with pastoral responsibility for guidance on monitoring colleagues' teaching activity. She sought to realise her interest in ensuring that her practice aligned with the expectations of OFSTED inspectors. The inspector conducted observations of two teachers using the OFSTED observation schedule with the headteacher in attendance. But an unintended consequence was to exacerbate the stress that her colleagues were already experiencing as they struggled to make a good start. The headteacher decided to postpone further observation and her plan to invite other staff to observe colleagues as part of their curriculum responsibility. Classroom observation threatened to undermine teachers' morale, when her priority was to sustain it.

She continued the effort she had begun during the implementation stage to promote the cultural transition among staff necessary for coherent practice to emerge, and among parents from both village communities needed to win their wholehearted support. An early attempt to foster identification with the new school was to arrange for the bishop of the diocese formally to open the new school at a ceremony where the students each performed something relating to reorganisation. One student stated how he had written to the LEA chief education officer during consultation on the initial proposal, pleading: 'Please don't close our school sir, close one of the duff ones.' But the cultural fragmentation resulting from the different pedagogic traditions followed by teachers from Farfield and the other staff persisted despite the headteacher's endeavours. She had succeeded at a joint meeting of both school staffs prior to reorganisation in gaining agreement to use the reading scheme adopted at Capston for all students (Chapter 6). After reorganisation, however, she noticed that not all teachers were abiding by the agreement and intervened in an attempt to ensure consistency of practice. As one offending teacher put it, 'She is trying to get me out of a rut but she's doing it in a nice way.' Similarly, she could not persuade staff from the two merged schools to agree whether material resources should be kept centrally or in the classrooms of teachers who were using them, nor what the purpose of displays of students' work should be and how often they should be changed.

An unanticipated factor that promised to facilitate cultural transition was the decision of the teacher from Farfield and the senior teacher to take VPR. They decided to take their chance before the new central government policy shift in 1997 effectively closed off this option. The headteacher and governors were presented with a new opportunity for *staffing the reorganised school* as a result of their departure at the end of the spring and summer terms respectively. There was also a need to appoint another teacher for the additional class for 9–10-year-old students for the 1997/8 academic year, to avoid a mixed-age class of the oldest students. The prospect of filling these posts from outside the merging schools gave the headteacher scope to bring in teachers who already shared her professional culture. It would help accelerate the transition towards a unified staff culture and stronger identification with Bigtree unhindered by memories of the pre-merger schools. The headteacher's capacity to act as a change agent depended on her having time to carry out the extensive managerial work involved. She successfully negotiated with governors for her exemption from any responsibility for a class to be extended for the second year.

Training and supporting school staff was an ongoing priority. Some activities had an internal focus, such as counselling individual colleagues and organising training days. Others concentrated on learning from experience elsewhere. The headteacher arranged for colleagues to visit comparable classes being taught in other schools, freeing them to do so by taking their class for the day. She also contributed to the further development of the self-help group of headteachers from growing schools in the area, who met regularly to exchange experience. She organised a joint session for all their staff to discuss how to carry out curriculum responsibilities in growing schools. *Contributing to new building and refurbishment* was a short-term task with long-term implications, ensuring satisfactory completion of the delayed building of new classrooms. Similarly, *redistributing furniture and equipment* was a top priority early on to create conditions for normal classroom operation. It soon became a priority for the newly appointed teacher of the oldest students, who found that little equipment had been purchased because staff had been unsure what would be required. She negotiated with the headteacher to use transition funding to help with the necessary purchasing. This task was repeated almost a year later ready for the expansion to a fifth class which would include 9–10-year-old students.

The urgency of *liaising with parents* derived from the negative perception among some from the village of Farfield (where Bigtree Primary School was located) that staff from Capston were, as one teacher suggested, 'coming here to take our school over'. The headteacher had to respond to complaints from individuals about staff who (like herself) had taught at Capston First. The teacher appointed from outside the two former first schools was also criticised for holding expectations of student behaviour and achievement that some parents judged to be too high. Cultural fragmentation affected parents too. The headteacher had anticipated pressure from parents from Capston who had lost the school in their village, but it did not materialise. For these parents, staff expectations of students in most classes remained as high as they had been at Capston. It was the beliefs and values of some Farfield parents about acceptable staff expectations of their children that were apparently transgressed. Complaints diminished as the situation evolved, suggesting that most parents had come to accept the new normality. The headteacher made herself and colleagues as accessible to parents as possible, organised formal parents' evenings and an open morning where parents could observe their children at work, and put time into preparing the first Bigtree Primary School prospectus.

Finally, *managing the curriculum* entailed the short-term endeavour to normalise educational provision in the new school and the longer-term concern to meet future OFSTED inspectors' expectations of staff practices. The headteacher encouraged each teacher to ensure that sufficient resources were available, especially for the older students. They consulted colleagues and drafted a curriculum policy for each of the subjects for which they were responsible.

Establishing routine organisation was shorter-term, agreeing on various procedures, including arrangements for supervising students during breaks and, for the headteacher, monitoring their implementation.

While institutionalisation of reorganisation at Bigtree was clearly still in progress by the end of the first year, the prospect of new staff appointments offered the possibility of a shift towards more unified practice and the associated staff professional culture in the coming months.

Implications of complexity for managing institutionalisation

LEA officials had realised their promotional interest in bringing about irreversible change in reorganised schools for each phase of the LEA initiatives when this stage was reached. But their interest extended further to ensuring that reorganisation did not compromise the quality of educational provision in reorganised schools. Rather, reorganisation should help to promote school improvement. Officials could point to many improvements in buildings and facilities but, as we have seen, the schools benefiting most tended to be the ones where reorganisation brought the most radical change, and so the greatest risk that institutionalisation might not go smoothly. Much of this complexity was experienced at school level by relatively few change agents with only modest experience of previous reorganisations. For them, the limits of agency in respect of the LEA initiatives were now very tight. There had been no option but to assimilate the structural changes brought by reorganisation and make them work in the post-reorganisation environment. Their longer-term institutional and individual professional survival depended on providing an education the quality of which would win the acceptance of parents and the approval of OFSTED inspectors.

The institutionalisation stage turned out to be quite *large-scale* for officials despite their diminished role compared with senior staff and governors in schools. They retained their long-term interest in promoting high-quality LEA-wide educational provision. Since they depended on change agents in schools to orchestrate institutionalisation they worked hard to support them. But the large number of schools in the combined phase 2 and 3 in the county meant that officials were stretched to address the post-reorganisation needs of staff and governors in the majority of schools in the LEA. By contrast, the strategy of five annual phases in the borough kept down the number of schools where a particular stage of reorganisation had been reached at any time. Officials' phase-wide monitoring was ongoing, as had to be their readiness to respond to problems emerging in individual institutions through troubleshooting activities. Specialists concerned with accommodation and facilities worked to finish any short-term tasks left incomplete by the reorganisation date. A complementary LEA-wide programme of more long-term training and support activities existed in both LEAs. Officials in the county embarked on a variety of new initiatives, targeting headteachers as key change agents in their quest to raise educational standards.

At school level, institutionalisation affected all staff to a varying degree. The balance of their reorganisation-related attention generally shifted rapidly away from making a new start towards their normal educational concerns, even in merged and expanding schools. Parents' reorganisation-related concerns also quite swiftly settled back to their normal pattern except where they continued to be dissatisfied with provision for their children. The tasks of keeping parents informed and responding to any expressions of concern were now the responsibility of headteachers and their colleagues. Inside their schools, headteachers adopted a monitoring, troubleshooting, and school-based support strategy for managing institutionalisation paralleling that of officials across all reorganised schools.

The *componential* character of institutionalisation was most complex in schools where the greatest changes had been implemented. Headteachers' metatask of orchestrating institutionalisation meant addressing a changing profile of task areas. At first they typically gave top priority to short-term tasks to get the post-reorganisation institution operating smoothly on a day-to-day basis. As these tasks were nearing completion the emphasis of the profile shifted towards longer-term tasks connected with educational provision, including the implementation of sub-innovations. Over time, orchestration increasingly focused on implementing the continuing flow of externally initiated reforms and associated LEA initiatives. Recently institutionalised practices connected with reorganisation became part of the context of ongoing work affecting the management of further changes.

Tables 7.1, 7.2, and 7.3 indicate how the institutionalisation stage remained *systemic* in so far as LEA officials' school monitoring and proactive and reactive support was carried out through a two-way flow of interaction across LEA and school levels. Officials' strategy was to use influence through the existing monitoring and support structures and new initiatives to channel institutionalisation activity in schools towards educational provision that inspectors valued. They also intervened where necessary to ameliorate consequences of reorganisation that they and headteachers perceived negatively, such as enduring cultural conflict between school staff from different pre-reorganisation institutions that might undermine the consistency and quality of practice.

The range of officials' support was designed to address just such a *differential impact* of institutionalisation on school staff and governors. Active steps were taken to identify the learning needs and occasional negative emotional response of particular individuals and groups and to target support accordingly. Most headteachers and senior staff employed their own monitoring and support strategies to identify and, where possible, meet the needs of other staff in their school or parents in their community. Headteachers and their senior staff colleagues were especially hard-pressed during early institutionalisation, dealing with the management tasks to get the reorganised school running smoothly. Officials attempted to sustain an overview of institutionalisation across each phase of schools as a basis for short-term troubleshooting, informing their efforts with later phases and developing their longer-term initiatives with an educational improvement focus. Staff and governors generally sustained a much more detailed overview about their school, the contribution of individual staff, and concerns of parents. They also reached out to other institutions where it suited their sectional interest in gathering and exchanging information that could inform institutionalisation of reorganisation in their school. But they interacted less frequently with officials over reorganisation issues as the residue of implementation tasks was completed.

The cumulative impact of initiation and implementation on parameters for institutionalisation were key features of the *context-dependency* of this final stage affecting the management strategies and access to resources of officials and school staff alike. Interaction with the continuing stream of central government policies and LEA initiatives associated with them increasingly required headteachers to combine institutionalising reorganisation with response to the evolving profile of impinging policy changes. Over time, the metatask of orchestrating institutionalisation became increasingly indistinguishable from that of coping more generally with multiple changes in the context of other ongoing work.

8 Get real!

Coping with complex educational change

We have traced how the characteristics of complex LEA reorganisation initiatives affected the activity of change agents in managing each of the three stages of the change process for different phases of reorganisation. They equally affected the response of users, many of whom were also change agents for some components. Central government ministers and civil servants realised their promotional interest in pressuring LEA officials and local councillors to bring about a significant reduction in surplus student capacity. Increasing the efficiency of local educational provision in this way contributed to keeping burgeoning public sector expenditure within bounds. Senior officials largely realised their promotional interest to be served by mounting the initiatives, and most headteachers of surviving schools realised their sectional interest in being empowered to manage a viable reorganised institution. Large-scale reorganisation did take place even though it ran counter to the sectional interests of many staff and parents at school level. By the time our fieldwork ended, institutionalisation was well under way in schools emerging from all phases across both LEAs.

The process of interaction culminating in these outcomes was interpreted as the pluralistic and unequal but reciprocal channelling and delimiting of individuals' agency inside deeper structural limits imposed by unquestioned assumptions and economic conditions. In Chapter 1 we claimed that much practical guidance on managing educational change overplays the extent of managers' agency and underplays its limits. Our account of reorganisation suggests that managers acting as change agents do indeed possess agency but that it is constrained by the agency of other change agents and users and by structural factors, the unwitting products of agency that set parameters for what is conceivable and attainable. Our normative position on practical guidance is that advice should not promise greater certainty and sure-fire success than managers of complex educational change are likely to have agency to deliver should they attempt to empower themselves by following it. If practical guidance is genuinely to be useful to managers in situations where some or all the characteristics of complexity we have identified are expressed, then prescriptions must surely reflect realistic assumptions about the extent and limits of managers' agency.

In the final chapter we work towards this 'knowledge for action' agenda. We draw on evidence from earlier chapters and offer additional illustrations to support our case that characteristics of complex educational change placed a ceiling on the potential manageability of reorganisation. It seems probable that some factors delimiting the capacity to manage complex educational change may be endemic to social interaction across a network of stakeholders and so not amenable to control.

First we take transformational leadership as a starting point for exploring the contribution of hierarchically distributed leadership to the management of reorganisation. This theory is taken as representative of the sorts of normative 'theory for action' that have been widely employed as a basis for practical prescription for school improvement. Delimitation of leaders' agency by policies instigated at a more central system level channelled those who were successful at LEA and school levels into expressing a restricted form of 'transformational' and 'transactional' leadership where they had little choice over the vision for change they espoused. We focus on LEA officials' successful leadership of stakeholders at school level on whom they depended to put into practice the proposed change for their institution. We also illustrate the consequences for one merger in the county LEA where the headteacher's leadership did not conform to the dominant approach. It supports our contention that leaders' agency in choosing how they led was channelled and delimited by the agency of others. If leaders chose to step outside the limits of acceptability to others, their agency stood to be constrained by the responses they provoked.

Second, we examine the endemic problem of contrasting and frequently incompatible perceptions of fair or unfair treatment, despite the best efforts of LEA officials to act equitably. These disjunctive perceptions reflected the diverse and often unforeseeable impacts of reorganisation on individuals and groups, their different and often contradictory values and priorities, and their varied awareness of how other stakeholders across the network were affected by reorganisation.

Third, we tentatively put forward a hierarchically ordered set of four change management themes suggested by our data. They may be generic at a high level of abstraction, with potential for guiding action to manage complex educational change elsewhere. We conclude by reflecting on the implications of our study for theory, research, policy, and practice.

Ambiguity and constraints on manageability

There is a long tradition of research and theorising behind the claim that a significant degree of ambiguity or uncertainty is endemic to organisational life (e.g. Hoyle 1986b; March 1988). Organisation members have to work hard at making sense of what is lived as a complex, disjointed, and confusing experience (Weick 2001). March and Olsen (1976) long ago defined internal organisational ambiguity in terms of experienced opaqueness connected with decision-making. The four kinds of ambiguity inherent in decision-making processes that they identified are exemplified in educational organisations. Goals tend to be inconsistent and ill defined; actions and their consequences are frequently difficult to ascertain; the institutional history is open to variable interpretation; and the attention organisation members will give to making particular decisions can be unpredictable.

The thrust of central government managerialist policies is arguably 'hyper-rational'. It is aimed at reducing ambiguity within and between organisations by specifying organisational goals and prescribing practices from resource management to the curriculum, pedagogy, assessment, and accountability measures in order to realise ministers' interest in improving national performance in the global economy. But, ironically, the educational reforms impinging on reorganisation and the legislative framework governing its course contributed greatly to the ambiguity besetting the very change agents whom ministers were pressuring to undertake LEA reorganisation initiatives. One certainty about complex educational change is that endemic ambiguity for managers and users of the change will be increased. The change process challenges habitual practices and beliefs of the large number of people in and around the range of organisations affected, raises the potential for unintended consequences of change agents' actions across a network of stakeholders associated with different organisations across system levels, and increases the unpredictability of achieving intended outcomes until they have happened.

Three prominent sources of ambiguity enhanced by the characteristics of complexity served to circumscribe the potential manageability of reorganisation. These sources encompassed internal organisational decision-making, as investigated by March and others, but also reached far beyond individual institutions or education system levels. First was individuals' variable but always *limited control* over other stakeholders and their responses and the structural factors that set parameters for agency. No one had absolute control over anyone else. Especially significant was the constraining impact of insensitive and even contradictory central government policies on change agents' room to manoeuvre at LEA and school levels. Second was individuals' equally variable but always *limited awareness* of what was happening. Awareness of reorganisation was unequally distributed across the network of stakeholders and could never be comprehensive, even for the chief education officers. Change agents' reliance on indirect means of communication, often through intermediaries, enhanced the potential for unintended consequences of actions of which their perpetrators might remain unaware. Third was the heightened salience of *contradictory beliefs and values* held by any individual or distributed among different groups of stakeholders. Where actions according to contradictory beliefs and values might have coexisted before without conflict by being kept separate, the change process could bring them together in the same interaction and so generate conflict (Wallace 1991a). Empirically, these sources of ambiguity operated together in bounding the agency of all stakeholders to some degree.

Tunnel vision and corrective action: external framing of leadership

Our evidence suggests that characteristics of complexity so severely limited officials' control over the change process that they virtually dictated the approach to leadership adopted in managing the LEA reorganisation initiatives. Ambiguity here concerned officials' enduring uncertainty over their ability to bring reorganisation about after a history of failed attempts on a smaller scale and in the new context of diminished authority.

Before we substantiate this claim it is necessary to clarify what we mean by leadership since there is no international agreement over the scope of the concepts of leadership and management or the relationship between them (Bolam 1999). It has become fashionable to distinguish leadership from management in North America. In the UK the term 'management' has been used for several decades to include what is increasingly being given the leadership cachet, especially by central government ministers and their agents. In our usage management is stipulated as the overarching term. Leadership is integral to the activity of managing change and represents a subset of the activities that it entails. The contribution of leadership is in stimulating and setting the direction for change, gaining acceptance among users for it, sustaining an overview of progress, and, if necessary, instigating pre-emptive or corrective action to maintain momentum in the chosen direction.

We also wish to distance ourselves from the individualistic, hortatory, and even heroic connotations accorded to leadership more generally in much normative theory and research of recent decades deriving directly or indirectly from North American private sector experience (e.g. Burns 1978; Bennis and Nanus 1985). According to popular image, leaders make things happen – their agency appears boundless. Mundane management (restrictively defined as 'doing things right') is subordinated to the nobler calling of leadership (expansively defined as 'doing the right things'). Effective leaders are seen to be those who have sufficient agency to come up with the big ideas, make their ethical decisions to set the direction for the organisation, and persuade others voluntarily to join them in pursuing shared goals that reach beyond any individual's self-interest (e.g. Starratt 1995; Sergiovanni 1996). Effective managers who see to the running of their organisation (including the successful implementation and institutionalisation of change) receive scant acknowledgement. The claim goes that (restrictively defined) management alone is not enough: managers could be doing the wrong things right, and leadership is necessary to point to the ethically rightful direction for management to follow.

But we suggest that the converse may equally hold: morally upstanding leadership is not enough. Leaders could be doing the right things wrong. There is much more which is essential to managing complex change than simply proclaiming a general direction and garnering support for it. Sophisticated and differentiated management activity is required to ensure that complex change gets further than a vision. Also, as we contend with reorganisation, agency to express leadership may be much more limited than these advocates imply. The direction may be set externally, whether or not those who find themselves acting as change agents agree that it is ethically right. Whoever sets the direction for change, it must be translated into coherent and enduring action on the ground, as the multiplicity of management tasks described in Chapters 5–7 illustrated.

The extent of leaders' agency will be contingent on the context, and will always be limited. Leadership never operates in a vacuum. As Bolman and Deal (1991: 408) neatly put it: 'things make leaders happen'. The evolving profile of managerialist central government public-sector efficiency and education reform policies was a major contextual variable in our research, both channelling the agency of those exercising leadership and delimiting what they could do. These policies were driven in turn by the national, international, and global economic forces highlighted in Chapter 2. Together, they made the central government drives happen to increase public-sector efficiency and raise educational standards that, in turn, stimulated the LEA reorganisation initiatives. Yet contingency is not without broad limits. Leaders do retain sufficient agency to make some choices governing their practice and that of the other stakeholders with and through whom their tasks are achieved. The range of practices is likely to be more or less deeply affected – but never entirely pre-determined – by contextual factors.

The leadership situation embodying things – not of leaders' choosing – that 'make leaders happen' represents a significant omission from popular normative models, notably the theory of transformational leadership (Burns 1978; Bass 1985). Little account is taken of contextual factors which vary but always in some way channel and delimit the agency of those who express leadership, whether transformational or otherwise, connected with a specific change or not.

Whose vision is it anyway?

Leadership for the LEA reorganisation initiatives was not only restricted in scope. It was also hierarchically distributed, consistent with research on schools (e.g. Hallinger and Heck 1999; Wallace and Hall 1994; Wallace and Huckman 1999) and Gronn's (2000) conception of organisational leadership as a variably distributed phenomenon. Gronn focuses primarily on what goes on inside individual organisations. Here change leadership was distributed systemically, expressed among change agents based at the three education system levels during different stages according to the distribution of authority within and between these levels. In this context, there was some agency to choose how to contribute inside parameters imposed by the direction set by central government ministers and their agents. The main thrust of LEA officials' leadership activity was directed not at practice in the LEA but towards stakeholders at the peripheral system level. The hierarchically distributed leadership expressed by officials across system levels had a major impact on the further hierarchical distribution of leadership at school level. Let us consider how officials' contribution as leaders matched up in terms of the normative theory of transformational leadership.

Several factors have been identified which typify forms of leader–follower relationship in different models of transformational leadership (Northcote 1997;

Leithwood *et al.* 1999). They build on the theory of Burns (1978), who distinguished *transactional* leadership (where leaders exchange rewards valued by followers in return for their support in achieving leaders' goals) from *transformational* leadership (where leaders attend to followers' needs and motivate them to transcend their self-interest in order to pursue a more altruistic goal). He regarded these two forms as alternatives, transformational leadership being more effective and morally uplifting for leaders and followers alike. Bass (1985) claimed that they were not alternatives but lay along a continuum from transformational, through transactional, to laissez-faire leadership. He identified seven factors associated with different forms of leadership along this continuum. At one end, *transformational leadership* encourages followers to reach beyond their self-interest to embrace some group goal advocated by leaders. It embodies:

- *idealised influence* – leaders are charismatic, acting as strong role models for followers who wish to emulate them, expressing high standards of ethical conduct which win followers' trust and respect and provide them with a sense of purpose
- *inspirational motivation* – leaders communicate high expectations, engaging followers in developing and making a commitment to achieving a shared vision whose compass extends beyond their immediate concerns
- *intellectual stimulation* – leaders encourage followers to be creative and innovative, to challenge their own and leaders' assumptions, and to engage in problem-solving
- *individualised consideration* – leaders create a supportive climate where they encourage followers to identify their diverse individual needs, facilitate their efforts to meet these needs and so promote their development.

In the middle of the continuum, *transactional leadership* is less concerned with followers' development or commitment than with creating situations where it is in their self-interest to do what leaders desire. This form of leadership operates through:

- *contingent reward* – leaders give specified rewards in exchange for followers' efforts, negotiating agreement about what needs to be done and the payoff for doing so
- *management by exception* – leaders offer corrective criticism, actively monitoring whether followers' actions comply with leaders' requirements, or more passively intervening only after problems have arisen.
  At the other extreme is *nonleadership*, expressed through:
- *laissez-faire* – a hands-off approach where leaders abdicate responsibility, avoid decisions, give followers no feedback, and make no effort to meet followers' needs.

Bass regarded transformational and transactional factors as complementary requirements for effective leadership. Transformational leadership generates enhanced commitment to a group-wide interest and the consequent extra effort necessary to bring about change; transactional leadership fosters ongoing work by meeting followers' basic needs linked with their sectional self-interests.

In our study, the agency of LEA officials was channelled from the first initiation stage towards a combination of transformational leadership – but restricted in the sense that their espoused vision about the need to reorganise provision to reduce surplus capacity was more or less thrust upon them by central government ministers – and transactional leadership. Both forms were required to channel users' agency and to delimit their response within parameters acceptable to officials. These users included the headteachers, senior staff, and governors who had to act as change agents during the implementation and institutionalisation stages if reorganisation was to succeed.

Why did LEA officials have so little choice over their approach to leadership of reorganisation? First, it is worth noting what they could *not* afford to choose because their agency was delimited by the tightly drawn boundaries of their systemic authority over stakeholders at school level. We have seen in Chapters 4–7 how authority over diverse components of the change was unevenly distributed between the three system levels such that for some components of reorganisation officials shouldered responsibility without authority. Even where LEA officials did have authority, they could be inhibited from making full use of it. Since the initiatives were so large-scale, officials were heavily dependent on other stakeholders whose expertise and co-operation they needed for implementation, yet who had the capacity to use influence to resist. Officials' dependence was especially acute for components where they had lost their previous authority. Here they were even more reliant on others' acquiescence or support.

We noted earlier that, since school staff were technically LEA employees, LEA authority existed, in principle, to publish proposals for the maximum number of school closures, to make all staff in these schools redundant, and to require them to apply for the smaller number of jobs that would exist in those institutions scheduled to survive reorganisation. The probable consequence would have been to alienate all school staff, their union representatives, and many parents who, together, had sufficient influence to undermine the initiative, whether through industrial action, by lobbying councillors who needed their votes, or by seeking GM school status. Officials' limited potential to control such a response precluded the feasibility of leadership requiring the heavy-handed exercise of such authority as they did possess.

Second, it is worth noting what officials could not afford to ignore. The large-scale character and differential impact of the initiatives meant that they affected many stakeholders who would have varied awareness of the promotional interest behind reorganisation and partially incompatible sectional interests reflected in their beliefs and values in respect of it. An alternative leadership strategy for lowering the potential for resistance was the opposite of enforcing authority: using both authority and influence to shape other stakeholders' beliefs and values so that their allegiance to incompatible sectional interests was tempered by acceptance of the wider promotional interest of officials (if you can't beat them, get them to join you). Achieving cultural hegemony was crucial if officials were to be empowered by the other stakeholders on whom they depended. This is the essence of restricted transformational leadership:

- *Idealised influence* promotes belief in the credibility of leaders and so willingness to accept their use of authority and influence. Officials acted as role models by adopting a 'professional approach' and capitalising on the legacy of their past authority. It was a far cry from the strongly affective charismatic approach of Bass's formulation, suggesting that the theory may be culturally relative and have limited applicability beyond North America.
- *Inspirational motivation* provides the means by which leaders articulate a vision and encourage followers to share it, broadening their horizons and promoting acceptance of leaders' promotional interest. Officials articulated and communicated a coherent vision for reorganisation and focused staff and governor support and development activity around it, but they hardly enjoyed unrestricted choice over its content. It had to be consistent with central government educational reform and economic policies, resulting in the administrative convenience of removing the first-middle-high school systems to achieve much of the required reduction in surplus capacity (Chapter 4).
- *Intellectual stimulation* invites followers' creative contribution to detailed planning and solving problems, empowering them as long as their actions are consistent with achieving the vision. There was little evidence of deliberate attempts to offer intellectual stimulation. The volume of inter-related components, coupled with the uncertainty generated by the potential to generate insurmountable resistance, gave officials more scope for intellectual stimulation than was comfortable throughout reorganisation. Problematic activities included involvement in developing and revising proposals, working with school staff and governors on implementation arrangements, and supporting their longer-term efforts to develop edu-cational provision after reorganisation.
- *Individualised consideration* symbolises the genuineness of leaders' concern for the well-being and development of followers while their needs are actually moulded to conform with leaders' promotional interest. Officials worked hard to be sensitive to an enormous diversity of individual and group needs, from calculating local provision and responding to 'special pleading' to consulting widely and responding to expressed needs for support with implementation and institutionalisation tasks in schools.

Promulgation of altruistic values was necessary to promote the culture of acceptance among other stakeholders, disposing them to contribute as officials desired and deflecting them as far as possible from the path of resistance. Officials had to establish and employ multiple channels of communication for dissemina-tion and feedback, generating a sense of being part of the same endeavour for mutual benefit.

Third, a complementary strategy takes us into the realm of transactional leadership. Officials sought a confluence of interests where other stakeholders' sectional concerns could be made to coincide sufficiently with the LEA-wide promotional interest (if you can't beat them, meet them half-way). Here officials could employ their authority over the distribution of resources that other stakeholders valued to align their respective interests. We have documented how they frequently led the negotiation of mutually acceptable deals over staffing and VPR offers, the stuff of *contingent reward*, where such stakeholders could secure resources they wanted in return for compliance with officials' requests. It is notable, in passing, that Bass's model of transformational leadership overplays the distinction between group goals (here the LEA-wide promotional interest in reorganisation) and individual self-interests (here sectional interests in securing or protecting what was perceived to be best for each individual, group, or school). Many occasions were engineered to find a confluence between self or sectional interests of stakeholders at school level and the group goal or promotional interest in reorganisation advanced by officials.

Fourth, *management by exception*, the second transactional leadership factor, was equally evident. Officials were ready to entertain other stakeholders' contribution to the LEA vision, problem-solving, consideration of their diverse sectional interests, or negotiated deals only where they stayed inside parameters that safeguarded the reorganisation initiatives as a whole. They continually monitored the perceptions and activities of other stakeholders through the many channels of communication. They arranged for pre-emptive or corrective action where they interpreted other stakeholders to be approaching the boundaries of these parameters or to have stepped outside them. During the initiation stage we saw how officials attempted to pre-empt parents and governors considering the GM escape route. Where such a counter-policy was instigated, they made strenuous efforts to dissuade parents from voting for GM status in the ballot required by central government legislation. The cultural thrust of officials' leadership to channel others' agency minimised the likelihood of such trans-gression, but they were ready to use their authority and influence to delimit others' agency by bringing them back into line. The veiled threat that officials in the borough might use their authority over VPR to penalise any governors who did not abide by informal agreements was generally enough to forestall any such move.

Whilst Bass implied that transactional leadership operates to maintain the status quo, it was actually integral to managing the change represented by reorganisation as a supplement to officials' restricted transformational leadership. Conspicuously absent was any hint of a laissez-faire approach. Far too much was at stake. Officials continued monitoring progress with institutionalisation in schools and were ready to intervene long after reorganisation was over. Uncertainty whether officials' desired longer-term outcomes for schools would be achieved was enduring. The normative theory of transformational leadership as formulated by Bass was thus only partially applicable to the contingency presented by this complex change. Use of power to shape culture through transformation to channel followers' agency there certainly was. But it was not in a direction of officials' choosing, and charisma played little part. More overt use of power through transactions was just as significant, both to channel followers' agency through the inducements of contingent reward and to delimit agency through management by exception. Therefore, this (or any other) normative 'theory for action' that ill fits contingent empirical circumstances by overplaying agency and the certainty of securing desired outcomes it implies is likely to offer unrealistic practical guidance that will have little potential to inform action on the ground.

The leadership contribution to managing a merger: a missing ingredient?

Restricted transformational and transactional leadership contributed also to the management of reorganisation at school level where mergers or expansion brought staff together from different institutions. Headteachers and, in larger schools, other senior staff had to attend to promoting cultural transition during the institutionalisation stage because of the fragmentation of the pre-reorganisation professional cultures to which staff belonged, where they had sometimes subscribed to incompatible beliefs and values. Transformation implied here the promotion of sufficient shared professional beliefs and values for coherent educational provision. Chapter 7 showed just how limited was change agents' control over cultural transition. In neither Hillside Secondary School nor Bigtree Primary School had a unified culture yet been achieved. Indeed, ambiguity was reflected in emergent balkanisation at Hillside. Only a change of staff held much promise of shifting the legacy of two contrasting pre-reorganisation staff cultures at Bigtree. Transactions were also an integral feature, whether through contingent reward – such as high school staff promotions at Hillside, or through management by exception – as where the headteacher's monitoring of the teacher at Bigtree revealed that the agreed reading scheme was not being followed and she subsequently took corrective action.

The significance of restricted transformational and transactional leadership was underscored at Ridge Primary School in the county, where the emphasis was more on transactional than transformational leadership, producing some undesired consequences. Under reorganisation proposals three first schools – Beacon, Highlane, and St Joan – were merged with Brook Middle School to form Ridge Primary. It was a split-site school housed on the former Brook Middle School site with an annexe in a village three miles away in the premises of the former Beacon First School (Table 1.4). Brook Middle was of comparatively recent origin, created during the earlier reorganisation in the 1970s. But the first schools were much longer established, each with its distinctive identity.

Three features of this reorganisation arrangement were likely to affect the experience of cultural transition for staff in the post-merger institution. First, the strong identities of the pre-merger schools meant that staff redeployed from them to the new school might retain strong allegiance to their pre-merger professional culture. Second, these staff knew each other to a varied extent and would have some beliefs about practice in the other pre-merger schools comprising their reputation amongst local teaching staff. Third, the creation of an annexe some distance from the main site would limit the amount of day-to-day contact between the staff working there and colleagues based at the main building.

The leadership approach adopted by the person appointed as headteacher of the merged school in shaping the course of cultural transition for staff would depend, in large part, on his or her professional beliefs and values informing choices of action. It would also be affected by these structural features, other processes and events surrounding the merger, and beliefs and values of other staff appointed to the new school with whom the headteacher would interact in launching the post-merger institution.

Contextual circumstances before the merger precluded much leadership activity being undertaken. Extra rounds of consultation during the initiation stage due to the exceptional number of schools merging had the consequence of compressing the implementation stage. The period from announcement of the Secretary of State's decision approving the merger to the reorganisation date was barely nine months. During this time, while the pre-merger schools remained open, much work had to be done to complete preparations for the change. They included setting up a temporary governing body, making all staff appointments, refurbishing what was to be the main site, and arranging for closure of the pre-merger schools.

The first appointment was that of the headteacher from a small school elsewhere in the county. Her new status as headteacher-designate did not give her authority over subsequent staff appointments for the merger. She was able to wield influence in tandem with the authority of the chair of governors over most appointments. But she had little choice over the redeployment of those staff from the merging schools who wished to work in the new primary school. They included the deputy head and another teacher from Brook Middle School. It proved impossible to bring the whole staff together until after the reorganisation date, because appointments were not completed until shortly beforehand. Most staff were preoccupied with preparing for the closure of their existing school. The headteacher-designate gave priority to the handover of her present, smoothly running school to her successor. In the limited time available to devote to planning for Ridge Primary she prioritised meeting parents and seeking to persuade them of the merits of the new school, determining the internal organisation, sorting out finances, and coping with the late completion of the refurbishment programme.

Aware that little had yet been done on creating school policies and curriculum planning, the headteacher-designate authorised two in-service training days for this purpose at the beginning of the term following reorganisation. She also encouraged future colleagues to meet those during the summer holiday with whom they would be working most closely and prepare provisional curriculum and lesson plans together.

The eleven teaching staff for the new school were drawn from no fewer than eight different schools, including five teachers from the four merging institutions.

Their pre-merger professional cultures would be fragmented at the beginning of the institutionalisation stage, individuals referring back to the beliefs and values of their past culture. Some form of new culture might emerge as they got to know each other and practices became established. The part played by the new headteacher proved pivotal in affecting the unanticipated direction taken by cultural transition during the first term.

Several factors prolonged the experience of cultural fragmentation. First, the original longer-term purpose for the two training days was overtaken by an uncontrollable short-term priority forced on the staff by late completion of refurbishment work. The start of term for younger students was delayed for three days. The classrooms could not be accessed by their teachers. In consequence these teachers and their colleagues who taught older students had to work all weekend sorting through resources and equipment from the pre-merger schools, then laying out each classroom. There was consensus among staff that the rushed beginning had left them 'on their knees before the teaching had even started'.

Second, the pressure to deal with day-to-day organisational issues meant that there was limited discussion of whole-school policies or curriculum plans at this early point. So individuals fell back on their pre-merger practices. One teacher who recalled the first weeks of term stated: 'That was very depressing . . . I think in a way we were all a bit like headless chickens running around to begin with.' When the headteacher subsequently used her authority to convene after-school meetings to establish coherent practice across both school sites, the extra work added to the already heavy pressure on other staff.

Third, some aspects of the headteacher's approach to managing the school ran counter to beliefs of the majority of other staff about how she should operate, perpetuating cultural fragmentation. The headteacher had a clear vision about the direction in which school policies and practice should go within the parameters set by central government reforms. Where she consulted other staff she employed her authority to delimit the contribution they could make. Consultation was bounded: the headteacher would put forward proposals and invite the comments of other staff rather than encouraging them to initiate or to play a part in shaping the debate. Though the headteacher did not actually prevent others from contributing, most felt inhibited from challenging her because they believed that she had authority to operate in this way.

The headteacher actively promoted major social events, aware of their symbolic importance in creating a positive image of the school among various stakeholders. She invested time in publicising the school, spending days away from it as she strove to raise additional funds from outside sources. A contrary belief held by several other staff was that she should have been in school at this early stage in its development, focusing on putting policies, curriculum plans, and the school development plan in place. They felt a strong need for her active support, including promoting the sense that they were all members of one staff team.

The headteacher recognised the importance of commending colleagues and expressing her appreciation, but it was not always her top priority because of other commitments. Some staff felt taken for granted.

Fourth, in this already fraught situation professional differences emerged between other staff, suggesting some incompatibility between the professional cultures of their pre-merger schools. One source of tension was the perception that not all of them maintained confidences. Individuals became guarded about the opinions they would express and to whom, one commenting: 'The atmosphere in our staffroom, it's all wrong – people don't have the trust to actually speak out . . . You feel you're rocking the boat [if you do].'

Emergent balkanisation

Other factors stimulated individuals to form subgroups where they felt affinity with colleagues. These subgroups coalesced in part around shared critical beliefs about individuals allied with other groups. First, the headteacher used her authority to empower a minority among other staff whose expertise she valued and publicly acknowledged. These individuals were taken into the headteacher's confidence and became perceived by their colleagues as a favoured group. But the creation of an in-group served to unite others through their sense of being outsiders. The favoured group formed a coalition whose members operated synergistically, each able to take initiatives in line with her professional beliefs.

One was a teacher appointed from the headteacher's previous school. Another acknowledged the distancing effect her actions had on colleagues: 'I tried to put a lot into this school. That perhaps alienated me from a lot of the staff.' She had used influence to achieve her interests by winning the support of the headteacher, subscribing to the belief that she must make the running:

> The difference between me and perhaps some other members of staff is that I'll go and tell her [the headteacher] . . . I believe that you have to stand up for what you believe in . . . I needed to know what [the headteacher] had in mind, and if she hadn't got much idea then I'd put something forward.

A few other staff perceived that they could not win the headteacher's respect and support, and so exerted influence by holding back from interaction with her. The perceived inequality of treatment transgressed the principle of fairness that other staff valued, one stating: 'You have to be seen to be even-handed.' The remainder lacked confidence to assert their views publicly.

Second, the headteacher made explicit her differential judgements about the quality of education provided in the pre-merger schools. One commented: 'I have got the feeling that all in the past must be forgotten and is of no consequence whatsoever.' Conversely, the headteacher employed her authority to impose practices from her own previous school.

Third, the deputy head, who had participated extensively in managing her pre-merger school, felt denied a meaningful managerial role at Ridge Primary. The headteacher had no prior experience of working with a deputy head, while the latter believed that what she had been previously empowered to do should also happen in the new situation. Their conflictual interaction contributed to lowering staff morale still further, especially where they publicly criticised each other. Despite her marginalisation the deputy head used influence by supporting disaffected colleagues and confronting the headteacher, becoming a figurehead for their resentments. But because the headteacher avoided delegating authority to the deputy, the latter could have little impact on the longer-term development of policies and practices.

Coalitions began to emerge, partly along pre-merger lines. One constituted the headteacher and others in her favoured group. They formed a subculture in so far as they shared complementary values. A second formed in reaction, consisting of the deputy head and two colleagues. Other staff belonged to less closely allied interest groups, some drawn together by what they held in common.

Cultural transition had shifted from prolonged fragmentation towards balkanisation. Coalitions were forming, their subcultures relating to pre-merger cultures which were more or less divergent. At the point fieldwork ended, the deputy head had just secured a headship elsewhere. Contradictory beliefs and values about the headteacher's leadership held by different staff were brought together in conflictual interaction. Her leadership was not received as transformational amongst those of her colleagues who became disaffected:

- There was little reported *idealised influence* – the headteacher's directive approach, absences from school and perceived favouritism were unacceptable to several teachers.
- *Inspirational motivation* was perceived by these teachers as the headteacher promoting her views rather than engaging in developing a shared vision about how to develop the school in compliance with central government requirements. Of the two teachers perceived to be favoured, one had worked with the headteacher before and apparently shared her beliefs and values while the other was prepared to express distributed leadership, especially where the headteacher did not have a clear preference.
- Opportunities for *intellectual stimulation* were offered differentially, the deputy head feeling marginalised while the teachers perceived to be favoured felt that they were empowered to take initiatives. Several teachers were inhibited from taking initiatives of which the headteacher might not approve.
- *Individualised consideration* was seen to be given only to the teachers perceived to be favoured while other staff felt that the headteacher had not fully acknowledged their needs or their workload.

The headteacher clearly possessed sufficient agency to choose her approach to leadership but not to make it work in ensuring the rapid transition towards a reasonably unified professional culture. Ambiguity due to the cultural conflict born of incompatible beliefs and values, exacerbated by the barriers to awareness following from the unwillingness of most disaffected staff to speak out, increased the unmanageability of the institutionalisation stage beyond that which may have been inherent.

The pathos of trying to play fair

Part of LEA officials' ethical stance embodied in their 'professional approach' was to operate with other stakeholders in accordance with the principle of equity. But this seemingly straightforward principle was highly problematic to enact. Ambiguity ensued from officials' limited control over other stakeholders' responses and the structural constraints imposed by externally instigated policies. Their aspiration to achieve equity for others was frequently unrealisable. Stakeholders based at school level were less aware than officials of the reorganisation initiative as a whole. These stakeholders constructed their interpretation of the principle of equity according to contrasting criteria, drawing on different sources of information in applying it to diverse situations. As a result their conceptions of equity reflected contradictory beliefs and values. One person's equitable treatment could be another's favouritism or victimisation.

We employ the label 'equity' to encompass the sentiments of 'fairness', 'fair play', and 'justice' expressed by informants. They lie within a dictionary definition of equity (Chambers 1998: 547). Characteristics of the complexity of reorganisation affected interaction according to incompatible conceptions of equity. It was most commonly articulated in two ways: in terms of fairness when invoked to justify a change agent's actions affecting outcomes for others; or in terms of unfairness when invoked by users to complain about the injustice of the intended or unintended consequences of others' actions on the person concerned.

Why was officials' attempt to act equitably subject to the pathos of a chronic discrepancy between aspiration and achievement? First, let us recall that large-scale reorganisation was inherently inequitable and officials did not possess sufficient agency to do more than ameliorate some of its more extreme manifestations. The accretion of past changes had left the legacy of a very unequal distribution of surplus student places in different schools, housed in buildings of varied age and quality. Officials could not accommodate all the diverse sectional interests of members of the many school communities affected because they were incompatible with downsizing local educational provision. Members of no school community wanted their school to close, but some schools would have to go where the surplus was greatest. The major inducement of new building and refurbishment could not be distributed according to need for improvement of the building stock but had to be directed towards enhancing capacity in a minority of the schools that would survive.

Second, members of these communities held partially incompatible beliefs and values about particular components of reorganisation within the limits of their assumptions about their entitlement and the possibility of alternative courses of action. Officials persuaded governors and headteachers of schools with staff vacancies to favour the interests of displaced teachers on permanent contracts over those appointed more recently on temporary contracts. This strategy was implicitly based on the principle of 'last in, first out'. But it brought the inequitable consequence of disadvantaging incoming teachers because they were able to secure only temporary employment. Understandably, they tended not to share a belief in this principle. Giving priority to redeploying displaced staff also compromised governors from using their authority to act according to the principle of 'selecting the best person for the job'. Yet no one questioned the assumption that loyalty should be shown towards displaced staff.

Germane to questions of equity were individuals' beliefs and values about the potential gains or losses embodied in the proposal for a particular school or sector of schools compared with their perception of gains or losses for some of the other schools in the LEA. Legal requirements dictated that the present job of staff with permanent contracts of employment in closing schools must terminate. They faced the possibility of redundancy. Staff on permanent contracts faced no such threat in schools that would only change character or expand. The headteacher of a closing middle school stated: 'What has happened in reality is that all those in middle schools are targeted for punishment – or the pain, shall we say. And everybody else is rather thoughtless about it.'

Third, reorganisation made a very differential impact on the people involved. The negative emotive force of proposals was greatest where stakeholders perceived their sectional interests to be most threatened. Many felt powerless where they were allowed little part in the relevant decisions, such as parents who wished to preserve their children's present school. The site supervisor (janitor) at Endale Middle endured several years of uncertainty, not only over his job but also over his home. He occupied a house on the middle school site. He would lose it if he were made redundant when the school was reorganised. A mere eight months before the reorganisation date, he had heard nothing about his future. He commented: 'I am still in this sort of limbo, this not knowing . . . Anything that has come back to caretakers is just filtered through on the grapevine.' The headteacher of another middle school in the borough was just old enough at 50 to be eligible for VPR. He had decided to go to avoid being made redundant. He was not ready to leave the teaching profession, yet did not have the enthusiasm to take on another headship:

> I am going to be so wounded and sad when this school shuts that I don't think six weeks later I could breeze into another school and say, 'Here I am, ten more years [of service], I'm your man.' . . . If I was younger I would be happy to go elsewhere. If I were slightly older retirement would be more appropriate.

Fourth, central to considerations of equity were the sources of comparison within criteria for judging fairness. Like was not always compared with like. Criteria and sources varied widely, producing incompatible judgements because awareness of the totality of the change beyond that part of direct concern was hierarchically distributed across system levels. Officials' well-intentioned actions with equity in mind could generate consequences that appeared inequitable to those at school level according to their view of equitable treatment. These consequences could remain hidden from their perpetrators because their knowledge of the impact of their actions at another system level was limited.

Equally, many stakeholders based at school level had little appreciation of the impact their actions could have on officials' efforts. School staff and parents had only a summary view of the reorganisation initiative but much greater knowledge of what was happening to their school and its community. The information on which they drew in making judgements about equity relied on sources from a few schools where they had contacts, rather than all schools affected. Another source of comparison could be schools in different phases of reorganisation which were not at the same stage. Staff in one area at the initiation stage could be facing possible redundancy while colleagues in another area at the institutionalisation stage could have already secured their future employment.

Fifth, during reorganisation the evolving profile of other innovations and unplanned changes squeezed resource parameters, as where central government cuts in budgets allocated to LEAs masked the savings made from removing surplus student places. Consequently, where staff and governors in schools had been led to expect an increase in their annual operating budget as a result of efficiency savings, they actually experienced a reduction. It was smaller than it would have been if the savings from reorganisation had not been made, but headteachers and governors could not tell this fact from the budget figures disseminated to them.

The wisdom of Solomon: redistributing computers from closing schools

The pervasiveness of ambiguity affecting perceptions of equity is exemplified by a contentious issue arising during implementation of the final phase of reorganisation in the borough. It shows how aspects of the complexity of reorganisation contributed to contradictory beliefs and values about equity and differential uses of power to promote or defend the incompatible sectional interests of two groups. The issue concerned the reorganisation over two years in the case-study pyramid of schools (Figures 1.1 and 4.3, Chapters 4 and 6). In their final year before closure, the middle schools would be three-quarters full since they no longer catered for the 9–10-year-old students who were retained in their first schools. The general principle was universally accepted that 'equipment should follow the children', so furniture and equipment for this age group should be transferred to the first schools. But there were different traditions of computer use: in first schools computers were allocated to classes, allowing one or two students access to them at any time; in middle schools a suite of computers was housed in a dedicated room where a half class of students could be taught together. The headteachers at the first schools feeding into these middle schools expected to receive one up-to-date computer for each class of 9–10-year-old students that, exceptionally, did not transfer at the beginning of this year. However, the middle school headteachers decided collectively that a full suite of computers was still required for the specialist teaching of their remaining half classes, even though the suite would be used for only three-quarters of the week. Fairness for them meant not compromising present middle school students' educational entitlement just because the schools were due to close.

The differential impact of reorganisation on the schools in this pyramid led to staff in the middle schools perceiving the issue as trivial compared with their preoccupation over their employment. As one middle school headteacher stated: 'I am dealing with people's livelihoods and they [first school headteachers] are arguing about a couple of computers.' But a first school headteacher regarded this view as 'a bit like sticking your head in the sand, because there is a problem'.

The middle school headteachers sent a few old computers to the first schools, a gesture perceived by the first school headteachers as unfair. Some wrote to the chief education officer to complain. They subscribed to the principle that 9–10-year-old students now being taught in first schools were entitled to the full range of educational resources that they would have enjoyed had they been taught in middle schools. Therefore they should receive a quarter of the up-to-date computers from the middle school suites. Each conception of equity relating to these computers appeared feasible and desirable to its advocates, but the two were mutually exclusive. Both factions employed the criterion that the entitlement of their students should be protected, but the foundations of that entitlement were incompatible. Protection of provision in the middle schools required the full suite of computers to be available on the fewer occasions during the week when half classes would use them. In first schools a quarter of the computers in these suites were needed for their additional classes of students.

LEA officials had no authority to intervene. Middle school staff had purchased the computers out of their devolved LMS budget. Middle school headteachers possessed sole authority to decide whether to retain the computers up to the reorganisation date. Yet the first school headteachers looked to officials to use their influence to resolve the conflict.

The official responsible for liaison with the first and middle schools made what turned out to be a wise move. He suggested at a headteachers' meeting that the middle school headteachers should relinquish the requested number of up-to-date computers and purchase new machines to replace them, financed through their LMS budget. He found a confluence between his promotional interest in smooth implementation of reorganisation across the pyramid and the seemingly irreconcilable interests of the different headteachers. He knew that all the computers would be needed after reorganisation and judged that the inroad the purchases would make on the middle schools' LMS budgets would be minimal. He was also aware that their budgets were healthy and that LEA resources would underwrite any possible shortfall when they closed. It was a negligible price to pay for restoring harmonious relationships between first and middle school staff during the very stressful year leading up to the reorganisation date. He resolved the conflict by empowering members of both factions to continue, separately, with their alternative traditions till the end of the year in line with their different professional cultures.

The ambiguity arising here from contradictory beliefs and values about the equitable distribution of computers was generated directly by reorganisation. The two normally separate traditions of computer use became mutually incompatible only as an unintended consequence of the earlier decision supported by all the headteachers to reorganise the pyramid over two years. Both traditions could not be sustained without an additional supply of computers, and the first school headteachers had limited control over their middle school counterparts because they had no authority to demand computers that belonged to the middle schools. So some resorted to influence by raising awareness of the issue at LEA level. Once the official was informed, he was able to draw on his knowledge of the overall budgetary situation in schools across the LEA, of which the headteachers involved had limited awareness, to broker a solution which alleviated this source of ambiguity.

Complex change management themes

Even if we accept that human capacity to manage complex educational change is bound to be limited and that a significant degree of ambiguity is endemic, the very important 'knowledge for action' question still remains: How may a network of stakeholders within and between system levels employ their agency within structural boundaries to maximise their capacity for managing complex educational change?

Here is our exploratory answer. Analysis of patterns across the multiplicity of tasks entailed in managing each stage of the LEA reorganisation initiatives suggested four broad change management themes. Their status is that of hypotheses or hunches. They were inductively derived from in-depth evidence, but only of one change in one country conceived by us as complex. The themes have face validity, and they might have applicability to other complex changes inside or outside the education sphere. But their applicability could be only at a high level of abstraction. The detailed expression of characteristics of complexity will be specific to the content and context of each change. Evidence from elsewhere suggests that context-dependency is likely to include not only interaction with other present and past changes but also the pervasive impact of particular national cultures (e.g. Hallinger and Kantamara 2000). Therefore we offer these themes as no more than evidence-informed starting points for reflection, as 'advance organisers' to frame planning, and a possible focus for training and other forms of practical support for change agents.

Table 8.1 illustrates how all five characteristics of complexity contributed to the highly differentiated and extensively but unequally distributed activity within each change management theme. There is a hierarchical order. The *metatask of orchestration* was the hub of the most strategic activity undertaken by those in formal positions, giving them the requisite authority through which the other three more specialised change management themes were steered. By this term we mean both more and less than leadership. More, because orchestration delves further into the detail through oversight of the multifarious activities necessary to keep the change on track. Less, partly because the scope for selecting a vision may be restricted but the need for steering a coherent change effort remains even where the vision is externally supplied, and partly because orchestration is more narrowly distributed than the notion of distributed leadership may imply.

Table 8.1 Indicative implications of complexity for change management themes

Characteristics of complexity	Change management themes			
	Metatask of orchestration	*Flexible planning and co-ordination*	*Culture building and communication*	*Differentiated support*
Large-scale	Establishing multiple communication links, identifying stakeholders' interests and minimising potential resistance	Planning to ensure expertise is available where and when needed, planning to minimise resistance and maximise support	Articulating a vision for change through diverse communication strategies, ensuring that coherent messages are disseminated	Identifying the range of existing expertise and facilitating its use to support others
Componential	Establishing interrelated structures and responsibilities to cover all components	Lock-step planning for multiple and sequential components, frequent updating of plans where later components are affected by earlier ones	Ensuring that change components are as consistent with the vision as possible, facilitating communication between those responsible for different components	Ensuring that the content of support strategies covers the range of components and their interrelationship
Systemic	Establishing and monitoring the effectiveness of cross-level linkages, seeking a confluence of interests between stakeholders	Facilitating co-ordination of planning between system levels by gathering and disseminating information between levels	Maximising cross-level support by nurturing a culture of acceptance and endorsement of change, encouraging frequent updating of information between levels	Designing support strategies for those involved at different levels, facilitating cross-level support
Differentially impacting	Monitoring the evolution of the range of impacts and taking responsive action where necessary	Predictive and responsive planning to take account of varied impacts and their evolution over time	Targeting strategies to promote a culture of acceptance on those with greatest power to resist, inviting and acting on feedback	Identifying the diversity of evolving needs and designing and updating a range of support strategies to meet them

| Contextually dependent | Predicting and monitoring the impact of other policies and changes and assimilating them, seeking to maximise resources within available limits | Taking account of the cumulative impact of early outcomes on subsequent plans, adjusting plans incrementally where other policies and changes impact | Monitoring the evolving balance between allegiance to the status quo and to change among different stakeholder groups | Monitoring and adjusting support strategies to ensure that diverse needs are met, designing support strategies within resource parameters |

There is also an implicit chronological order. The groups of stakeholders based at different system levels who were responsible for orchestration shifted with each stage of the change process, following the overall flow of interaction across the network of stakeholders (Figure 3.1). From the beginning of the first initiation stage it fell to the CEO and a small group of senior officials and councillors at LEA level, prompted and approved by central government ministers and senior civil servants and the legislative and financial framework setting parameters for reorganisation. From the beginning of each implementation stage, orchestration became shared across system levels with the headteacher or headteacher–designate, a small group of senior staff in larger institutions, and the chair of the permanent or temporary governing body. From the date of reorganisation, it became the exclusive province of the latter group throughout the institutionalisation stage. Orchestration included instigating change management activity, creating and sustaining favourable conditions for the change to happen, setting up management structures and delegating responsibilities, monitoring progress, and taking corrective or adaptive action where necessary and feasible to keep the change process on track, especially in response to the evolving profile of interacting policies and other ongoing work.

The componential nature of reorganisation meant that even orchestrators could not escape coping with ambiguity. There were so many factors whose combined interaction was beyond any individual's understanding, let alone control, that no orchestrator could achieve a comprehensive overview, though it could be maximised through constant monitoring. Other characteristics of complexity shaped orchestration activity, as where the large number of people affected meant that multidirectional communication channels had to be forged between them to ensure that they formed a network with mutual linkages.

Orchestration guided activity under the other three change management themes, many requiring specialist expertise and so much more widely distributed within and between system levels. *Flexible planning and co-ordination* involved thinking through what needed to be done at LEA and school levels for the initiatives as a whole and for each stage, taking account of contextual parameters such as the inducement to borrow from central government to finance desirable building and refurbishment, and the interrelationship between plans. The approach to planning reflected the tension between retaining flexibility, as in an evolutionary approach (Louis and Miles 1990), and retaining overall coherence through longer-term cycles, as in more traditional approaches such as strategic planning (Steiner 1979). It conformed to the notion of 'flexible planning' for change in a relatively turbulent environment (Wallace and McMahon 1994). Planning connected with reorganisation was a medium-term predictive process for the change as a whole, for one or more phases and for the stages of the process, updated year-on-year as dictated by the annual financial planning cycle. It was also highly incremental. Planners responded iteratively to new information about progress and spasmodically and often unpredictably occurring factors, such as a delay in central government decisions on submitted proposals for phases 2 and 3 in the county. At school level, we have seen how bad weather frequently delayed completion of building work towards the end of the implementation stage, necessitating adjustment of plans for moving into the new accommodation. Coping with this tension meant that, at heart, planning was a more or less continual process of creation, monitoring, and adjustment inside the broad longer-term thrust.

Characteristics of complexity similarly shaped the distribution of planning activity and its content. Plans had to be made and co-ordinated for the multiplicity of interrelated components differentially affecting schools and the people connected with them, coupled with ensuring that the necessary diversity of expertise would be available to deal with each component. Critical path planning for implementation had to be co-ordinated closely between LEA officials and school staff since much preparation for reorganisation was a cross-level affair. Officials were much exercised during the implementation stage with trying to ensure that all displaced staff from closing schools gained redeployment in surviving schools or premature retirement. Their effort entailed much prompting of headteachers and governors to create or reconfigure the staffing structure and appoint the staff needed for their school.

The heavy emphasis on *culture building and communication* throughout the change process was deeply affected by all characteristics of complexity. Indicatively, at the initiation and implementation stages the large-scale and systemic characteristics of reorganisation implied that information must be disseminated to a large number of people in school communities and feedback sought from them. Dependence on the acquiescence or endorsement of stakeholders at central government and school levels meant that LEA officials had to try to achieve cultural hegemony by promulgating consistent messages within a vision of the benefits that reorganisation would bring, and also to pre-empt any potential resistance. The differential impact of reorganisation proposals on stakeholders' sectional interests enabled officials to capitalise on the favourable culture in expanding high schools while seeking to gain acceptance elsewhere. Once firm proposals were approved, headteachers and governors were dependent on their colleague staff to carry out implementation tasks alongside their normal work. If institutionalisation was to extend as far as improvement efforts directed towards shared goals, headteachers were dependent on their staff pulling together. The differential impact of reorganisation on individual staff members in schools that were a product of merger meant that the staff culture was fragmented when merged institutions opened. Most headteachers and their senior colleagues worked hard to promote a new school-wide professional culture embracing improvement consistent with headteachers' educational values. Most had made some progress even though by the time our fieldwork ended their achievements had so far fallen short of their aspirations.

An enormous amount of *differentiated support* had to be provided for the people who needed it, and at the right time. Forms of support spanned provision of expertise, finance, and physical resources such as new building, training, and individual counselling. Characteristics of complexity had a profound impact on the way this variety of provision was managed. Let us take two instances. First, the contextually dependent character of support followed from the fact that the aggregate of past changes, including a previous reorganisation initiative and, over time, cumulative experience with early phases of the present initiatives, had produced a pool of expertise among officials. The evolving profile of central government and LEA policies facilitated and constrained what could be done. Second, the differential impact of the proposals for those stakeholders affected meant that the needs-identification process and provision of support strategies, such as preparatory briefing and training, had to be updated during each stage of reorganisation. By the time institutionalisation of the final phase had proceeded for a year or so, the focus of officials' support had turned from reorganisation as such towards school improvement in the post-reorganisation context.

Beyond hyperrationalisation and hyperconceptualisation?

To conclude, our research indicates how patterns were detectable in the 'dynamic complexity' of the reorganisation initiatives. They may prove to have wider implications for managers who act as change agents and for those who support the development of their practice. Our approach was to develop 'knowledge for understanding' by analysing just what it is that makes managing complex change so complex through linking both the small picture of subjective meaning and the big picture of delimiting structural factors. We aimed to develop a sounder basis for realistic 'knowledge for action' than either 'hyperrational' formulations that under-emphasise complexity, its inherent ambiguity, and the limits of agency, or 'hyperconceptual' formulations that 'over-reach' the limits of applicability of a metaphor between disparate phenomena – frequently with little empirical backing. Realistic practical guidance building on this foundation will have to be conceived in terms of general tools for reflection rather than detailed checklist prescriptions. The research on reorganisation suggests that complex educational changes are likely to be both relatively unmanageable and deeply contingent on their content and context. If reorganisation was contextually dependent, other complex educational changes will be self-evidently diverse. Therefore broad themes, with plenty of room for creative interpretation in their context of use, are as close to prescription as we believe is appropriate, given the nature of the phenomenon and the limited knowledge base.

Research on a single instance of complex educational change is just as self-evidently no more than a point of departure for understanding of what, by definition, is a multifaceted phenomenon whose forms of expression are multiple. We were able to identify two hierarchically ordered typologies: the characteristics of complexity and their detailed constituents with management implications; and the change management themes topped by the metatask of orchestration. In our study, expression of both the characteristics and change management themes evolved over time according to the stage reached by the change process for each phase of reorganisation. Fullan's typology of stages stood up well as the frame for chronological mapping.

Further investigation is needed on different complex educational changes in different local and national contexts to test how far the characteristics, their constituents, and the change management themes identified here do have wider applicability and how far they would bear further elaboration and refinement. It may be an ambitious 'intellectual project' to aim to develop a stronger empirical basis for practical guidance on strategies for managing complex educational change of diverse content in equally diverse national and cultural contexts. But it is surely no longer viable to rely on simplistic slogans and metaphors, out of touch with the reality of complex educational change that change agents are struggling to manage. Figure 8.1 is an analytical grid based on our two typologies and the stages of the change process. We offer it as one way of framing further research that builds on our study. It may also be useful as a practical planning and monitoring aid for orchestrators of complex educational change. It is a three-dimensional matrix, adding the three stages of the change process to the two-dimensional matrix (see Table 8.1) comparing the five characteristics of complexity and the four change management themes. Research or planning and monitoring could be framed by considering the relationship between chosen categories within and between each of the three dimensions that forms a cell of the matrix. In this way it is possible to plot what does or does not happen or what should happen by investigating or thinking through:

- in any one dimension, what is embodied in any category or how the contents of two or more categories relate to each other (e.g. among the change management themes what the management tasks of orchestration are or should be, or how the management tasks of orchestration do or should link with the management tasks encompassed by each of the other three themes)
- in any two dimensions, how the content of one or more categories in the first dimension does or should relate to the content of one or more categories in the second dimension (e.g. how the componential nature of a change does or should impact on the management tasks of orchestration, or how the componential nature of a change does or should affect the combination of management tasks among all the change management themes)
- in the three dimensions, how the content of one or more categories in each

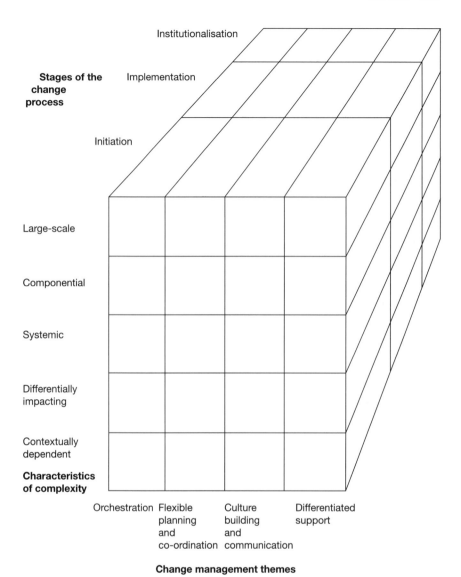

Figure 8.1 Relationship between characteristics, management themes, and stages of complex change

dimension relates to the others (e.g. how the componential nature of a change does or should affect the management tasks of orchestration during the initiation stage, or how the componential nature of a change does or should affect the management tasks of orchestration and who does or should carry them out during the initiation and implementation stages).

The research also has implications for theory-building. Attempting to understand complex educational change as a process necessitates a conceptualisation that is sophisticated enough to grasp the small phenomenological picture and the big sociopolitical picture and also to grasp the dynamics of their interrelationship. Our theoretical orientation had to be eclectic to build sufficient conceptual bridges between different formulations embracing different parts of the small and big pictures and their linkage. Our pluralistic perspective followed the lead of Hargreaves (1983) and Giddens (1984) in connecting agency and structural limits through the notion of 'relative autonomy'. We also drew on the earlier work of Wallace and colleagues on combining cultural and political perspectives within the pluralistic perspective and on the interface between policy implementation, mediation, and the management of multiple innovations in the context of other work. Our eclecticism had the advantage of enabling us to ask bridging questions and to synthesise the answers in describing and explaining what we found. But conceptual bridgework does have the disadvantage of making for intellectual complexity and ambiguity. Working with such a range of concepts and the way they articulated with each other was difficult. The alternative would be a more reductionist and therefore simplistic account, capturing less of the phenomenon. So eclecticism seems a path worth taking but we are very aware of the attention that must be paid to stipulative definitions so that concepts are mutually complementary and together provide a coherent orientation.

Implications of the research for policymakers at the national level seem as clear as their attention to these implications is unlikely, given the structural pressures driving their public-sector reform agenda. So we will be brief. There does appear to be some room to manoeuvre, despite these pressures, for policymakers to make more or less effort to maximise the coherence between the policies developed inside their education and other relevant departments and to minimise the kind of mutually inhibiting impact of their reciprocal interaction that we saw with reorganisation. The past UK Conservative central government was heavily criticised by the Audit Commission (1996) for the contradiction between pressure on LEAs to reorganise to remove surplus student capacity and the promotion of the GM schools sector. Since 1997 incoming New Labour government ministers have changed the reorganisation policy so that the decision to approve proposals is taken locally, and have also abolished the GM sector. They have coined the slogan 'joined up government' as a symbol of their determination to bring greater coherence.

Room to manoeuvre is nevertheless limited because of the ambiguity endemic to the policy process. Ministers and their agents have limited control over the content and implementation of policies, limited awareness of the consequences of their actions at other system levels, and contradictory beliefs and values leading to disjunction between policies that 'joining up' cannot remove. Ambiguity can be reduced, and ministers stand to achieve more of their aspirations for implementation if policymaking is more joined up. But some 'policy pathos', the chronic shortfall between these aspirations and their achievement, will remain.

The complexity of educational change is unlikely to become any simpler, and so more manageable, in the foreseeable future.

Our findings support the contention of Clarke and Newman (1997) that system–changing policies contributing to the managerialist project to 'roll out' state power between central government and the peripheral system level have multiplied the sites where sufficient agency exists to mediate these policies. Devolution of authority to the school level at LEA expense left LEA officials and councillors short on authority. But they remained long on influence through their 'professional approach', seeking cultural hegemony and capitalising on the enduring cultural legacy of their past authority, marked by habitual deference among newly empowered school staff and governors. Managerialist policies had not yet replaced the old professional culture that spanned LEA and school system levels with a managerialist culture. At the time of writing LEAs still constitute a significant 'lump' in the British state with some very modest reinstatement of their authority.

The injunction in the heading of this chapter to 'get real' about complex educational change implies accepting that it is beyond the agency of policy-makers, change agents, or users alike to eliminate ambiguity from the change process. Some amelioration is certainly possible at the edges, and strategies such as joined up government and orchestration of complex change may help to reduce ambiguity – up to a point. But human agency does have limits. The impact of policies within the managerialist project on reorganisation bears witness to the irony of trying too hard to reduce ambiguity. An unintended consequence has been to create more of it. Given the nature of politics and the assumptions and economic conditions that drive politicians to act as they do, we can safely predict that in the education sphere change agents and users will continue to be expected to cope with complex educational change under conditions which are not of their choosing.

Meeting the 'knowledge for action' agenda means finding feasible ways of supporting change agents and users with managing complex educational change within the limits of human agency. Developing their coping capacity is as much about making a degree of ambiguity tolerable and manageable as it is about maximising the coherence of change strategies and orchestrating the change process. That, realistically, is where their empowerment lies.

References

Audit Commission (1984) *Obtaining Better Value in Education: Aspects of Non-teaching Costs in Secondary Schools*, London: Her Majesty's Stationery Office.

Audit Commission (1986) *Towards Better Management of Secondary Education*, London: Her Majesty's Stationery Office.

Audit Commission (1988) *Surplus Capacity in Secondary Schools: A Progress Report*, London: Her Majesty's Stationery Office.

Audit Commission (1990) *Rationalising Primary School Provision*, London: Her Majesty's Stationery Office.

Audit Commission (1996) *Trading Places: The Supply and Allocation of School Places*, London: Audit Commission.

Audit Commission (1997) *Trading Places: A Management Handbook on the Supply and Allocation of School Places*, London: Audit Commission.

Bacharach, S. and Lawler, E. (1980) *Power and Politics in Organisations*, San Francisco: Jossey-Bass.

Bass, B. (1985) *Leadership and Performance beyond Expectations*, New York: Free Press.

Bennis, W. and Nanus, B. (1985) *Leaders: Strategies for Taking Charge*, New York: Harper & Row.

Berger, P. and Luckmann, T. (1967) *The Social Construction of Reality*, Harmondsworth: Penguin.

Bolam, R. (1975) 'The management of educational change: towards a conceptual framework', in V. Houghton, R. McHugh, and C. Morgan (eds) *Management in Education*, London: Ward Lock.

Bolam, R. (1999) 'Educational administration, leadership and management: towards a research agenda', in T. Bush, L. Bell, R. Bolam, R. Glatter, and P. Ribbins (eds) *Educational Management: Redefining Theory, Policy and Practice*, London: Paul Chapman.

Bolman, L. and Deal, T. (1991) *Reframing Organisations: Artistry, Choice and Leadership*, San Francisco: Jossey-Bass.

Bower, M. (1966) *The Will to Manage: Corporate Success through Programmed Management*, New York: McGraw-Hill.

Briault, E. and Smith, F. (1980) *Falling Rolls in Secondary Schools: Part One*, Windsor: NFER Publishing Company.

Brown, P. and Lauder, H. (1996) 'Education, globalisation and economic development', *Journal of Education Policy* 11, 1: 1–25.

Burns, J. M. (1978) *Leadership*, New York: Harper & Row.

Bush, T., Coleman, M. and Glover, D. (1993) *Managing Autonomous Schools: The Grant Maintained Experience*, London: Paul Chapman.

Caldwell, B. and Spinks, J. (1988) *The Self Managing School*, London: Falmer Press.

Chambers, W. and R. Ltd (1998) *The Chambers Dictionary*, Edinburgh: Chambers Harrap Publishers Ltd.

Clarke, J. and Newman, J. (1997) *The Managerial State*, London: Sage.

Dale, R. (1986) 'Perspectives on policy making', Part 2 of Module 1 of Open University course E333 *Policy Making in Education*, Milton Keynes: Open University Press.

Davies, B. (1997) 'Re-engineering and its application to education', *School Leadership and Management* 17, 2: 173–85.

Deakin, N. and Parry, R. (1993) 'Does the Treasury have a social policy?', in N. Deakin and R. Page (eds) *The Costs of Welfare*, Aldershot: Avebury.

Department for Education (1992) *Choice and Diversity: A New Framework for Schools* Cm 2021, London: Department for Education.

—— (1994) *Circular on the Supply of School Places* Circular 23/94, London: Department for Education.

Department of Education and Science (1965) *The Organisation of Secondary Education* Circular 10/65, London: Department of Education and Science.

Dunleavy, P. and Hood, C. (1994) 'From old public administration to new public management', *Public Money and Management*, July–September, 9–16.

Fidler, B. with Edwards, M., Evans, B., Mann, P. and Thomas, P. (1996) *Strategic Planning for School Improvement*, London: Pitman Publishing in association with The British Educational Management and Administration Society.

Firestone, W. and Louis, K. S. (1999) 'Schools as cultures', in J. Murphy and K. S. Louis (eds) *Handbook of Research on Educational Administration* (2nd edn), San Francisco: Jossey-Bass.

Foster, C. and Plowden, F. (1996) *The State under Stress*, Buckingham: Open University Press.

Fullan, M. (1993) *Change Forces: Probing the Depths of Educational Reform*, London: Falmer Press.

—— (1999) *Change Forces: The Sequel*, London: Falmer Press.

—— (2001) *The New Meaning of Educational Change* (3rd edn) New York: Teachers College Press.

Fullan, M. with Stiegelbauer, S. (1991) *The New Meaning of Educational Change* (2nd edn), London: Cassell.

Giddens, A. (1976) *New Rules of Sociological Method*, London: Hutchinson.

—— (1984) *The Constitution of Society*, Cambridge: Polity.

Gleick, J. (1988) *Chaos: Making a New Science*, London: Heinemann.

Griffiths, A. (1971) *Secondary School Reorganisation in England and Wales*, London: Routledge & Kegan Paul.

Gronn, P. (2000) 'Distributed properties: a new architecture for leadership', *Educational Management and Administration* 28, 3: 317–38.

Hallinger, P. and Heck, R. (1999) 'Can leadership enhance school effectiveness?', in T. Bush, L. Bell, R. Bolam, R. Glatter, and P. Ribbins (eds) *Educational Management: Redefining Theory, Policy and Practice*, London: Paul Chapman.

Hallinger, P. and Kantamara, P. (2000) 'Educational change in Thailand: opening a window onto leadership as a cultural process', *School Leadership and Management* 20, 2: 189–205.

Hargreaves, A. (1983) 'The politics of administrative convenience: the case of middle schools', in J. Ahier and M. Flude (eds) *Contemporary Education Policy*, London: Croom Helm.

—— (1992) 'Cultures of teaching: a focus for change', in A. Hargreaves and M. Fullan (eds) *Understanding Teacher Development*, London: Cassell.

Horgan, J. (1997) *The End of Science*, London: Little, Brown and Company.

Hoyle, E. (1986a) 'The management of schools: theory and practice', in E. Hoyle and A. McMahon (eds) *The Management of Schools*, London: Kogan Page.

—— (1986b) *The Politics of School Management*, London: Hodder & Stoughton.

Kogan, M. (1975) *Educational Policy Making: A Study of Interest Groups and Parliament*, London: George Allen & Unwin.

—— (1978) *The Politics of Educational Change*, London: Fontana/Collins.

Laumann, E., Galskiewicz, L., and Marsden, P. (1978) 'Community structure as inter-organizational linkages', *Annual Review of Sociology* 4: 455–84.

Leithwood, K., Jantzi, D., and Steinbach, R. (1999) *Changing Leadership for Changing Times*, Buckingham: Open University Press.

Lindblom, C. (1983) 'Comments on Manley', *American Political Science Review* 77, 2: 384–6.

Louis, K. S. and Miles, M. (1990) *Improving the Urban High School: What Works and Why*, New York: Teachers College Press.

McDonnell, L. and Elmore, R. (1991) 'Getting the job done: alternative policy instruments', in E. Odden (ed.) *Education Policy Implementation*, Albany, NY: State University of New York Press.

Mackinnon, D., Statham, J., and Hales, M. (1996) *Education in the UK: Facts and Figures* (revised edn), London: Hodder & Stoughton.

March, J. (ed.) (1988) *Decisions and Organisations*, Oxford: Blackwell.

March, J. and Olsen, P. (1976) *Ambiguity and Choice in Organisations*, Bergen: Universitetsforlaget.

Merriam, S. (1988) *Case Study Research in Education*, London: Jossey-Bass.

Meyerson, D. and Martin, J. (1987) 'Cultural change: an integration of different views', *Journal of Management Studies* 24: 623–47.

Miles, M. and Huberman, M. (1994) *Qualitative Data Analysis* (2nd edn), London: Sage.

Minsky, M. (1985) *The Society of Mind*, New York: Simon & Schuster.

National Audit Office (1986) *Department of Education and Science: Falling School Rolls*, London: Her Majesty's Stationery Office.

Nias, J., Southworth, G., and Yeomans, R. (1989) *Staff Relationships in the Primary School*, London: Cassell.

Nice, D. (1992) *County and Voluntary Schools* (8th edn), Harlow: Longman.

Nohria, N. (1998) 'Is a network perspective a useful way of studying organisations?', in G. Robinson Hickman (ed.) *Leading Organisations: Perspectives for a New Era*, London: Sage.

Northcote, P. (1997) *Leadership: Theory and Practice*, London: Sage.

O'Donnell, G. (1985) *Mastering Sociology*, London: Macmillan.

Osborne, D. and Gaebler, T. (1992) *Reinventing Government: How the Entrepreneurial Spirit is Transforming the Public Sector*, Reading, MA: Addison-Wesley.

Pollitt, C. (1993) *Managerialism and the Social Services* (2nd edn), Oxford: Blackwell.

Ranson, S. (1990) *The Politics of Reorganising Schools*, London: Unwin Hyman.

Saran, R. (1973) *Policy Making in Secondary Education: A Case Study*, Oxford: Oxford University Press.

Sergiovanni, T. (1996) *Moral Leadership: Getting to the Heart of School Improvement*, San Francisco: Jossey-Bass.

Southworth, G. (1998) *Leading Improving Primary Schools: The Work of Headteachers and Deputy Heads*, London: Falmer Press.

Stacey, R. (1992) *Managing the Unknowable: Strategic Boundaries between Order and Chaos*, San Francisco: Jossey-Bass.

—— (1996) *Strategic Management and Organisational Dynamics* (2nd edn), London: Pitman Publishing.

Starratt, R. (1995) *Leaders with Vision: The Quest for School Renewal*, Thousand Oaks, CA: Corwin Press.

Steiner, G. (1979) *Strategic Planning: What Every Manager Must Know*, New York: Free Press.

Taylor-Gooby, P. and Lawson, R. (1993) 'Where we go from here; the new order in welfare', in P. Taylor-Gooby and R. Lawson (eds) *Markets and Managers: New Issues in the Delivery of Welfare*, Buckingham: Open University Press.

Wallace, M. (1991a) 'Contradictory interests in policy implementation: the case of LEA development plans for schools', *Journal of Education Policy* 6, 4: 385–99.

—— (1991b) 'Coping with multiple innovations: an exploratory study', *School Organisation* 11, 2: 187–209.

—— (1992) 'The management of multiple innovations', Module 1, Unit 3, Part 2, Open University Course E326 *Managing Schools*, Milton Keynes: Open University.

—— (1996a) 'Policy interaction and policy implementation: a case of school merger under duress', *Educational Management and Administration* 24, 3: 263–75.

—— (1996b) 'A crisis of identity: school merger and cultural transition', *British Educational Research Journal* 22, 4: 459–73.

—— (1998a) 'Innovations in planning for school improvement: problems and potential', in A. Lieberman, M. Fullan, and D. Hopkins (eds) *International Handbook of Educational Change*, Dordrecht, The Netherlands: Kluwer Academic Press.

—— (1998b) 'A counter-policy to subvert education reform? Collaboration among schools and colleges in a competitive climate', *British Educational Research Journal* 24, 2: 195–215.

—— (1999) 'Combining cultural and political perspectives: the best of both conceptual worlds?', in T. Bush, L. Bell, R. Bolam, R. Glatter, and P. Ribbins (eds) *Redefining Educational Management: Policy, Practice and Research*, London: Paul Chapman.

—— (2000) 'Integrating cultural and political theoretical perspectives: the case of school restructuring in England', *Educational Administration Quarterly* 36, 4: 608–32.

Wallace, M. and Hall, V. (1994) *Inside the SMT: Team Approaches to Secondary School Management*, London: Paul Chapman.

Wallace, M. and Huckman, L. (1999) *Senior Management Teams in Primary Schools: The Quest for Synergy*, London: Routledge.

Wallace, M. and McMahon, A. (1994) *Planning for Change in Turbulent Times: The Case of Multiracial Primary Schools*, London: Cassell.

Wallace, M. and Weindling, D. (1999) 'Overview of a group of research projects with relevance to school management', in T. Bush, L. Bell, R. Bolam, R. Glatter, and P. Ribbins (eds) *Redefining Educational Management: Policy, Practice and Research*, London: Paul Chapman.

Weick, K. (2001) *Making Sense of the Organisation*, Oxford: Blackwell.

Whitty, G., Power, S., and Halpin, D. (1998) *Devolution and Choice in Education*, Buckingham: Open University Press.

Wise, A. (1983) 'Why education policies often fail: the hyperrationalisation hypothesis', in V. Baldridge and T. Deal (eds) *The Dynamics of Organisational Change in Education,* Berkeley, CA: McCutchan.

Index